Using Quicken

Stephen Nelson

CORPORATION

LEADING COMPUTER KNOWLEDGE

Using Quicken®

Copyright © 1989 by Que® Corporation

Library of Congress Catalog No.: 89-62242

ISBN 0-88022-474-6

92 91 90   8 7 6 5 4

Interpretation of the printing code: the rightmost double-digit number is the year of the book's printing; the rightmost single-digit number, the number of the book's printing. For example, a printing code of 89-1 shows that the first printing of the book occurred in 1989.

Using Quicken covers Versions 2 and 3.

ABOUT THE AUTHOR

Stephen Nelson

Stephen Nelson, a certified public accountant, provides financial consulting and computer-based financial modeling services to a variety of firms and investors—principally in the areas of real estate and manufacturing.

Nelson's past experience includes a stint as the Treasurer and Controller of Caddex Corporation, a venture-capital-funded start-up software development company and an early pioneer in the electronic publishing field, and, prior to that, as a senior consultant with Arthur Andersen & Co. There, Steve provided financial and systems consulting services to clients in a variety of industries.

Steve has authored over 30 articles on financial management and modeling for national publications, including *Lotus Magazine* and *INC Magazine*. Steve is the author of Que's *Using DacEasy* and the author and architect of *Business Forecasting and Planning with Microsoft Excel*, a collection of spreadsheet templates published by Microsoft Press.

Nelson holds a Bachelor of Science in Accounting from Central Washington University and a Master's in Business Administration with a finance emphasis from the University of Washington.

Publishing Manager

Lloyd J. Short

Product Director

David Maguiness

Production Editor

Kelly D. Dobbs

Editors

Sara Allaei
Mary P. Arthur
Fran Blauw
Richard Turner
Alice Martina Smith

Technical Editor

Alan L. Gray, CPA

Editorial Assistant

Stacie Lamborne

Book Design and Production

Dan Armstrong   Cindy Phipps
Brad Chinn   Joe Ramon
David Kline   Dennis Sheehan
Jennifer Matthews   Peter Tocco
Jon Ogle

Composed in Garamond and Excellent No. 47
by Que Corporation

ACKNOWLEDGMENT

I would like to thank Mari Latterell, product manager at Intuit, for taking the time to review this manuscript and for her helpful comments and suggestions.

CONTENTS AT A GLANCE

TABLE OF CONTENTS

5   Using the Register 117

6   Using the Register Menu Options 139

II Maintaining Your Accounts

TRADEMARK
ACKNOWLEDGMENTS

Que Corporation has made every effort to supply trademark information about company names, products, and services mentioned in this book. Trademarks indicated below were derived from various sources. Que Corporation cannot attest to the accuracy of this information.

Hewlett-Packard is a registered trademark and LaserJet is a trademark of Hewlett-Packard Co.

IBM is a registered trademark of International Business Machines Corporation.

Lotus, 1-2-3, and Symphony are registered trademarks of Lotus Development Corporation.

Microsoft and MS-DOS are registered trademarks of Microsoft Corporation.

Quicken is a registered trademark and Billminder, CheckSaver, Tax Reform Analyzer, and Transfer Utility are trademarks of Intuit.

WordPerfect is a registered trademark of WordPerfect Corporation.

Introduction

If you are reading this introduction, one of the following three statements is probably true:

- ❏ You are considering the installation of a personal or small-business accounting package like Quicken.

- ❏ You have decided to install Quicken and want a little extra help.

- ❏ You already are using Quicken and want a reference source that goes beyond the information provided in the user's manual.

In any of these cases, *Using Quicken* will help. In this text, you find a wealth of information on Quicken Version 3 and on managing your personal or small-business finances.

When you finish reading this introduction, you will know what Quicken Version 3 is and whether the program suits your needs. This introduction also identifies the chapters that cover each of the pieces that make up the whole of Quicken.

What Is Quicken?

Quicken is a computer-based bookkeeping system you can use to manage your personal or business finances. Used in the simplest way, Quicken maintains your check register for you—deducting payments and adding deposits to your checking account balance. Quicken eliminates the possibility of you overdrawing your account because of an arithmetic error. The real value of the package, however, stems from several other features

1

the program provides. First, Quicken enables you to use your computer and printer to generate checks—a real time-saver if you find yourself writing many checks at home every month.

Second, Quicken enables you to use the information stored in your check register to report on your income and outgo, track tax deductions, and compare your actual income and expenses to what you originally budgeted. Third, Quicken can be used to perform bookkeeping for most personal and business assets and liabilities including personal investments, business receivables, personal credit lines and mortgages, and business payables. With these extra features, individuals can track and manage their finances closely and many small businesses can use Quicken as a full-fledged accounting package. (Quicken enables you to generate personal and business income statements, balance sheets, and cash-flow statements.)

When To Use Quicken

Answering the question "When should you use Quicken?" depends on whether or not you are using the program for personal or small-business purposes. If you are considering Quicken for personal use, four factors indicate that Quicken represents a good investment of your time and money:

1. When check writing and checking-account record keeping take more time than you want to spend. Quicken does most of the work related to keeping your check book: recording transactions, writing checks, reconciling account balances, and maintaining the check register. Because Quicken does the work for you, the program saves you a tremendous amount of time.

2. When you need to track your tax deductions carefully. Quicken tracks the amounts you spend on tax-deductible items. At the end of the year, totaling your charitable contribution deduction is as simple as printing a report.

3. When you want to budget income and expense amounts and compare what you earn and spend with what you budgeted. Budgets, contrary to their reputation, are not equivalent to financial handcuffs that prevent you from enjoying life. Budgets are tools that enable you to identify your financial priorities. They help you monitor your progress in organizing your financial life so that you meet your financial objectives. Quicken makes budgeting easy.

4. When you want to monitor and track personal assets, such as investments, and personal liabilities, such as your mortgages and credit card debt.

If you are considering Quicken for business, three factors indicate that Quicken represents a good investment of your time and money and a reasonable accounting alternative:

1. You do not need or want to use a small-business accounting package that requires double-entry bookkeeping. Packages such as DacEasy, Peachtree, and others require that you use double-entry bookkeeping. Although this procedure is a powerful and valuable tool, if you are not familiar with double-entry bookkeeping, you probably can spend your time in better ways than learning accounting methods. Quicken provides a single-entry, easy-to-use accounting system.

2. You do not need a fancy billing and accounts receivable system. Quicken enables you to perform record keeping for accounts receivable. If you have less than two dozen transactions a month, Quicken provides a satisfactory solution. If your transaction volumes exceed this amount, however, you may want to consider a full-fledged accounts receivable package that prepares invoices, calculates finance charges, and easily handles high volumes of customer invoices and payments.

3. You do not need an automated inventory record-keeping system. Although Quicken enables you to set up other assets such as inventory, the program does not enable you to track the number of units of these other assets—only the dollars. With inventory, however, you not only need to know the dollars of inventory, you need to know the number of units of inventory. Suppose, for example, that you sell snow skis. You need to know the number of pairs of skis you have as well as the dollar value of your snow ski inventory.

About This Book

Using Quicken is divided into 3 parts and 12 chapters. (If you read the book from cover to cover, you may notice repetition in some places—inevitable when the book also needs to work as a reference.)

Part I—Transactions

Chapter 1, "Getting Started with Quicken," guides you through the steps you need to take before you start using Quicken, including ordering any preprinted forms you will need, deciding which Quicken options to use, learning to use the system, picking a starting date, and installing the software. Chapter 1 describes each of these steps in detail.

Chapter 2, "Selecting Accounts and Changing Settings," describes two additional tasks you need to complete to start using the package: using the Change Settings menu within Quicken to finish the installation and setting up one or more bank accounts to write checks.

Chapter 3, "Writing and Printing Checks," describes one of Quicken's core features—the capability to print checks. Chapter 3 includes instructions for completing the Write Checks screen, where you provide the information Quicken needs to print a check, and instructions for recording, reviewing, editing, and printing checks.

Chapter 4, "Using the Write Checks Menu Options," describes how to use the function keys available on the Write Checks screen to speed up the check writing process. The chapter includes information on the Edit Find, Quick Entry, and Activities function key options. Although the information in Chapter 4 is not essential to operating Quicken, this information makes using the **Write and Print Checks** option even faster.

Chapter 5, "Using the Register," discusses the fundamental financial tool you probably use now—your check register. The check register records your every financial move and the cash balances that remain after each transaction. This chapter describes the basics of using Quicken's check register to make the whole process easier. These basics include how to complete the Check Register screen, how to record various types of transactions in the check register, how to review and edit check-register transactions, and how to print the check register.

Chapter 6, "Using the Register Menu Options," describes using the Edit Find, Quick Entry, and Activities function key options—tools you can use to record checking account transactions in your check register. Recording transactions in Quicken's check register is easy and fast, especially when you learn to use the check register function keys.

Part II—Maintaining Your Accounts

Chapter 7, "Using Categories and Classes," discusses one of Quicken's optional and most powerful features—the capability to categorize and classify your spending. The categories make determining tax deductions, the amounts spent for various items, and the types of money that flow into your bank accounts easy. The classes also enable you to look at specific groups of categories, such as just personal expenses or business expenses. Chapter 7 defines Quicken's categories and classes, describes why and when you should use them, shows the predefined categories provided within Quicken, and explains how to use these categories. Chapter 7 also outlines the steps for adding, deleting, and modifying your own categories and classes.

Chapter 8, "Reconciling Your Bank Account," discusses one of the important steps you can take to protect your cash and the accuracy and reliability of your checking account and banking records. This chapter first reviews the reconciliation process in general terms and then describes the steps for reconciling your accounts in Quicken, correcting and catching errors, and printing and using the reconciliation reports that Quicken creates.

Chapter 9, "Protecting Your System," describes the steps you can take to protect your system and the money it counts. The first part of the chapter outlines procedures for protecting yourself from check forgery and embezzlement. The second part of the chapter outlines the ways you can minimize human errors with the Quicken System.

Part III—Advanced Features

Chapter 10, "Accounting for Other Assets and Liabilities," describes some of the special features that Version 3 of Quicken provides for personal use including tracking cash, other assets such as investments, credit card liabilities, and other liabilities such as a mortgage. Chapter 10 also describes the new features that Version 3 of Quicken provides for business users, including how to use Quicken to account for business receivables and payables, other assets and liabilities, and how to generate a business balance sheet.

Chapter 11, "Using Quicken's Reports," shows you how to sort, extract, and summarize the information contained in the check register and gain even better control over and insight into your income, expenses, and cash flows. Chapter 11 describes each of the six report options and when and how you use them.

Appendixes

Using Quicken also provides two appendixes.

Appendix A, "A Review of Budgeting," discusses one of Quicken's most significant benefits—budgeting and monitoring your success in achieving a budget. This appendix reviews the steps for budgeting, describes how Quicken helps with budgeting, and provides some tips on how to budget more successfully. If you are not comfortable with the budgeting process, Appendix A should give you enough information to get started. If you find budgeting a rather unpleasant exercise, the appendix also provides some tips on making budgeting a more positive experience.

Appendix B, "Using This Book with Version 2," outlines the differences between Quicken Version 2 and Version 3. With this appendix, you should be able to use this book for either version of Quicken.

Appendix C, "Using Quicken in Your Business," covers some of the special techniques and procedures to use Quicken for business accounting. This appendix begins by discussing the overall approach for using Quicken in a business. Then, the following seven basic accounting tasks are detailed: invoicing customers, tracking receivables, tracking inventory, accounting for fixed assets, preparing payroll, job costing, and tracking loans and notes.

Appendix D, "Tips for Specific Business Situations," provides income tax accounting tips as well as tips for professionals, restaurant managers and owners, retailers, and nonprofit organizations.

Transactions

Includes

Getting Started with Quicken

Selecting Accounts and Changing Settings

Writing and Printing Checks

Using the Write Checks Menu Options

Using the Register

Using the Register Menu Options

1

Getting Started
with Quicken

Using a new computer-based accounting system presents unique chal-lenges and opportunities, particularly if you have used manual sys-tems in the past. Accounting systems, even simple ones like Quicken, automate repetitive steps. Accounting, like other processes, must be per-formed in a certain way with steps performed in a certain order. Getting the cart before the horse is easy—and usually happens in several places.

Getting started with a new system often turns into a major headache. By applying some of the tactics that others have learned through trial and error, you can ease considerably the installation of any computer-based accounting system, including Quicken. Getting Quicken up and running is easiest if you follow certain steps in a certain order. This chapter describes these steps in the order you should take them:

1. Deciding which Quicken features to use

2. Ordering any preprinted forms you need

3. Learning to use the system

4. Picking a start-up date

5. Installing the software

6. Operating the software

Spend a few minutes to review the next few sections, and you should save yourself from common mistakes like ordering the wrong preprinted forms, failing to verify that the new system can perform necessary tasks, or installing features you do not use.

Deciding Which Features To Use

You must decide which of seven accounting or record-keeping features you want to use:

1. Register

2. Check writing

3. Billminder

4. Reconciliation

5. Categories and classes

6. Balance sheet generation

7. Budgeting and variance analysis

Table 1.1 describes each feature, lists any prerequisites a feature has, and identifies the chapters in this book that cover that feature.

Table 1.1
Summary of Quicken Features

Feature	Description	Prerequisite	Chapter(s)
Register	Records checking account transactions and balances; also enables you to track other assets and liabilities		5 and 6
Check writing	Prints checks	Register	3 and 4
Billminder	Reminds you of bills that should be paid	Register Check writing	1
Reconciliation	Reconciles your check register account balance to the bank statement balance	Register	8
Categories and classes	Enables you to add up similar transactions or groups of transactions	Register	7

Table 1.1—*continued*

Feature	Description	Prerequisite	Chapter(s)
Balance sheets	Enables you to track the assets you own like receivables or investments and liabilities like payables or mortgages; also calculates your personal or business net worth	Register	10
Budgeting and variance analysis	Enables you to compare what you spent with what you budgeted	Register Categories	11

You have to use the register feature because it represents the foundation of the system. As table 1.1 shows, every other feature relies on the register.

The check writing feature is a real time-saver, although the time savings does not come cheap. (You spend roughly between $30 and $50 for 250 computer check forms.) Nonetheless, having your computer print checks is something you may want to consider—particularly if you currently prepare more than two dozen checks each month.

The Billminder reminds you of bills you are supposed to pay. When you turn on your computer or when you enter Quicken, you are reminded that bills must be paid. This handy feature can save you the price of Quicken and this book many times over by eliminating or minimizing late-payment fees.

The reconciliation feature makes explaining differences between your records and the bank's records a snap. If you use a checking account, not reconciling the account is almost inexcusable. Reconciling helps you understand the differences between the bank's ending balance on the monthly statement and your current register balance.

Categories enable you to track your income and expenses. With classes, you can add another dimension to your categorization of income and expense amounts by grouping related categories together. Use categories when you want to track how much you spend on items such as housing, food, entertainment, and so on. You need to use categories if you want to budget or if you want Quicken to add up tax-deductible expenses for the year.

Classes are more applicable to business uses of Quicken. You want to use classes to keep track of income and expense by geographical location, by job or project, or by department.

The balance sheets feature enables you to perform record keeping for other assets besides cash and for other liabilities. Personal assets include home and investments. Personal liabilities include mortgage or credit card debt. Business assets include accounts receivable and equipment. Business liabilities include a bank loan or credit line. By performing the record keeping for assets besides cash and liabilities, Quicken can produce balance sheets that enable you to calculate and track your personal or business net worth.

Ordering Preprinted Check Forms

If you decide to use Quicken to print checks, you must order check forms for every bank account for which you want to print checks using your computer. The cheapest and easiest source of check forms is Intuit, the manufacturer of Quicken. (No, I'm not getting any money from Intuit to say this; and yes, I checked each of the other major check-form printers.)

By completing and mailing the order form included in the Quicken package, Intuit prints check forms with your name and address at the top of the form and the bank and account information at the bottom of the form. Do not worry about the bank accepting your new checks.

CPA Tip: When deciding where to start numbering your computer check forms, consider two things: First, you will want to start the computer-printed check form numbers far enough away from your manual check numbers so that they do not overlap or duplicate and cause confusion in your record keeping and reconciliations; second, you may find it helpful to start numbering your computer-printed check forms with a number that shows you at a glance whether you wrote a check using Quicken or manually.

When you select check forms, you make a series of choices related to color, style, or lettering, and decide whether the check form is multipart or has voucher stubs. Table 1.2. summarizes your options.

Table 1.2
Summary of Quicken Check Form Options

Name	Colors	Form Size (inches)	Number of Parts	Comments
Prestige Antique	Tan	3.5 x 8.5	1	Antique refers to parchment background; printed three to a sheet.
Prestige Standard	Gray	3.5 x 8.5	1 or 2	You can choose blue, green, or maroon accent strip; printed three to a sheet.
Prestige Payroll/ Voucher	Gray	7.0 x 8.5	1 or 2	You can choose blue, green, or maroon accent strip. Larger form size due to voucher stub.
Standard	Blue or Green	3.5 x 8.5	1, 2, or 3	Printed three to a sheet.
Voucher/ Payroll	Blue or Gray	7.0 x 8.5	1, 2, or 3	Larger form size due to voucher stub.
Laser	Blue or Green	3.5 x 8.5	1	8.5 x 10.5 sheets—each with 3 check forms—fit into printer paper tray.
Laser Voucher/ Payroll	Blue or Green	3.5 x 8.5	1 or 2	8.5 x 11 sheets—each with 1 check form—fit into printer paper tray.
Wallet-size Computer	Blue or Green	2 5/6 x 6	1 or 2	2-inch check stub so that overall form width is 8.5 inches

You are on your own when you select the color, size, and the style of lettering you want. This discussion, however, provides a couple of hints about the number of parts your check form should have and whether or not your check form should have a voucher stub or remittance advice.

The number of parts in a check form refers to the number of printed copies. A one-part form means that only the actual check form that you sign is printed. A two-part form means that a carbon copy of the check is printed at the same time as the original. With a three-part form, you get two copies in addition to the original.

Multipart forms probably are not necessary for most home uses. In a business, however, the second and third parts can be attached to paid invoices as a fast and convenient way of keeping track of which checks paid which invoices. An extra copy of the check form may be valuable to keep in your check register until the canceled check comes back from the bank. In this way, you have all your checks in one place. The third copy also can be placed in a numerical sequence file to help you identify the payee better than if you had only the check number.

One precaution to consider if you use multipart forms is that the forms may wear out your impact printer's head (the points that hit the printer ribbon and cause characters to be printed). Check your printer's multipart form rating by referring to your printer manual. Verify that your printer is rated for at least the number of parts you want to print.

The voucher stub, also called the remittance advice, is the blank piece of paper about the same size as the check form and is attached to the check form. Voucher stubs provide extra space for you to describe or document the reason for the check. You also can use this area to show any calculations involved in arriving at the total check amount. You may, for example, use the voucher stub space to describe how an employee's payroll amount was calculated or to define the invoices for which that check was issued. As with multipart forms, voucher stubs probably make more sense for business use rather than home use.

If you are not sure which check forms to choose, try Quicken's starter kit. The starter kit costs about $35 as of this writing, includes 250 checks, and gives you a chance to experiment with preprinted check forms.

Learning To Use Quicken

Accounting and record keeping with Quicken are easy. Before using Quicken for personal or small-business accounting, invest some time learning Quicken and figuring out how to get the program to work for you. You can approach the learning process in several ways.

Read the Quicken user's manual and this book—or at least the chapters that apply to those parts of the program you think you will use. Understanding the underlying accounting principles and the software's operation is essential if you are to enjoy all the benefits that Quicken provides. Reading this book and the Quicken user's manual gives you a sturdy foundation on which to build.

Talk to other Quicken users in your locality. You probably can find Quicken users just down the street. Formal and informal users' groups are excellent support groups. Other users often are working through the same problems that you are encountering and, hopefully, are enjoying the same benefits you are seeking. The store that sold you Quicken, the store or computer consultant who helps you with your hardware and software, or the CPA who prepares your annual financial statements or tax return may be able to direct you to Quicken users' groups.

Spend some time experimenting with the software. Try different transactions, explore the menus and screens, and pore over the reports. Far from being wasteful or superfluous, this activity (called a *user test*) produces important benefits. Experimenting increases your confidence in the system, gives you experience in working with live business or family data, and most importantly, enables you to confirm that an option can accomplish the needed tasks.

Picking the Conversion Date

Picking the conversion date is another critical decision you must make before you can enjoy the many advantages of an automated accounting system. The *conversion date* is the day on which you plan to stop using your old manual system and begin using your new Quicken system. The less you expect from Quicken, the less important the conversion date is. You must finish a series of steps before you can begin using the system. Some of these tasks have been described already: you must decide which options you want to use; if you have elected to print checks with Quicken, you need to order and receive your checks, and you need to learn the system.

If you are going to use the categories or the budgeting features, also consider the issue of a clean accounting cutoff point for the date you begin record keeping with Quicken. From the conversion date forward, Quicken provides your accounting information. Before the conversion date, your old accounting system must provide your accounting information. Pick a natural cutoff date that makes switching from one system to another easy. The best time to begin using any accounting package is usually at the beginning of the year. All the income and expense transactions for the new year are recorded in the same place. Picking a good cutoff date may seem trivial, but having your tax deductions for one year recorded and summarized in one place is handy.

If you cannot start using Quicken at the beginning of the year, the next best time is at the beginning of the month. If you start at the beginning of a month, you must combine your old accounting or record keeping information with Quicken's information to get totals for the year. When calculating tax deductions, for example, you need to add the amounts Quicken shows to whatever your old system shows. Your old system may not be anything fancy—perhaps a shoe box full of receipts. Watch for a couple of things when you choose an accounting cutoff point. You may put the same income or expense transaction in both systems and, therefore, count the transaction twice when you add the two systems together to get the annual totals. You may neglect to record a transaction because you think that you recorded the transaction in the other system. In either case, your records are wrong. To begin using Quicken at the beginning of the month, spend some time summarizing your accounting information from the old system. Make sure that you do not include the same transaction (income received or an expense paid) twice. This repetition can occur if you pay the expense once using the old system and then again using Quicken.

You probably can guess that, for the same reasons, the worst time to begin using Quicken is in the middle of month. With no natural cutoff point, you are likely to count some transactions on both systems and forget to record others in either system.

The less you expect from Quicken, the less important an issue the conversion date is. If you don't use Quicken to summarize income and expense transactions or monitor how well you are sticking to a budget, and all you really want is a tool to maintain your checkbook and produce checks, the conversion date isn't as important.

Installing the Software

To use Quicken, you must meet the following minimum hardware requirements:

- ❏ IBM personal computer or compatible
- ❏ 320K of memory for Version 3; 256K of memory for Version 2
- ❏ Two floppy disk drives or one floppy disk drive and a hard disk
- ❏ MS-DOS or PC-DOS Version 2.0 or higher

❏ Any printer (except one that uses thermal paper)

❏ An 80-column color or monochrome monitor

Table 1.3 lists the Quicken Program and Data Files.

Table 1.3
Program and Data Files

File	Description

Included on the program disk:

Q.EXE	Quicken program
Q.HLP	On-line help file accessed with F1
BILLMIND.EXE	Program to check for checks, batches due
QCHECKS.DOC	Blank supplies order form
INSTALL.EXE	Installation program (not copied to the hard or floppy disk used as your program disk)
CONVERT.COM	Quicken 2 data file conversion program
PRINTERS.DAT	Printer driver file
HCAT.QMT	Predefined home category list
BCAT.QMT	Predefined business category list
TCAT.QMT	Predefined category list including categories from HCAT.QMT and BCAT.QMT

Quicken creates the following files:

Q.CFG	Configuration and set-up information
Q3.DIR	List of account descriptions and check due dates

Assuming that you use an account group named QDATA, Quicken also creates the following files:

QDATA.QDT	Data file for account group
QDATA.QNX	Data file index for account group
QDATA.QMT	Memorized transaction list for account group
QDATA.QDI	Dictionary file for account group

The steps for installing the Quicken system vary depending on whether your computer uses only floppy disks or has a floppy and a hard disk drive. Refer to the appropriate section that follows to install Quicken on your system.

Installing Quicken on a Hard Disk System

You should know a few things about the Quicken hard disk installation program, INSTALL, before you use the program. INSTALL creates a directory named QUICKEN3 on your hard disk in which the program files are stored. Your data files also are stored in the QUICKEN3 directory unless you change the system settings (described in Chapter 2).

INSTALL also creates a batch file named Q.BAT so that all you have to do is type *Q* at the C> prompt to run QUICKEN. If you already have a Q.BAT file (if you have been using Quicken Version 2), INSTALL renames the old file Q2.BAT. If you decide to use the Billminder option, the INSTALL program adds a line to the end of your AUTOEXEC.BAT file that runs the Billminder program every time you start your computer. (INSTALL does not destroy the old AUTOEXEC.BAT file; the program renames the file AUTOEXEC.B00 in case you want to retrieve or re-use the original file.) If you want to use the old version of your autoexec file, you can use a word processing program to remove the Billminder line, or you can delete the new AUTOEXEC.BAT file and rename AUTOEXEC.B00 as AUTOEXEC.BAT using the DOS RENAME command. (Your DOS user's manual describes how to rename files.)

INSTALL also verifies that the CONFIG.SYS file's BUFFERS statement equals or exceeds 10 and that the FILES statement equals or exceeds 10. (INSTALL resets these statements because Quicken runs with several files open and performs many reads from the hard disk. For more information on the CONFIG.SYS file and the BUFFERS and FILES statements, see your DOS manual.) If you do not have a CONFIG.SYS file, INSTALL creates one with the appropriate BUFFERS and FILES statements. If the CONFIG.SYS file you currently have does not have these statements, INSTALL adds them. If the statements exist, but are set to less than 10, INSTALL increases the statement settings to 10.

To install Quicken on a hard disk system, do the following:

1. Turn on your computer and monitor. Make sure that the correct system date and time are set. (Type *DATE* at the C> prompt.) DATE is the DOS command for setting the system date. Refer to your DOS user's manual if you need help using the DATE command.

2. Place the Quicken help disk in drive A. (If you have a 3.5 inch disk, the help and program portions of Quicken are on the disk.) Type *A:INSTALL* and press enter.

3. The introductory Install screen, shown in figure 1.1, appears. Press
   Enter, and Quicken displays the screen you use to specify on which
   disk you want to install Quicken, as shown in figure 1.2. (Press F2
   to change the display on your monitor from monochrome to color
   of from color to monochrome.)

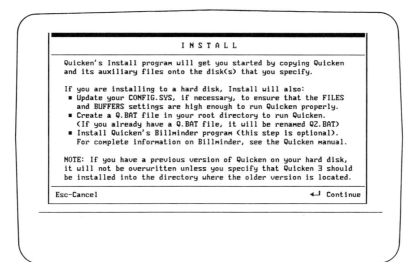

Fig. 1.1.

*The
introductory
screen.*

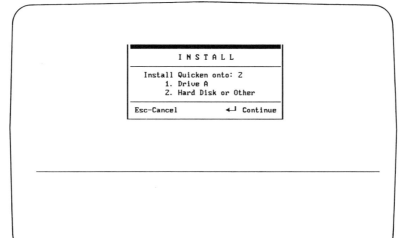

Fig. 1.2.

*Quicken asks
which disk to
use.*

4. Select 2 to designate a hard disk installation and press Enter to continue. Quicken displays the specify directory location screen shown in figure 1.3. The default directory that Quicken creates and installs itself into is \Quicken3. If you want to use some other directory, you specify so here by typing the default directory. When the correct directory is displayed, press Enter. (Version 2 of Quicken stores files in the directory, C:\QUICKEN2. Do not specify the directory as C:\QUICKEN2 because you will overwrite these records.)

Fig. 1.3.

Quicken asks which directory to install itself onto.

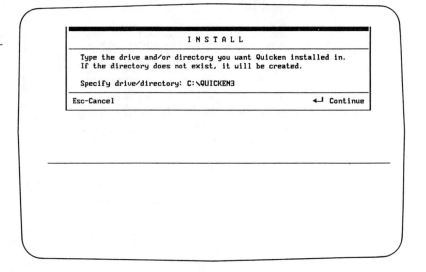

```
                        I N S T A L L

     Type the drive and/or directory you want Quicken installed in.
     If the directory does not exist, it will be created.

     Specify drive/directory: C:\QUICKEN3

   Esc-Cancel                                         ↵  Continue
```

5. Upon completing the installation, Quicken asks whether or not you want the Billminder option installed as shown in figure 1.4. Press Enter to answer yes or ESC to answer no. Quicken completes the first part of the installation and prompts you to insert the program disk in drive A as shown in figure 1.5. Billminder alerts you that you have entered checks that need to be printed. (See Chapter 2 for more about the Billminder option.)

After you insert the program disk and press Enter, Quicken continues with the installation. Quicken tells you when the installation is complete by displaying the screen shown in figure 1.6. To return to the C> prompt, press Enter.

6. To begin using Quicken, type *Q* at the C> prompt. Before displaying the Main menu, Quicken may ask if you have a color or a monochrome monitor. Type *1* for yes or *2* for no. (Figure 1.7, which also is used when installing Quicken on a floppy disk system, shows the screen Quicken uses to ask you this question.)

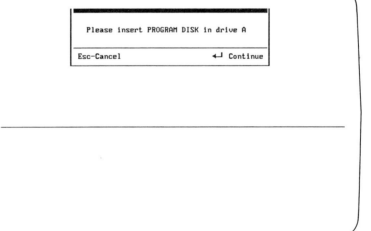

```
                    Installing Quicken Billminder

  Quicken's Billminder is a program that notifies you, as your computer
  starts up, if you have Quicken checks or scheduled transactions due.

  If you request the Billminder, it will be copied to the root directory
  of your hard disk and a line will be added to your AUTOEXEC.BAT file.

  Do you want Billminder to be installed (Y/N)? Y

  Esc-Cancel                                          ↵ Continue
```

Fig. 1.4.

Quicken asks if you want to install Billminder.

```
           Please insert PROGRAM DISK in drive A

  Esc-Cancel                        ↵ Continue
```

Fig. 1.5.

Quicken asks you to insert the program disk.

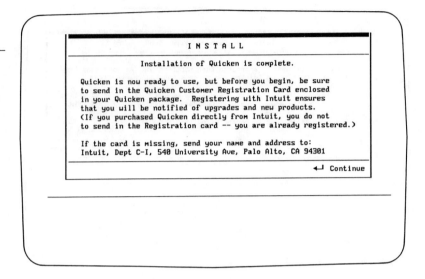

Fig. 1.6.

Quicken tells you when the installation is complete.

Installing Quicken on a Dual Floppy Disk System

To install Quicken on a floppy disk system, do the following:

1. Place your DOS disk in drive A and turn on your computer and monitor. Make sure that your system has the correct date and time set. (Type *DATE* at the A> prompt.) Then format three blank floppy disks. (Refer to your DOS manual for information on the FORMAT command if you are not sure of how to format.) Label the first disk *Quicken program copy*; label the second disk *Quicken help copy*, and label the third disk *Quicken data disk*. (If you have a 3.5 inch disk, the program and help portions of Quicken are on one disk.)

2. Place the Quicken help disk in drive A and the disk you formatted and labeled *Quicken help copy* in drive B. Copy the Quicken help disk in drive A to the Quicken help copy disk in drive B by typing *COPY A:*.* B:* at the A> prompt and pressing Enter. Repeat these steps to make a copy of the Quicken program disk.

3. After the copies are complete, remove the Quicken program disk from drive A and put the program and help disks someplace safe. Move the Quicken help copy disk to drive A and the Quicken data disk to drive B.

4. To start Quicken from the help copy disk, type *Q* and press Enter. (In the future, you also start Quicken this way.)

If Quicken cannot determine what kind of monitor you use, you see the screen shown in figure 1.7. To respond to the monitor question, type *1* to indicate a color monitor or *2* to indicate a monochrome monitor.

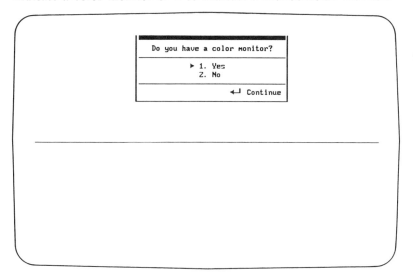

Fig. 1.7.

Quicken asks whether your monitor is color or monochrome.

If you did not set the date, Quicken asks for the correct date. To enter the correct date, type today's date in MM/DD/YY format (for example, 11/26/90). After you respond to these queries, press Enter. Quicken's Main menu appears as shown in figure 1.8.

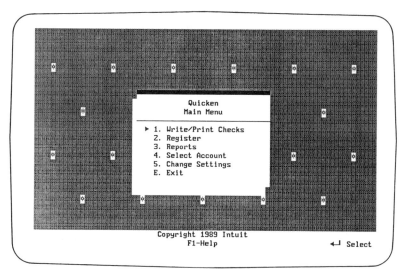

Fig. 1.8.

Quicken's Main menu appears after you specify a monochrome or color monitor.

Setting Up Accounts

You need to do one more thing to complete your installation of Quicken: Set up a bank account upon which to write checks. If you want to create personal or business balance sheets or use multiple bank accounts, you also need to set up additional accounts for other checking accounts, assets, or liabilities. Chapter 2 describes how to set up other accounts. Chapter 10 outlines the steps for working with these other accounts and for creating personal and business balance sheets.

From Quicken's Main menu, select the **Register** option by typing *2* or by using the down-arrow key to highlight the option and then pressing Enter.

The First Time Setup screen appears next (see fig. 1.9). By this point, you need to decide whether or not you want to use the standard categories predefined by Quicken or your own categories. If you do, you can direct Quicken to use one or both of the predefined category lists. Type *1* if you want to use Quicken's home categories. Type *2* if you want to use Quicken's business categories. If you want to use both, type *3*. If you want to use neither, type *4*. (Chapter 7 describes Quicken's categories in more detail.)

Fig. 1.9.

The First Time Setup screen.

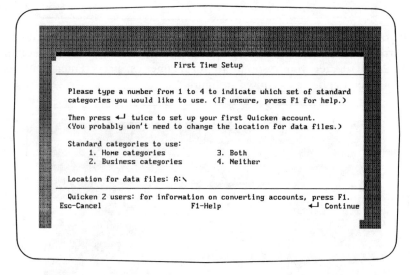

You also can specify the data directory Quicken should use to store your records. For hard disk users, the default directory is QUICKEN3. For floppy disk users, the default directory is just B:\. If you want to use a different directory, you can do so by specifying that directory on the First Time Setup screen.

Quicken Version 2 users may want to convert the Quicken 2 files before continuing. To convert the files, place the original Version 3 Help disk in drive A, type *A:CONVERT*, and press Enter. Quicken walks you through the necessary steps to convert your files. You are asked to supply the file name for the new files. The default file name is QDATA. (Do not use the same name as your Version 2 files.)

After you complete the First Time Setup screen, press Enter, and the Set Up New Account screen appears (see fig. 1.10). This screen provides several fields that you need to fill with information including account name, account type, the starting account balance, the starting date, and account description.

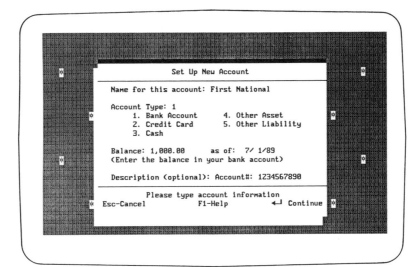

Fig. 1.10.

The Set Up New Account screen.

The name field can be up to fifteen characters long and use any characters except [,], /, and :. You also can include spaces. In the Account Type field, you indicate whether the account is an asset or a liability and what kind of asset or liability. Because you are setting up a bank account, the account type should be 1. You also need to give Quicken the starting account balance. For a bank account, this amount should be the current account balance according to your records. (In Chapters 10 and 11, you discover how and why you use the other account types to create whole or parts of balance sheets and the rules for setting starting balances.) The as of date should be the date on which the balance you entered is correct. Filling in the Description field is optional, but gives you an additional 21 characters to describe an account.

When you finish entering information for the Set Up New Account screen, press Enter. Quicken completes the installation and displays the Register screen shown in figure 1.11. The only information showing is the balance forward transaction Quicken recorded to set your opening balance. (The register is described in more detail in Chapter 5.)

Fig. 1.11.

The Register screen.

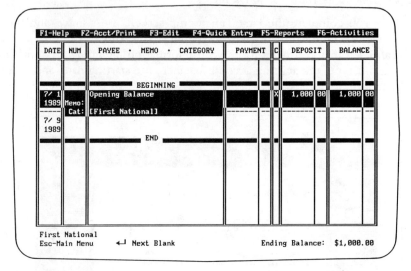

To exit from the Register screen, press Esc. Quicken returns you to the Main menu. If you also need to create another bank account, use the **Select Account** menu option. This option is described in Chapter 2.

Operating the Software

Quicken uses the following four general operating conventions:

1. On-line help

2. Using and selecting menu options

3. Collecting data on-screen

4. The on-line calculator

So that you know how to use these conventions from the start, they are described in the following sections.

Using Help

Think of Quicken's Help feature as a user's manual stored in your computer's memory. You can access this manual from anywhere in Quicken by pressing F1. Quicken's Help is context-sensitive, meaning that the program not only provides the manual, but opens the manual to the correct page. If you select **Help** from Quicken's Main menu, for example, you receive information about the Main menu options (see fig. 1.12).

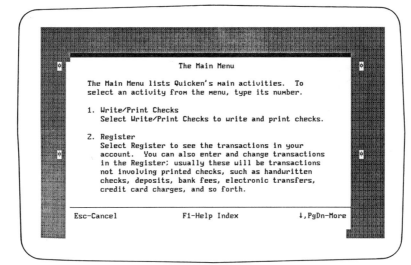

Fig. 1.12.

The Help screen with information about Quicken's Main menu.

Often, the information provided by the Help key takes more than one screen. Use the PgDn key to see the next page or pages of information. You can use the PgUp key to see the preceding page or pages of help information. After you read the help information and are ready to return to the program, press Esc. Quicken returns you to where you were when you pressed the Help key.

If you press F1 twice, you access the Select Help Topic screen that acts as an index of 46 topics on which you can get help (see fig. 1.13). To select a topic, move the selection triangle so that it marks that topic and press Enter.

Fig. 1.13.

*The Select Help
Topic screen.*

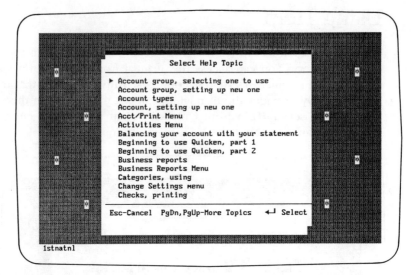

Using and Selecting Menu Options

Quicken provides the following four ways to select menu options:

❑ Typing the number of the option

❑ Highlighting the option and pressing Enter

❑ Using the shortcut keys

❑ Using the function keys

The first way to select an option from a menu is to type the number of the option you want to execute or access. If you want to select the **Write/ Print Checks** option from the Main menu, for example, you can type *1*.

The second way to select menu options is to use the cursor-movement keys to highlight the appropriate menu selection. If you press the up- and down-arrow keys, the small triangle to the left of the menu option numbers moves up and down. When the small triangle is next to the menu option you want to select, press Enter to access that option.

The third way to select menu options is to use one of the shortcut key combinations. Not every menu option has a shortcut key, but most of the options you use regularly do. To execute a shortcut, hold the Ctrl key and press the appropriate letter key. Chapter 5 describes how you can select a menu from the Register screen, select the **Delete transaction** option from the menu, and confirm that you want to delete a transaction by pressing Enter. Performing those three actions represents one way to delete a transaction. You also can press the Ctrl key and D to accomplish the same thing. Quicken shows you the shortcut keys (for example, Ctrl-D) behind the options (see fig. 1.14).

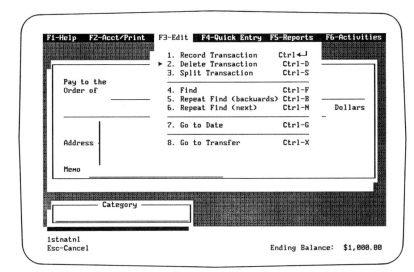

Fig. 1.14.

Ctrl-D is the shortcut key combination to delete a transaction.

Shortcut keys are described more in the chapters discussing the associated menu options. For now, remember that shortcut keys are another way to execute menu options and that they save time.

To exit any menu or screen and return to the preceding, higher level of the menu, press Esc.

From Quicken screens, such as the Write Checks screen (described in Chapter 3) and the Register screen (described in Chapter 5), you have another method of selecting menu options: you can press one of the function keys. Function-key options fall into one of two groups: function keys that access an option you may have moved to from the Main menu and keys that provide options related to entering information on-screen.

As an example of the first group of function-key options, pressing F5 from the Write Checks screen accesses the Reports menu shown in figure 1.15. You also can move to the Reports menu by selecting the **Reports** option from Quicken's Main menu as shown in figure 1.16.

The first group of function-key options may seem confusing at first, but this group of shortcuts enables you to jump around the Quicken menu structure. (Menu maps at the back of the book diagram the Quicken menu structure.)

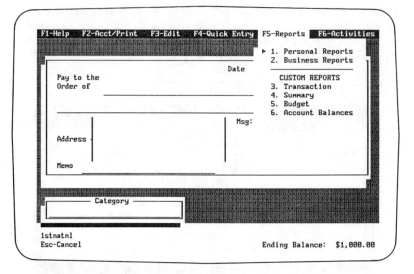

Fig. 1.15.

*F5 is one way
to access the
Reports menu.*

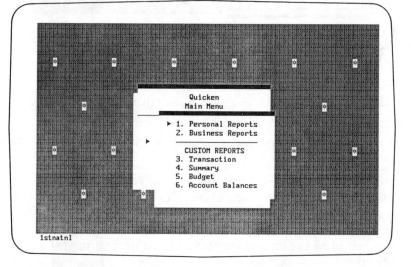

Fig. 1.16.

*Quicken's Main
menu also
accesses the
Reports menu.*

You also access the second group of function-key options (those keys that
provide options related to entering information on-screen) from one of
the Quicken screens. In fact, you can access these options from a screen
only by using a function key. You can access two groups of options this
way: the Edit and the Quick Entry options under the **Write/Print Checks**
and **Register** options on the Main menu. F3 accesses the Edit menu
options shown in figure 1.17, and F4 accesses the Quick Entry menu

options shown in figure 1.18. These options provide tools you can use to make the screen that the options are related to easier to use. (Chapters 4 and 6 describe the applicable menus and their options.)

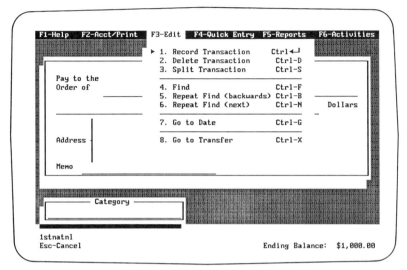

Fig. 1.17.

F3 accesses the Edit menu options.

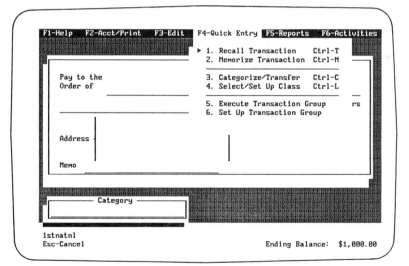

Fig. 1.18.

F4 accesses the Quick Entry menu options.

Collecting Data On-Screen

Collecting data on-screen involves moving between fields, entering and editing fields, and saving your work. Quicken provides you with a variety of ways to accomplish any of these tasks. The following sections explain these three actions.

Moving between Fields

Quicken provides a variety of ways to move between fields. You can move from field to field by pressing Enter. You can move to the next field by pressing Tab and to the preceding field by pressing Shift-Tab. You also can move between fields using the arrow keys. Pressing Ctrl-← moves the cursor to the beginning of the preceding field and pressing Ctrl-→ moves the cursor to the beginning of the next field.

Entering and Editing Data On-Screen

Entering or editing a field of data is as easy as moving between fields. To enter data into a field, type the appropriate characters. Whether Quicken accepts only numeric or alphabetic and numeric data depends on the field you are entering. Refer to the chapter pertaining to the screen you are using for more information.

Generally, however, type dollar amounts as numeric data by using the number keys on your keyboard. Do not enter the dollar symbol or any punctuation characters because Quicken adds these symbols for you. If an amount represents a negative number, however, precede the number with a minus sign, as in −1.47. Quicken assumes that the number is an even dollar amount, unless you use a decimal when entering the number. For example, entering 1245 displays as $1,245.00, and entering 12.45 displays as $12.45.

Most of the remaining data stored in the system (data other than dollar amounts) can be alphabetic, numeric, or both. Where alphabetic characters are allowed, you can use upper- or lowercase characters.

You can edit or change an entry in a field by retyping the field's contents or by using the arrow keys to position the cursor on the characters you want to change. To delete characters, use the Backspace or Del key. The Backspace key removes the character preceding the cursor location; the Del key removes the character at the cursor location. To add characters in existing text, press the Ins key and type the needed characters. To add characters to the end of the text, position the cursor at the end of the text using the right-arrow key and type the remaining characters.

If you are editing a date field, Quicken provides a special editing capability. By pressing the + key, you can add one day to the date; by pressing the − key, you can subtract one day from the date. (If the date is only the month and year—as in a few places in the Quicken system—you can move the date ahead one month by pressing the + key and back one month by pressing the − key.)

Saving Your Work

When you finish entering data on-screen and want to save the data, you have three ways to save your work:

❏ Pressing F10

❏ Pressing Enter from the last field on-screen

❏ Pressing Ctrl-Enter

If you are recording a check, Quicken displays a blank Write Checks screen so that you can enter another check. If you are recording a transaction in the register, Quicken displays the next empty row in the register so that you can record another transaction.

Using the Calculator

One of the tools new to Version 3 of Quicken is the on-line calculator that you can use by pressing the shortcut key combination Ctrl-O. Figure 1.19 shows the Calculator screen.

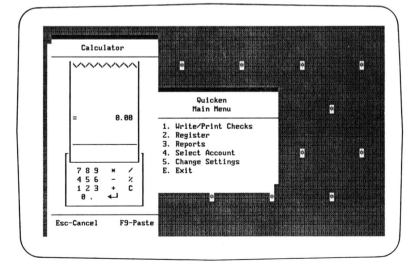

Fig. 1.19.

Ctrl-O accesses the on-line calculator.

Quicken verifies that the Num Lock is on so that you can use the numeric keypad to enter numbers. If the Num Lock key is off, Quicken temporarily toggles the key on while you are using the calculator.

Use the on-line calculator as you do a regular calculator. For example, to add three invoices for $12.87, $232.01, and $49.07 and subtract a $50 credit memo, you press the following keys:

$$12.87 + 232.01 + 49.07 - 50$$

Then, press Enter or the equal sign, =. Quicken performs the math and displays the results as shown in figure 1.20.

Fig. 1.20.

Using the calculator.

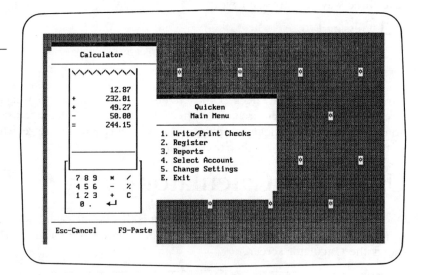

To clear the on-line calculator, press C. To multiply numbers, use the asterisk. To divide numbers, use the slash. If you want to add or subtract a percentage from a number, the on-line calculator also provides a percent key. For example, to add 25% to 200, press 200 + 25% and then Enter. Quicken calculates and displays the result shown in figure 1.21.

You can press Esc to exit the on-line calculator. If you are calculating an amount to enter as a value in a screen field, you also can press F9, and Quicken enters the calculation result into the field that the cursor was on when you pressed Ctrl-O.

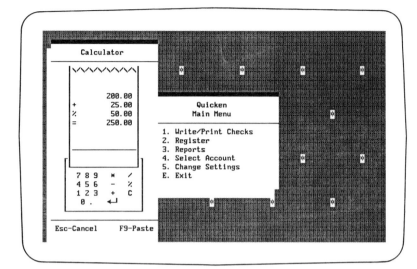

Fig. 1.21.

Using the percent key.

Chapter Summary

This chapter described the steps for readying your business or family for a new computer-based accounting package. The chapter also provided the procedures for installing the software on your computer. The steps to preparing your business or family included deciding which options to use, ordering any check forms you need, learning to use the system, and picking an appropriate conversion date. In this chapter, you also learned some basics of Quicken operations, such as how to use the Help feature, choose menu options, enter and edit data on-screen, and use the on-line calculator.

2

Selecting Accounts and Changing Settings

After installing Quicken, you need to take two additional steps to start using the package: setting up one or more bank accounts and using the Change Settings menu to fine-tune the installation.

Selecting and Setting Up Accounts

You need to set up bank accounts for each checking and savings account. You also need to set up additional accounts to perform record keeping for other assets and liabilities. Other personal assets include investments and your home, and liabilities may include credit card debt, credit lines, and mortgages. Other business assets include accounts receivable, and liabilities include bank loans and accounts payable. To set up accounts and to edit or delete accounts you previously set up, you need to choose **Select Account** from the Main menu.

Setting Up Another Account

To set up a bank account, choose the **Select Account** option from Quicken's Main menu (see fig. 2.1). Quicken then displays the Select Account to Use screen shown in figure 2.2.

Fig. 2.1.

The Quicken
Main menu.

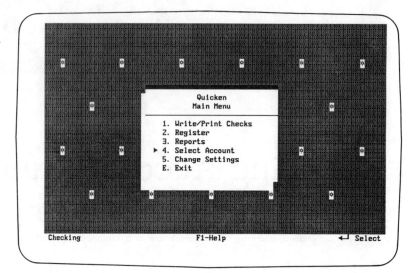

Fig. 2.1.

*The Quicken
Main menu.*

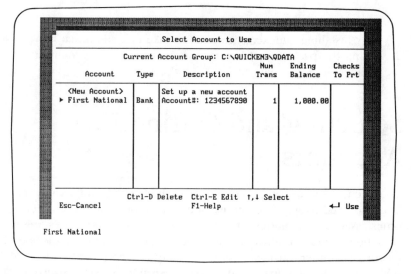

Fig. 2.2.

*The Select
Account to Use
screen.*

To add another account, select the ‹New Account› entry on the Select
Account to Use screen by using the arrow keys. Then, press Enter. The Set
Up New Account screen appears as shown in figure 2.3.

When installing Quicken, you completed the Set Up New Account screen
to define the bank account upon which you write checks.

The account name field can contain up to 15 characters, except brackets
([ ]), a slash (/), or a colon (:).

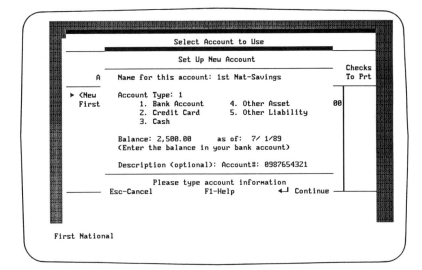

Fig. 2.3.

The Set Up New Account screen.

If you are setting up a personal or business bank account, you specify the account type as 1. If you are setting up an account to keep track of what you spend and what you owe on a credit card, specify the account type as 2. If you are setting up an account to keep track of on-hand cash, such as petty cash or the amount of money in the cash register, specify the account type as 3. If you are setting up an account to keep track of some other asset, such as investments, specify the account type as 4. If you are setting up an account to keep track of some other liability, such as a mortgage loan, specify the account type as 5.

For bank accounts, the balance should correspond with your records as of the conversion date. For cash, the balance should be the total of the actual cash you are holding. For other assets, the balance should be the cost of the asset or its market value. (Businesses usually account for their assets as cost and not market value.) For credit cards and other liabilities, record the balance as the amount owed.

The optional description field provides space for another 21 characters to further describe the account. Figure 2.3 shows a complete Set Up New Account screen that you might use to describe a savings account.

Editing and Deleting Accounts

You also can use the Select Account to Use screen to edit and delete accounts. To edit an account, select the account you want to change and press Ctrl-E. Quicken then displays the Edit Account Information screen that enables you to edit only the account name and description (see fig. 2.4).

Fig. 2.4.

*The Edit
Account
Information
screen.*

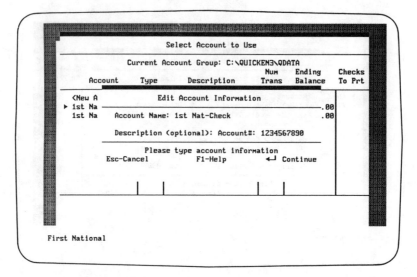

To delete an account previously set up, select the account you want to delete from the Select Account to Use screen and press Ctrl-D. Quicken warns you that the account is about to be removed and asks you to confirm your decision by typing *YES*. Figure 2.5 shows the warning screen. Caution should be used as you may delete an account containing transactions.

Fig. 2.5.

*Quicken warns
you that an
account is
about to be
removed.*

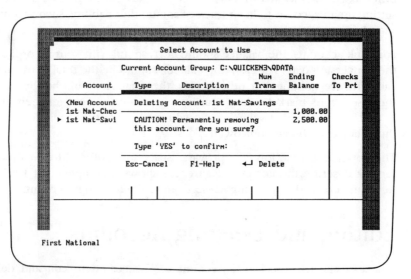

If you decide not to delete the account, press Esc to return to the Select
Account to Use screen.

Changing Settings

The Change Settings menu, shown in figure 2.6, provides a set of six
options that enable you to fine-tune Quicken's installation and operation.

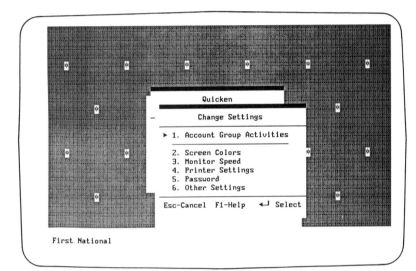

Fig. 2.6.

*The Change
Settings menu.*

Using the Account Group
Activities Menu

The Account Group Activities menu, shown in figure 2.7, provides five
options you can use to manage accounts by grouping similar accounts
together, backing up and restoring accounts, and specifying where a
group of accounts should be stored on disk.

Fig. 2.7.

*The Account
Group Activities
menu.*

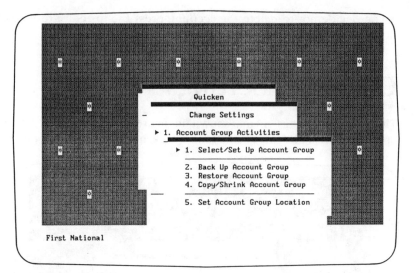

Selecting and Setting Up Account Groups

A feature new to Version 3 of Quicken is its capability to group accounts and then transfer amounts between accounts within the group. For example, when you want to move money from a savings account to a checking account to pay bills, you need to record the transfer in only one account. Quicken knows to record the transfer in the other account as well and does so.

If you are using credit card, asset, and liability accounts, you may make some of the following transfers:

1. Making a credit card payment with a check decreases the checking account balance and decreases your credit card debt. This transfer of cash from a bank account to the credit card company reduces your liability.

2. Making a mortgage payment with a check also decreases the checking account balance and decreases your mortgage principal. This transfer of cash from your bank account to the mortgage company reduces your mortgage balance.

3. Withdrawing money from your savings account to purchase shares in a mutual fund decreases your savings account balance and increases your investment account balance. This transfer moves cash from your savings account to your investment account.

The following rules govern money transfers between accounts:

1. To make transfers between accounts, the accounts must be part of the same account group.

2. All the accounts you want to appear on a balance sheet must be part of the same account group.

Chapter 10 describes the steps for creating personal and business balance sheets. Quicken, unless you direct otherwise, places all the accounts you create in the same group, QDATA.

To set up an account group, choose the first option on the Account Group Activities menu, **Select/Set Up Account Group**. The screen shown in figure 2.8 is displayed.

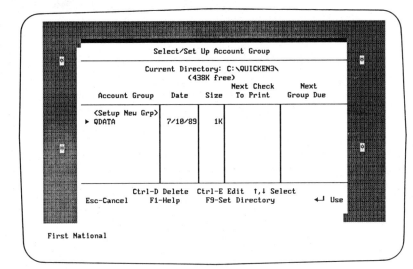

Fig. 2.8.

The Select/Set Up Account Group screen.

Identifying the Current Directory

Quicken displays all the groups within a directory on the Select/Set Up Account screen. Figure 2.8, for example, shows all the groups in the directory C:\QUICKEN3\. To see groups in another directory, press F9. The Set Account Group Location screen is displayed (see fig. 2.9). You can use this screen to specify some other directory to look in for account groups.

Fig. 2.9.

The Set Account Group Location screen.

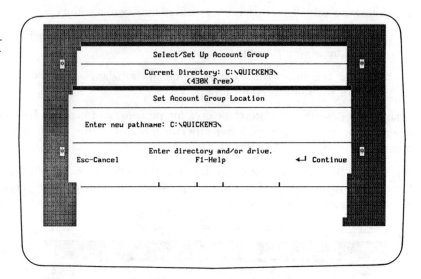

If you are using a hard disk system for Quicken, you probably keep your files in the QUICKEN3 directory on drive C of your hard disk. The installation program specifies that directory for the Quicken program and data files.

If you are using a two floppy disk system for Quicken, you probably keep your data files on the floppy disk in drive B. Quicken leaves the directory specified as B:. If you are using a one floppy disk system (data files are stored on the Quicken program disk in drive A), the directory needs to be specified as A:.

You can change the directory, but whatever you enter into this field needs to be a valid DOS path name. (The drive letter must be valid and followed by a colon.) Directories and subdirectories already must have been created. (The hard disk installation program creates the directory QUICKEN3.) If you use a directory and subdirectory together, they must constitute a valid path. The subdirectory specified, therefore, must be in the directory specified. (For more information on directories, subdirectories, and path names, see your DOS user's manual.)

The current directory also shows the amount of disk space available for data files. Figure 2.8 shows that 438K is free—just under half a megabyte of space is available on the hard disk. Quicken allows you up to 65,353 transactions. The practical limits, however, are much lower than that. (You record transactions in your register. Common transactions include checks, deposits, interest income, and bank service fees.) You probably are not going to generate more than a few hundred transactions each year if you use Quicken at home or more than a few thousand transactions if you use Quicken for a small business.

If you store your bank account data files on a floppy disk, disk space becomes a concern. A 360K, 5.25 inch disk allows space for about 3,000 transactions, and a 720K 2.5 inch disk, allows space for about 6,000 transactions.

Using the Account Group Field

The Account Group field shows the DOS file name of the account groups in the current directory. QDATA is the group Quicken sets up during installation. Other account groups you set up using this screen also appear in this field.

Using the Date Field

The Date field identifies the date the account group was set up. Figure 2.8, for example, shows that the account group, QDATA, was created on 7/10/89. The dates Quicken displays actually are the DOS file dates shown if you use the DIR C:\QUICKEN3 command to list the files in the C:\QUICKEN3 directory.

Using the Size Field

The Size field shows the combined sizes of the files that store information for an account group. In figure 2.8, QDATA's size is only 1K, because no transactions have been entered into the account.

Using the Next Check To Print Field

Chapter 3 describes how to use the Write Checks screen to enter information for the checks you want to print. If you already have entered information onto this screen, the earliest date you entered for a check to be printed would appear in the Next Check To Print field. This field enables you to keep track of the checks you need to print.

Using the Next Group Due Field

Quicken enables you to set up groups of checks that you can enter simultaneously using the Write Checks screen and a function key option. If you are using transaction groups, described in Chapters 4 and 6, the date of the next transaction group would appear in the Next Group Due field. See the discussions of the **Set Up Transaction Group** and **Execute Transaction Group** function-key options in Chapters 4 and 6 for more information on what transaction groups are and how they work.

Adding, Editing, and Deleting Account Groups

To add another account group, select the ‹Setup New Group› option and press Enter. Quicken displays the Create An Account Group screen on which you enter the group name that Quicken uses for the file name. (You must use a valid DOS file name.) You also need to tell Quicken whether you want to use either or both of the predefined home or personal category lists and the directory location for the group. Figure 2.10 shows the Create An Account Group screen completed to define a separate group for business accounts.

Fig. 2.10.

The Create An Account Group screen.

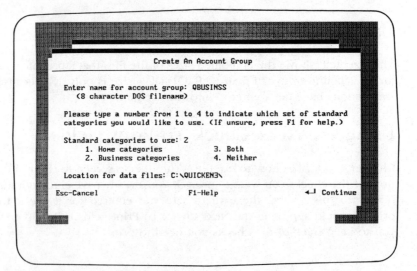

If you are setting up a new group, you also need to decide whether or not you want to use categories. Using Quicken's predefined categories is easier than creating your own. You can use one of the standard category lists by typing *1* if you are using Quicken at home or *2* if you are using Quicken for a business. If you want to use Quicken for home and business accounts, type *3*. If you do not want to use Quicken's standard categories, type *4*.

CPA Tip: If you are going to use Quicken for personal and business accounts, segregate your business record keeping from your personal record keeping. The best approach is to set up separate account groups: one for your business and another for your personal use. This approach makes generating balance sheets easier.

You also can specify the disk and directory location. The default location for an account group is C:\QUICKEN3, but you can specify a valid disk and path name with the name for the account group. Figure 2.11 shows the Select/Set Up Account Group screen with the new account group, QBUSINSS.

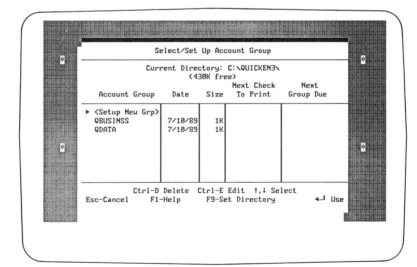

Fig. 2.11.

The Select/Set Up Account Group screen showing the new group, QBUSINSS.

To edit an account group, select the group you want to modify and press Ctrl-E. Quicken displays the Rename An Account Group screen, shown in figure 2.12, that enables you to modify the name used for a group.

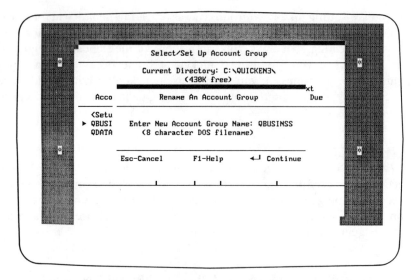

Fig. 2.12.

The Rename An Account Group screen.

To delete an account group, select the group and press Ctrl-D. Quicken displays the Deleting Account Group screen shown in figure 2.13. To delete an account, type *YES* and press Enter. To cancel the delete operation, press Esc.

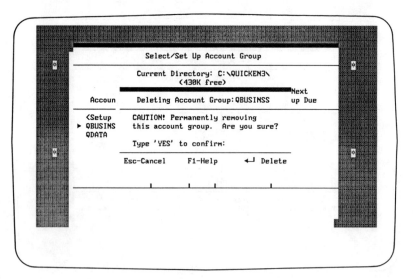

Fig. 2.13.

The Deleting Account Group screen.

Working with Multiple Groups

If you want to create and use additional groups, you first need to tell Quicken which group you are working with. On the Select/Set Up Account Group screen, mark the account group you want to use and press Enter.

You also need to set up accounts for any new groups you create. When you first select a new group on the Select/Set Up Account Group screen, Quicken prompts you for data to set up one account with the Select Account to Use and Setup New Account screens, shown earlier as figures 2.2 and 2.3. You can enter one or more accounts following the steps described earlier in the section, "Selecting and Setting Up Accounts."

Backing Up and Restoring Account Groups

The **Back Up Account Group** and **Restore Account Group** options on the Account Group Activities menu work together to protect your data. Use backup procedures to copy your accounting information in case your original files are lost or damaged. You can use restore procedures to recover your accounting information if the original files become lost or damaged.

Backing Up An Account Group

The **Back Up Account Group** option prompts you to insert the backup disk in the appropriate drive and then displays the screen shown in figure 2.14. This screen is similar to the Select/Set Up Account Group screen —only the title is different. (If you need a field-by-field description of this screen, see "Selecting and Setting Up Account Groups" earlier in this chapter.)

The steps for backing up your account groups are essentially the same whether you are using a hard disk or floppy system. To select an account group to back up, move the selection triangle so that it is to the left of the account group you want to back up and press Enter. Quicken copies the selected account group to the backup disk.

If the account group you are trying to back up does not fit on the disk, an error message alerts you that the disk is full and you should press Esc to cancel. Quicken then displays the warning message Account not backed up. When you successfully back up a bank account, Quicken displays the message Account Group backed up successfully.

Fig. 2.14.

The Select Account Group to Back Up screen.

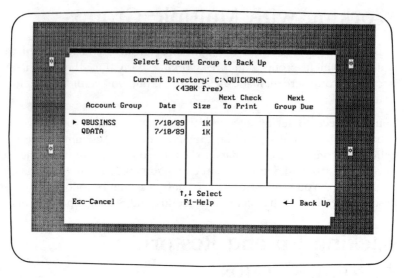

You need to make two important decisions about backing up. First, you must decide how often you need to back up. Opinions vary regarding how frequent is frequent enough. You generally should back up your data files after completing any session in which you enter or change accounting data. For example, when you finish installing the software and entering your first set of account transactions, you should back up your files. Most people back up their account records daily, weekly, or monthly.

After you become familiar with restoring account group procedures and have worked with Quicken for a while, you can better estimate how often you need to back up your account groups. If you discover that backing up your files requires as much effort as re-creating six months of record-keeping, for example, you may decide to back up your accounting files only every six months.

Second, you need to decide how many old backup copies you should keep. Usually, two to three copies are adequate. (This rule of thumb is called the grandfather, father, and son scheme.) Suppose that you back up your account groups every day. On Thursday, someone—no one admits it—accidentally deletes the group. If you keep two old backup copies in addition to the most recent backup copy, you have backups from Wednesday, Tuesday, and Monday. If the Wednesday copy is damaged (an unlikely, but possible situation), you still have the Tuesday and Monday copies to restore. The more recent a backup copy, the easier data is to recover, but using an old backup copy is easier than recovering an account group without a backup copy.

Store the backup copies of your account group in a safe place. Do not keep all the backup copies in the same location, if possible. If you experience a fire or if someone burglarizes your business or house, you may lose all your copies—no matter how many backups you keep. Store at least one copy at an off-site location. If you are using Quicken at home, perhaps you can keep a backup copy in your desk at work; if you are using Quicken for a small business, keep a backup copy at home.

Restoring the Backed-Up Files

Eventually, someone accidentally will delete or destroy an account group. Your computer may malfunction; someone may spill the contents of the pencil sharpener or a cup of coffee on the floppy disk containing the Quicken data files. To retrieve the data you copied with the **Back Up Account Group** option, you essentially step through the same process in reverse. Select the **Restore Account Group** option. Quicken prompts you to insert the backup disk in drive A and then displays the Select Account Group to Restore screen (see fig. 2.15). This screen mirrors the Select Account Group to Back Up screen. Select the account group you want to restore from your backup disk and press Enter.

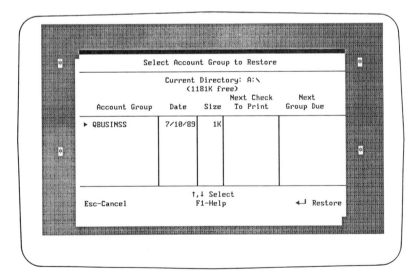

Fig. 2.15.

The Select Account Group to Restore screen.

Because you cannot restore the currently selected account group, you need to select another group. If you do try to restore the currently selected group, the message shown in figure 2.16 alerts you to this error.

Fig. 2.16.

*Quicken alerts
you if you
attempt to
restore the
currently
selected group.*

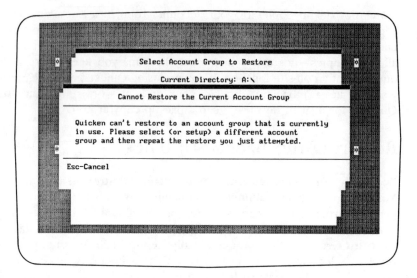

If you originally set up only one group, you need to set up a second, dummy account group that you can select as the current group before you use the restore option.

Before Quicken restores the account group files from your backup disk, the program warns you that an existing account is about to be overwritten.

This message gives you a last chance to stop before the actual file restoration. If you want to abort the restore operation, press Esc. If you want to continue the restore operation, press Enter. When the restore operation finishes, Quicken displays the message, Account Group restored successfully.

You can press Enter to return to the Select Account Group to Restore screen. To return to the Account Group Activities menu, press Esc.

After you restore all your data files, you may notice a small problem. If you have worked with the files since the last backup, the restored versions differ from the damaged files. The second part of recovering from damaged or destroyed data files involves re-entering all the account transactions you entered since the time you backed up. Back up the account group before proceeding further.

CPA Tip: If some disaster befalls data files that you didn't back up, you essentially must go through each of the steps described in Chapters 1, 2, and 7. You need to reinstall the software (described in Chapter 1), fine-tune Quicken's operation using the Change Settings options (described later in this chapter), and redefine any categories that you want to use (described in Chapter 7). After you complete the recovery, back up your files before proceeding further.

Using the Copy/Shrink Account Group Option

The fourth option on the Account Group Activities menu is **Copy/Shrink Account Group**. You must use the **Select/Set Up Account Group** option to select an account before copying it. If you do not, Quicken displays a warning message.

After you select the **Copy/Shrink Account Group** option, Quicken displays the Copy Account Group screen shown in figure 2.17.

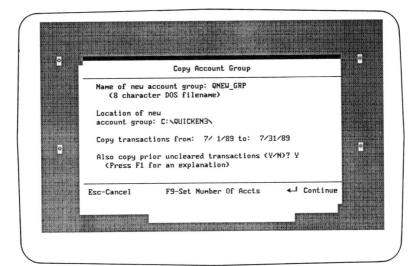

Fig. 2.17.

The Copy Account Group screen.

You fill in four fields to complete the Copy Account Group screen. These four fields ask for the name of the new account group, the location of the new account group, the copy transactions from and to dates, and if you also want to copy prior uncleared transactions.

Naming a New Account Group

The name field enables you to specify the DOS file name of the new account group. The name must be a valid DOS file name. (If you are unsure of DOS file-naming conventions, see your DOS user's manual.)

Specifying the Location of a New Account Group

The Location of new account group field enables you to specify a different directory in which the copied account group is stored. The only rule is that the disk and directory you specify must be a valid path name.

Using the Copy Transactions From and To Date Fields

In these fields, you type the ranges of dates for which you want transactions copied. If you want no transactions copied, set the date range as one that includes no transactions—such as November 1, 1950 to November 1, 1950.

Using the Also Copy Prior Uncleared Transactions Field

Prior uncleared transactions are transactions—mainly checks and deposits—that occurred before the copy from date but have not yet been recorded by the bank. Because you need these prior uncleared transactions to reconcile your bank account, press Y for yes if you are going to reconcile your bank account and N for no if you are not going to reconcile your bank account.

CPA Tip: Reconcile your bank account every time you receive a bank statement. Doing so provides a way of catching and correcting mistakes you and your bank may make in your account.

After you completely fill the fields with the appropriate information, press Enter. Quicken makes a copy of the account group in the specified location with the specified name.

Quicken, as a default, limits the number of accounts in the new copied group to 64. Pressing F9 accesses the Set Maximum Accounts In Group screen that enables you to increase the limit to as many as 255 accounts. Quicken warns you if you try to set the number of accounts greater than 255. Figure 2.18 shows the Set Maximum Accounts In Group screen.

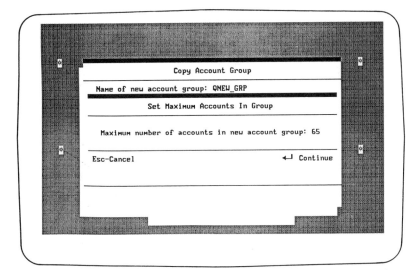

Fig. 2.18.

The Set Maximum Accounts In Group screen.

Setting the Account Group Location

The **Set Account Group Location** option on the Account Group Activities menu accesses the Set Account Group Location screen (shown in figure 2.9) and enables you to direct where Quicken looks for account groups. You enter the disk and directory that describes a valid path name that you want Quicken to use to look for account groups.

Using the Other Change Settings Options

The Change Settings menu has five more options other than **Account Group Activities**: **Screen Colors**, **Monitor Speed**, **Printer Settings**, **Password**, and **Other Settings**. (The Change Settings menu is shown in figure 2.6.) Because the easiest time to change settings is when you begin using Quicken, these options also are described here.

Changing Screen Colors

Selecting the **Screen Colors** option displays the Change Color Scheme screen that gives you five color sets to choose from, as shown in figure 2.19.

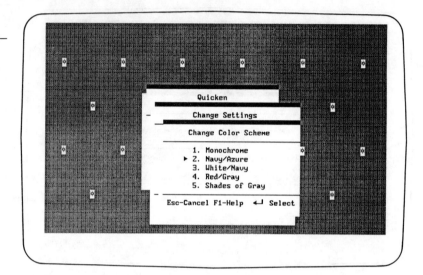

The default color scheme for a monochrome monitor is **Monochrome**, but you also should try **Shades of Gray** to see which works best for you. If you have a monochrome monitor and the screen display is unclear, you probably have the monitor type defined as color.

The default color scheme for a color monitor is **Navy/Azure**, but you should try each of the color schemes to see which works best. If you are color blind, for example, you may find that one of the other color schemes is easier to see.

Changing Screen Update Speed

The **Monitor Speed** option on the Change Settings menu enables you to choose between slow and fast for the screen update speed. Quicken initially assumes that you want the fast option. If Quicken ascertains that your monitor update speed should be fast, the program will not let you change the setting to slow.

Unfortunately, your monitor may not be able to handle the fast speed setting. You may see little flecks and patches—sometimes called snow—on-screen. If you notice snow on your monitor, set the monitor speed to slow.

Adjusting Printer Settings

The Change Printer Settings submenu, shown in figure 2.20, provides three options: **Check Printer Settings**, **Report Printer Settings**, and **Alternate Printer Settings**. Each of the three options is the same—except for the titles.

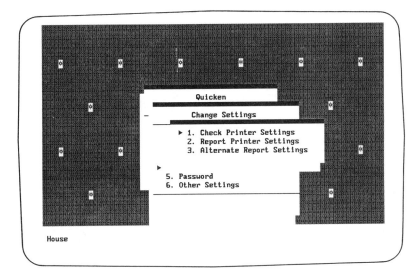

Fig. 2.20.

The Change Printer Settings submenu.

If you select any of the three options, Quicken displays the Printer List screen from which you choose your printer (see fig. 2.21). To choose a printer from the list, highlight your choice by using the up- and down-arrow keys. After you select the correct printer, press Enter. Quicken displays the Check Printer Settings screen, shown in figure 2.22. If you cannot find your printer on the list, select **Unlisted Printer**.

If you selected a printer from the printer list, Quicken correctly fills out the Printer Settings screen. If you cannot find your printer on the list and selected the undefined printer option, however, you need to use the Printer Settings screen to describe your printer.

Fig. 2.21.

The Printer List screen.

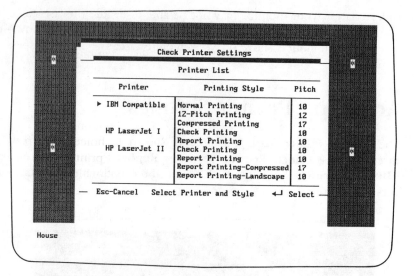

Fig. 2.22.

The Check Printer Settings screen.

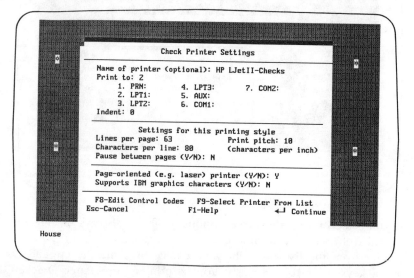

On this screen, you use the following eight fields to describe your printer: Name, Print to, Indent, Lines per page, Printer Pitch, Characters per line, Pause between pages, and Control Codes.

Naming the Printer

The printer name field is optional, but use this field to describe a printer in more detail. Figure 2.22, for example, shows HP LJetII-Checks.

Choosing a Communications Port

The Print to field tells Quicken which communications port should be used to send checks and reports to the printer. The PRN, LPT1, LPT2, and LPT3 options refer to parallel ports. The AUX, COM1, and COM2 options refer to serial ports.

You probably should select LPT1 as the Print to option, but check with your computer and printer manuals. If you have a choice, choose a parallel port, because parallel connections mean that the printer and computer can talk to each other at the same time—in parallel, which usually results in faster communication.

When you choose a serial port, the computer can send information to the printer only when the printer is not sending information back to the computer. The printer can only send information to the computer when the computer is not sending information back to the printer. With a serial port, your computer and printer take turns communicating with each other.

Indenting

In the Indent field, you tell Quicken how many characters it should move in from the left margin of the form to begin printing. Each time Quicken begins printing a line, the program tabs this many characters to the right. Enter a number from 0 to 80, but be careful that you do not enter a number so large that Quicken does not have room to print. For laser printers, you can use an indent setting equal to 0. For other impact printers, start with an indent setting equal to 0, but you may need to increase this setting if Quicken starts printing too far on the left of your paper. (If Quicken prints off the page on the right of the paper, reduce your indent setting.)

Using the Lines Per Page Field

You need to tell Quicken how many lines you want printed on a page. Quicken assumes that 6 lines equal an inch. If you are using 11-inch paper, therefore, set this value to 66. If you are using 14-inch paper, set this value to 84.

To tell if the Lines per page setting is correct, compare where Quicken starts printing on successive pages. If printing does not start at the same distance from the top of the page, you need to adjust the Lines per page setting. The setting is too large if Quicken starts printing lower on the second page than on the first. Your setting is too small if Quicken starts printing higher on the second page than on the first.

Setting Print Pitch

The Print pitch field specifies how many characters your printer prints in an inch. Typical pitch, or characters per inch, settings are 10, 12, and 15. Check your printer manual to determine your printer's pitch. You also can use a ruler to measure the number of characters including blank spaces printed on an example of the printer's output.

Using the Characters Per Line Field

The Characters per line field shows how many characters fit on a line. This setting usually equals 80 if your pitch, or characters per inch, setting is 10. The characters per line usually equals 96 if your pitch setting is 12. For condensed print, the pitch usually is set to 17 characters per inch.

Pausing between Pages

The Pause between pages field, which you set to Y for yes and N for no, tells Quicken whether it should stop after printing a full page so that you can insert a new piece of paper or adjust the printer. If you need to insert a new sheet of paper every time Quicken completes printing a full page, set the toggle to Y.

Using a Page-Oriented Printer

Printers that use individual sheets of paper are, from Quicken's perspective, page-oriented. The most common page-oriented printer is a laser printer. Because Quicken needs to know if your printer is page-oriented, you need to enter *Y* for yes and *N* for no.

Supporting IBM Graphics Characters

If available on your printer, Quicken uses IBM graphics characters in headings on reports. You need to inform Quicken about the availability of IBM graphics characters by entering *Y* for yes and *N* for no in the appropriate field.

Entering Control Codes

Control codes are special sequences of letters, numbers, and other keyboard characters that cause your printers to perform in a specific manner or style (such as using a condensed pitch). To use printer control codes— sometimes called printer setup strings or escape sequences in printer user's manuals—press F8.

The screen shown in figure 2.23 appears. Use this screen to send a control code to the printer before you print a report, each time Quicken starts printing a new page, after you print a report, and if you have a laser printer and want to insert checks sideways.

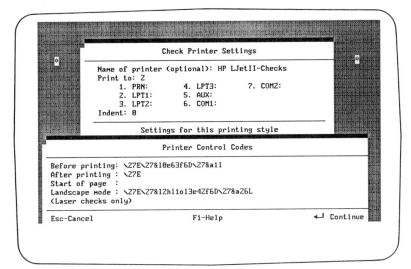

Fig. 2.23.

The Printer Control Codes screen

Figure 2.23 shows printer control codes that begin with \27. Your printer manual shows the control codes appropriate for your printer.

Using Passwords

Selecting the **Password** option from the Change Settings menu displays the menu shown in figure 2.24. You can use two types of passwords in Quicken: main and transaction date passwords.

The main password provides access to an account group. If you want each account group to have a password, you need to set up a password for each group. If you select the **Main Password** option, Quicken displays the Set Up Password screen shown in figure 2.25.

Fig. 2.24.

The Password menu.

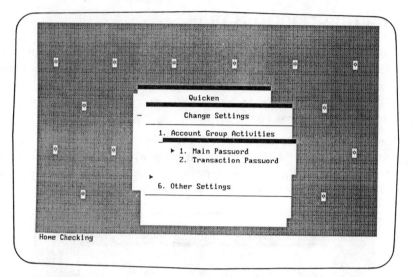

Fig. 2.25.

The Set Up Password screen.

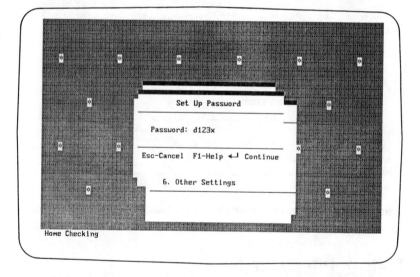

To define a main password, type the combination of letters and numbers you want to use as a password. You can use up to sixteen characters. After setting the password, Quicken will ask you for the password before letting you view or modify transactions in any of the accounts within the group. Figure 2.25, for example, shows that the main password is set to d123x. The next time you try to access the Write Checks, Register, or Reports screen for the account group with the password d123x, Quicken requires that you enter the password. Figure 2.26 shows the screen on which you type the password. As an additional precaution, Quicken does not display the password you type. Quicken does not distinguish between the use of upper- and lowercase letters in establishing or using passwords.

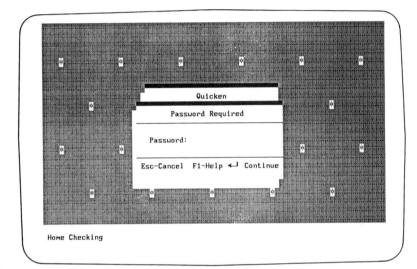

Fig. 2.26.

Entering the main password.

If you want to change or remove the password, reselect the **Main Password** option. Quicken displays the Change Password screen shown in figure 2.27. Type the old and new passwords and press Enter. You now can use the new password. If you no longer want to use passwords, leave the New Password field blank as shown in figure 2.27.

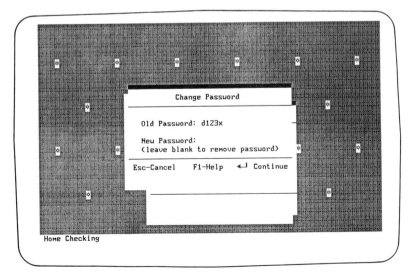

Fig. 2.27.

The Change Password screen.

You can require transaction date passwords to make changes to accounts before a certain date. These passwords are useful if you want to restrict or limit transactions recorded or modified for prior months. To define a transaction password, select the **Transaction Password** option. The screen shown in figure 2.28 is displayed.

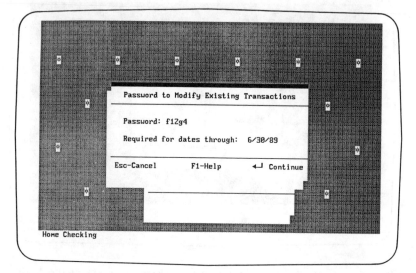

Fig. 2.28.

The Password to Modify Existing Transactions screen.

On this screen, you enter the password and the date through which the transaction password is required. Figure 2.28 shows the password, f12g4, required for entering or modifying transactions dated through 6/30/89. If you want to record a transaction dated 6/30/89, Quicken requires that the transaction password be entered on the screen shown in figure 2.29.

Quicken does not display the password as you type it. If you want to change a transaction password, reselect the Transaction Password menu and type the old and new passwords. You also can specify a new transaction date to use (see fig. 2.30).

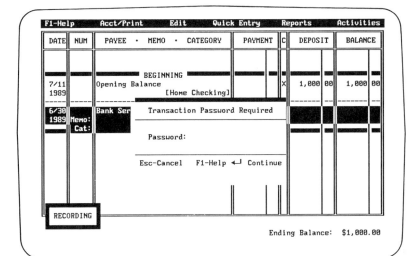

Fig. 2.29.

Entering the transaction password.

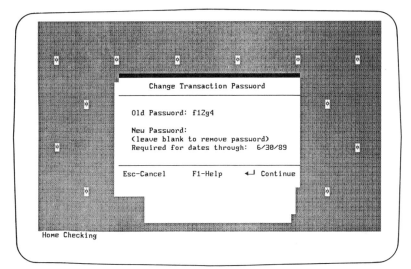

Fig. 2.30.

The Change Transaction Password screen.

CPA Tip: You should consider the following three conventions when using passwords:

1. Make sure that you do not lose your password. If you lose your password, you lose your data. Record your password in a safe place in case you need to refer to a written record.

2. If you are worried about someone accessing or modifying your account group information and want to use passwords to prevent this, use nonsensical passwords. Passwords that make no sense are more difficult to guess.

3. Be sure that you do not use some seemingly clever password scheme such as using month names or colors as passwords. If you set the main password as blue, after someone knows the main password, it is not going to take that person long to figure out the transaction password even if it is chartreuse or mauve.

Fine-Tuning with Other Settings

The Other Settings screen, shown in figure 2.31, enables you to tinker with twelve other settings. You can fine-tune Quicken to operate in the fashion you find most helpful. The settings on this screen are described in the following sections.

Fig. 2.31.

*The Other
Settings screen.*

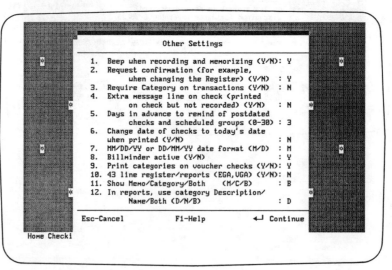

Using the Beep When Recording and Memorizing Switch

With the beep switch, you can turn off the beep noise that Quicken makes when the program records and memorizes transactions. You may want to consider this option if you enter a lot of transactions. You also use this switch to turn on the beep noise if you previously have turned the beep off. Press N if you want to turn off the beep noise; press Y if you want to turn on the beep noise.

Using the Request Confirmation Switch

Use the Request confirmation switch to turn off the pop-up confirmation messages that display to give you a second chance before executing many Quicken operations. Because the confirmation messages may save you from accidentally doing something you would rather not do, you probably want to set this switch to Y. To turn off the confirmation messages, set this switch to N.

Using the Require Category on Transactions Switch

The Require Category on transactions switch causes a reminder message to appear if you enter a transaction without a valid category. You do not have to use categories if this switch is set to Y, but you have to confirm that you do not want to use a category. If you plan to use categories, you should set this switch to Y for yes. (Chapter 7, "Using Categories and Classes," describes in detail the categories feature.)

Using the Extra Message Line on Check Switch

The Extra message line on check switch adds another line before the address box on your checks. This line increases the amount of information you can use to describe a check. Because the extra message line does not show through the window in the Quicken envelopes, do not use this line as an extra address line. Use the message line to annotate or describe a check further, such as with the invoice or account number you are paying. If you want to print an extra message line, press Y; if you do not want an extra message line, press N.

If you set the switch to Yes, another field appears on the Write Checks screen. This optional extra message field is located above the signature field and to the right of the first address line.

Selecting the Days in Advance for Postdated Check Reminders

The Days in advance to remind of postdated checks and scheduled groups setting specifies the number of days in advance that Quicken reminds you of postdated checks and scheduled transaction groups. The number of days can be from 0 to 30. Quicken reminds hard disk users slightly differently than floppy disk users. Because of this difference, the rules for specifying the days in advance setting also differ.

Hard disk users are reminded of postdated checks and scheduled transaction groups every time they turn on the computer. If you are a hard disk user, therefore, you should set the days in advance to one less than the number of days between times you turn on your computer. For example, if you use your computer every other day, the difference in days between use is two. One number less than two is one. Therefore, you should set the days in advance as one. Whenever you turn on your computer, you are reminded of the bills that should be paid that day and the bills that can be paid the next day, but that need to be paid today because you will not use your computer tomorrow.

Floppy disk users follow a slightly different procedure. Floppy disk users are reminded of postdated checks and scheduled transaction groups on the Quicken Main menu. Quicken reminds floppy disk users, therefore, only when the Quicken program is started. If you are a floppy disk user, set the days in advance field to one day less than the number of days between times you use Quicken. If you use Quicken on a weekly basis, for example, every Saturday morning, set the days in advance field to 6. You always are reminded every Saturday morning of the bills to be paid for the next six days.

Changing the Date of Checks to Current Date When Printed

When the Change date of checks to today's date when printed field is set to Y, Quicken prints checks with the check date shown as the current system date. When the check date you entered is different than the check printing date, the check's date is changed.

Selecting the Date Format

The date format field specifies whether the date format used in Quicken should be month/day/year or day/month/year. If you want the date for the first day of June 1989 to appear as 6/1/89, for example, press M for month first. If you want the date for the first day of June 1989 to appear as 1/6/89, press D for day first.

Using the Billminder Active Switch

The Billminder active field enables you to determine whether or not Quicken reminds you of postdated checks and transaction groups. If you want to use the Billminder feature, set this switch to Y for yes.

Printing Categories on Voucher Checks

The Print categories on voucher checks switch determines whether or not category information is printed on the voucher portion, or remittance advice, of a check. (This field obviously does not apply unless your checks have voucher stubs.) You do not need the category field information printed on the voucher stub unless someone you pay a check to needs to know which income or expense categories the check affects. If you decide not to use the category fields to record categories and instead use them for information such as the invoices a check pays, you can have this information printed on the voucher stub.

Using the 43-Line Register

If your computer uses an Enhanced Graphics Adapter (EGA) monitor and card, you can set the 43 line register/reports field to Y for yes, which doubles—from six to twelve—the number of lines Quicken displays in the register. If you have an EGA monitor, try the option. You should find that having more register information on-screen is helpful. If the compressed version of the register strains your eyes, set the toggle back to N.

Displaying Information in the Register

The Show Memo/Category/Both field determines which information appears on the memo line of the check register when the transaction is not selected. You have three choices: M designates that only the memo should appear; C designates that only the category should appear; B designates that both the memo and category should appear. Because you do not have enough room to fully display the memo and category fields, if you select B, Quicken abbreviates the two fields.

Displaying Information in Reports

The `In reports, use category Description/Name/Both` field determines whether the category name, category description, or both appear on reports. You have three choices: D designates that only the description appears; N designates that only the name appears; B designates that both the name and description appear. D is the default setting and the one you probably want to use.

Chapter Summary

This chapter described the two additional steps you may need to take after you install Quicken. You learned how to set up one or more accounts and account groups and how to use the Change Settings menu to fine-tune the installation.

3

Writing and Printing Checks

With Quicken's check printing feature, you can write checks and pay bills faster and more efficiently than you ever thought possible. You can pay bills faster because Quicken provides a collection of short-cuts and timesaving techniques that automate and speed check writing and bill paying. You can pay bills more efficiently because Quicken helps you keep track of the bills coming due and provides categories with which you can classify the ways you are spending your money.

This chapter describes the basics of using the **Write/Print Checks** option on the Main menu. Included in this chapter are discussions of the following topics:

- ❏ The geography of the Write Checks screen
- ❏ Completing the Write Checks screen
- ❏ Recording checks
- ❏ Reviewing and editing checks
- ❏ Using the Acct/Print menu options

The Write Checks Screen

You use the Write Checks screen, shown in figure 3.1, to collect the information you use to print check forms. After collecting the information, Quicken records the check in the check register. You then can print the check. To access the Write Checks screen, select the **Write/Print Checks** option from Quicken's Main menu. The fields you fill in to complete the Write Checks screen are described next.

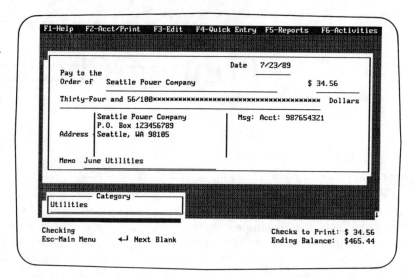

Reviewing the Geography of the Write Checks Screen

The Write Checks screen can be broken into three parts: the menu bar at the top of the screen, the check form, and the information bar at the bottom of the screen.

The menu bar shows the function keys you use from the Write Checks screen to access menus. F2 accesses the Acct/Print Checks menu and is described later in this chapter. F3, F4, and F6 access the Edit, Quick Entry, and Activities menus described in Chapter 4. F5 accesses the Reports menu described in Chapter 11.

The second part of the screen is the actual check form you complete to have your checks printed. The steps for completing the form are described in the next section, "Completing the Write Checks Screen."

The third part of the Write Checks screen is the information bar at the bottom of the screen. This bar shows several pieces of information, including the account you currently are using, descriptions of what the Esc and Enter keys do, the checks to print total, and the ending balance in the account. Figure 3.1 shows the bank account as Checking, the Checks to Print total as $34.56, and the ending balance as $465.44.

Completing the Write Checks Screen

Completing the Write Checks screen involves filling up to seven fields: date, payee, amount, address, message, memo, and category. You already know most of the process because the steps for completing the Write Checks screen parallel those for manually writing a check. The only real difference is that Quicken's Write Checks screen makes the process easier. The fields you fill to complete the Write Checks screen are described below.

Using the Date Field

The Date field is the check date in a month/day/year format. The first time you use Quicken, the program fills the Date field with the system date. After you write your first check using the Write Checks screen, Quicken fills the Date field with the last date used. To edit the date, you have two choices. First, you can move the cursor to the part of the date—month, day, or year—you want to change and type over what is already on-screen. Second, you can use the + and − keys to change the date one day at a time. Each time you press the + key, Quicken moves the date ahead one day. Each time you press the − key, Quicken moves the date back one day. When you finish editing the date, press Enter, and Quicken moves the cursor to the payee field.

CPA Tip: Businesses and individuals often receive discounts for paying bills early. Consider early payment in setting the check date. Not taking early payment discounts is an extremely expensive way to borrow money from the vendor. Suppose that a vendor normally requires payment within 30 days but allows a two percent discount for payments received within 10 days. If you pay within 30 rather than 10 days, you pay the vendor a two percent interest charge for paying 20 days later. Because one year contains roughly 18 20-day periods, the two percent for 20 days equals approximately 36 percent annually.

Although you may need to borrow this money, you probably can find a much cheaper lender. As a rough rule of thumb, if a vendor gives you a one percent discount for paying 20 days early, you are borrowing money from him at about 18 percent annual interest if you do not pay early and take the discount. A three percent discount works out to a whopping 54 percent per year.

Using the Pay to the Order of Field

The Pay to the Order of field is where you enter the name of the person or business, called the payee, that the check pays. Type in the field the name you want to appear on the check. Because you have space for up to 40 characters, you should not have any problem fitting in the payee's name. In fact, you should have room to enter *and* and *or* payees. (An *and* payee, for example, is Vader Ryderwood and Russell Dardenelle. Both Vader and Russell must endorse such a check to cash it. An *or* payee is entered as "Vader Ryderwood or Russell Dardenelle" and requires Vader or Russell to endorse the check to cash it.) After you complete the payee field, press Enter, and the cursor moves to the amount field.

Using the Amount Field

The amount field shows the amount of the check. You can use up to 10 characters to input the amount. Quicken enables you to enter only numbers, commas, and periods in the amount field. Quicken enters commas if you do not and if room is available for them. The largest value you can enter in the amount field is 9999999.99. Because this number is a little hard to read without commas (the number is $9,999,999.99), you probably want to use commas. If you use some of the 10 characters for commas, the largest value you can enter is 999,999.99.

When you complete the amount field and press Enter, Quicken writes out the amount on the next line of the check—just as you do when writing a check manually. To save space, Quicken may abbreviate Hundred as Hndrd, Thousand as Thsnd, and Million as Mill.

Using the Address Field

The optional Address field provides five, 30-character lines. If you use envelopes with windows and enter the payee's address in this field, the address shows in the envelope window. You save time that otherwise is spent addressing envelopes.

Assuming that you are using the Address field, you need to type the payee's name on the first line. Quicken provides a shortcut for you. If you type ′ (apostrophe) or ″ (double quotation mark), Quicken copies the name from the Pay to the Order of field. (Because the Pay to the Order of field has space for 40 characters and the address lines have only 30 characters, this shortcut may cut off up to the last nine characters of the payee's name.)

Using the Message Field

If you set the extra message line switch to yes, the cursor moves to the extra message line field after you complete the first address line. (The extra message line switch is on the Change Settings menu under the **Other Settings** option and is described in Chapter 2.) This field gives you another 24 characters for additional information you want printed on the check, such as an account number for a credit card or a loan number for a mortgage. Because this information does not show through an envelope window, do not use the line for address information.

Using the Memo Field

Memo is the sixth field you fill on the Write Checks screen. Using the Memo field is optional, but can be useful in several ways. You can use this field as you use the extra message line to further describe the reasons for a check, such as "May rent," or you can use the line to tell the payee your account number or loan number.

Using the Category Field

You use the Category field to describe the category into which a check falls, such as utilities expense, interest expense, or entertainment. You also can use the Category field to describe the class into which a check falls. (Categories and classes are described in Chapter 7.)

Quicken provides a listing of the most typical categories for home or business use to enable you to quickly categorize your most frequent transactions. You access the predefined list by pressing Ctrl-C.

To use the Category field to describe a category, enter the name you used to define the category. Figure 3.1 shows the completed Write Checks screen with the Category field filled with the name, Utilities. To use subcategories, enter the category name followed by a colon followed by the subcategory name. Figure 3.2 shows the Category field filled with the category-subcategory combination, Utilities: Electric.

To use classes, enter a slash followed by the class name. You can use classes with or without categories. Figure 3.3 shows the class name North used to further define the check to Seattle Power.

Fig. 3.2.

Separate subcategories from categories with a colon.

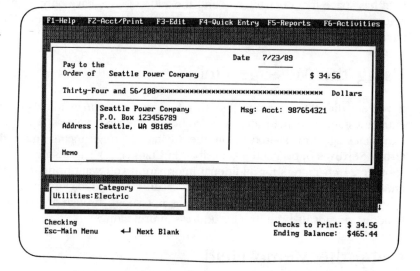

Fig. 3.3.

Classes are designated with a slash and can follow categories.

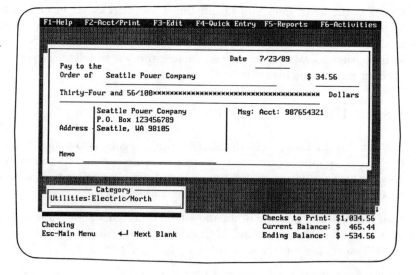

You even can use subclasses by following the class name with a colon and a subclass name. Figure 3.4 shows the subclass name NW.

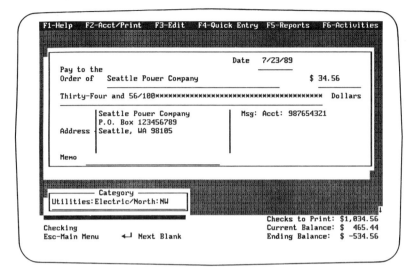

Fig. 3.4.

Subclasses can be used to further define classes.

If you enter a category that Quicken does not recognize because you have not used the category before, Quicken alerts you that the category cannot be found and provides you with the two options shown in figure 3.5.

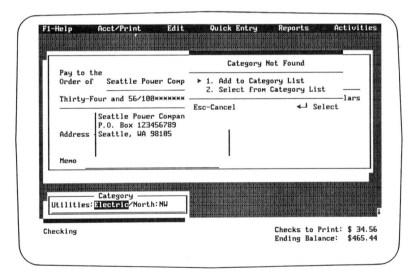

Fig. 3.5.

The Category Not Found screen.

The first option enables you to add the new category to the Category List. If you select this option, another screen appears on which you enter the income, expense, or subcategory code, and an optional description (see fig. 3.6).

Fig. 3.6.

The Set Up Category screen.

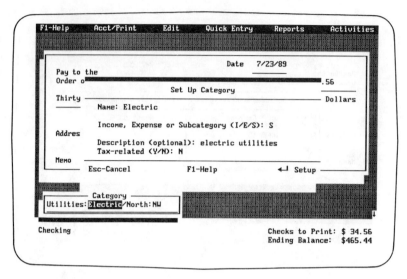

The second option in figure 3.5 enables you to select an already used category from the list as shown in figure 3.7.

Fig. 3.7.

The Category and Transfer List screen.

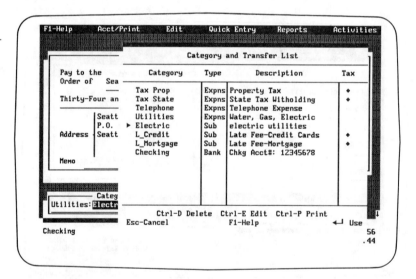

If you use the **Select from Category List** option, Quicken finds the category that most closely matches what you entered in the Category field—a handy feature if you are not sure how to spell a category name correctly.

If you use a class that Quicken does not recognize because you have not used the class before, Quicken alerts you and provides you with the two options shown in figure 3.8.

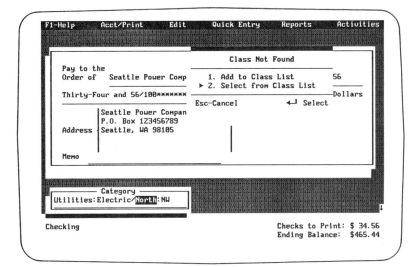

Fig. 3.8.

The Class Not Found screen.

The first option enables you to add the new class to the Class List. If you select this option, another screen appears on which you enter the class description (see fig. 3.9).

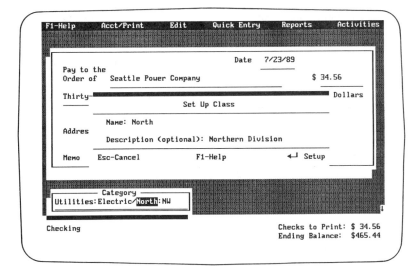

Fig. 3.9.

The Set Up Class screen.

The second option enables you to select an already used class from the list shown in figure 3.10.

Fig. 3.10.

The Class List screen.

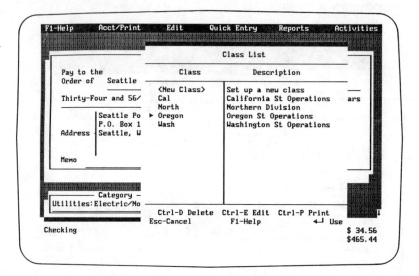

If you are having problems with the memo field—for example, if Quicken keeps expecting you to use a category but you decided you did not want to use categories—you probably set the required categories flag on the Change Settings menu's **Other Settings** option to Yes. If you do not require categories, you need to return to the Change Settings menu's **Other Settings** option and change the required categories setting to No. (Chapter 2 describes each of the options on the Change Settings menu.)

Using the Category Field To Record Transfers

You also can use the Category field to record transfers from one account to another. Suppose that you are writing a check for deposit to your savings account in another bank. Obviously, the check is not an expense—you are transferring funds from one account to another. You can identify such transfers by entering the account name in brackets in the Category field as shown in figure 3.11.

If you record a transfer, Quicken records the transfer in both accounts. In the sample transaction shown in 3.11, a payment of $1,000 is recorded for the checking account and, at the same time, a deposit of $1,000 is recorded for the savings account.

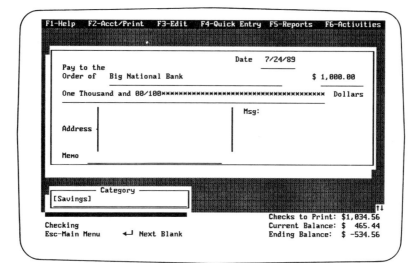

Fig. 3.11.

Transfers can be recorded in the Category field.

Recording the Check

You can record the check several ways after completing the fields. If you are on the last field, Memo, you can press Enter, or you can press Ctrl-Enter or F10 to record the check from any field. (You also can select **Record transaction** from the Edit menu on the Write Checks screen. Chapter 4 describes this and each of the Edit menu options.) After you press Ctrl-Enter or F10, Quicken displays the prompt shown in figure 3.12 and asks you to confirm that you want to record the check. If you select **Record transaction**, the check is recorded.

Whichever method you choose to record a check, you briefly see a flashing message in the lower left-hand corner of the screen that says, RECORD-ING. (If you use a very fast computer, you may not be able to read the message because it appears and disappears so quickly.) When Quicken finishes recording the check, your computer beeps, and the recorded check scrolls off the screen. A new, blank check form hidden by the preceding check is left on-screen—ready to be filled.

Reviewing and Editing Checks

You can return to, review, and edit the checks you create with the **Write/ Print Checks** option until you print them. (After printing, you need to use the Main menu's **Register** option described in Chapters 5 and 6.)

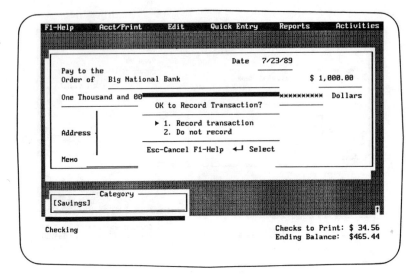

Fig. 3.12.

*The OK to
Record
Transaction?
prompt.*

You can use the PgUp, PgDn, Home, and End keys on the Write Checks screen to move through the checks you have created but not yet printed. PgUp displays the preceding check; PgDn displays the next check; Home displays the first check; End displays the last check.

Quicken arranges by date the checks you have created with the Write Checks screen but have not printed. Those checks with the earliest dates are listed first, and those checks with the latest dates are listed last. Checks with the same date are arranged in the order you entered them. To edit a check you already have recorded, press PgUp or PgDn to move to the check you want to change and then edit the appropriate fields.

If you decide you want to delete a check, press Ctrl-D while the check is displayed. (You also can select **Delete Transaction** from the Edit menu on the Write Checks screen. Chapter 4 describes the Edit menu options.)

Postdating Checks

With Quicken, you can enter postdated checks. The Billminder feature uses postdated checks to determine which bills the program should remind you of. (The Billminder feature is described in Chapter 2.) If you enter postdated checks, Quicken adds the current account balance to the information bar at the bottom of the Write Checks screen. The current balance is the checking account balance—not including postdated checks. Figure 3.11 shows a check dated 7/24/89 to Big National Bank. If the system date is 7/23/89, the check is considered postdated. Quicken, therefore, displays the current balance. Notice that the difference between the ending and current balance is $1,000, the amount of the only postdated check—the one written for Big National Bank.

If you decide to use the Billminder feature, Quicken uses postdated checks to remind you of bills you should pay and checks you should print.

Using the Acct/Print Menu

The Acct/Print menu has six options as shown in figure 3.13.

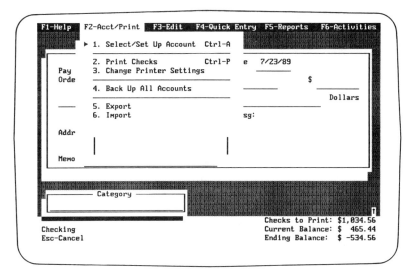

Fig. 3.13.

The Acct/Print menu.

The **Select/Set Up Account** option is the same as the Main menu option **Select Account** and is described in Chapter 1. The **Change Printer Settings** option operates the corresponding options on the Change Settings menu accessed from the Main menu. The **Back Up All Accounts** option is the same as the **Back Up Accounts** option on the Account Group Activities menu accessed by choosing **Change Settings** from the Main menu.

The **Export** option creates an ASCII file from transactions in the check register. The **Import** option retrieves transactions stored in an ASCII file and records the transactions in the check register. Only the second, fifth, and sixth Acct/Print menu options are described in this chapter because the other options are described in Chapter 1.

Printing Checks

The **Print Checks** option (Ctrl-P) displays a screen you use to print checks created with the **Write/Print checks** option. Before you select **Print Checks**, load your check forms. Load the check forms into your printer in the same way that you load regular paper. If you are using an impact printer, insert the continuous form checks into the printer as you would insert continuous form paper. If you are using a laser printer, place the check form sheets in the printer paper tray, as you would regular sheets of paper. (As Chapter 1 points out, you use continuous form checks for impact printers and check form sheets for laser printers.)

The Print Checks screen, shown in figure 3.14, displays two messages that give you information about the checks ready to be printed and provides three fields for you to use to control the printing of your checks. The two messages tell you how many checks you have to print and how many checks are postdated. Figure 3.14 shows that you have two checks to print and that one check is postdated.

Fig. 3.14.

The Print Checks screen.

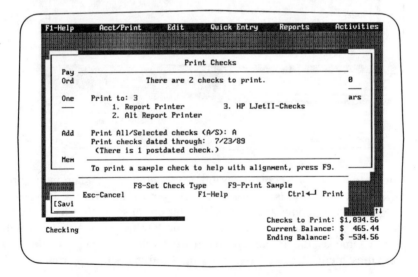

You use three fields and two function keys to control the check printing. The three fields are Print to, Print All/Selected Checks (A/S), and Print checks dated through. You also can use F8 (Set Check Type) and F9 (Print Sample). These three fields and two function keys are described in the following paragraphs.

Using the Print to Field

The Print to field in figure 3.14, which you answer by pressing a 1 or a 3, selects the printer you want to use to print the checks. If you add printer names with the **Change Printer Settings** option accessed from the Change Settings menu, you see those printers listed on this screen.

Using the Print All/Selected Checks Field

To print all the checks entered on the Write Checks screen, leave this field set to A for All. If you want to print only some of the checks, however, press S. Quicken then displays the Select Checks to Print screen shown in figure 3.15 from which you can select the checks you want to print.

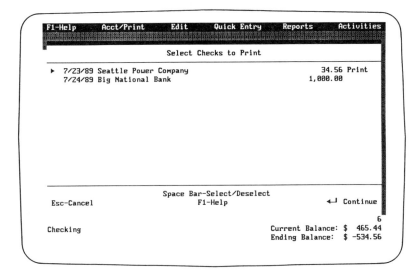

Fig. 3.15.

The Select Checks to Print screen.

To select a check you want printed, use the arrow keys to move the selection triangle. When the selection triangle is next to the check you want to print, press the space bar to select the check. To deselect a check previously marked for printing, press the space bar again.

Using the Print Checks Dated Through Field

The Print postdated checks through field accepts a date through which you want Quicken to print postdated checks. Suppose that today is 5/10/89 and that the checks waiting to be printed are dated 5/10/89,

5/11/89, and 5/12/89. (The number of postdated checks appears below the Print postdated checks through field.) If you set the date of this field as 5/11/89, Quicken prints the checks dated 5/10/89 and 5/11/89. The program, however, does not print the check dated 5/12/89.

Using F9—Print Sample

You also can press F9 to print a sample check. Using this function key prints one check form with the fields filled. Sample checks are essential for vertically and horizontally aligning checks if you are using an impact printer. (If you use a laser printer, you do not need to use this feature.) Figure 3.16 shows the sample check printed by Quicken.

Fig. 3.16.

A sample check.

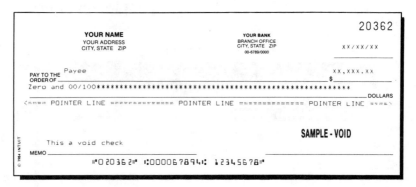

The Date field is filled as XX/XX/XX. The Pay to the Order of field is filled with Payee. The amount fields are filled with XX,XXX.XX and Zero and 00/100***.... The Memo field is filled with the phrase, This is a void check.

Quicken also prints a pointer line as shown in figure 3.16. The pointer line enables you to tell Quicken how the check form is vertically aligned. Quicken uses this information to vertically align the check forms. To use this alignment capability, enter the number from the check form's tractor pin-feed strips that the pointer line points to. Only even numbers show on the pin-feed strips. The odd numbers are identified by hash marks.

On the sample check shown in figure 3.16, for example, the pointer line points to 24. You type *24* in the Position number field on the Type Position Number screen shown in figure 3.17. Press Enter, and Quicken calculates where it should start printing on the next check form to ensure the correct vertical alignment.

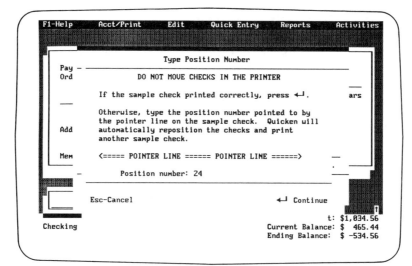

Fig. 3.17.

The Type Position Number screen.

You also need to horizontally align the check form. To horizontally align the check, manually adjust the check form in the printer to the right or left. You may decide, for example, that the fields shown in figure 3.16 are a little too far, perhaps an eighth of an inch, to the left. In that case, you manually move the check forms over to the left an eighth of an inch. Quicken prints the next check with its check form spaces filled an eighth of an inch to the right compared to the preceding check form. Figure 3.18 shows a sample check to Big National Bank printed with the vertical and horizontal alignment correct.

Fig. 3.18.

A sample check made payable to Big National Bank.

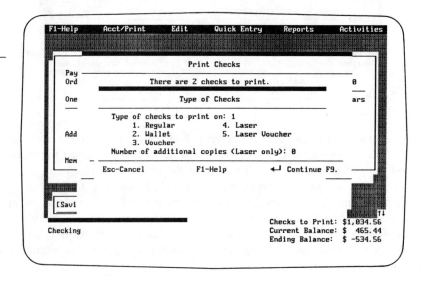

Using F8—Set Check Type

You can press F8 to access the Set Check Type screen that you use to tell Quicken what kind of check form you are using. Figure 3.19 shows the Type of Checks screen used to specify the type of check form. 1 designates regular checks; 2 designates wallet checks; 3 designates voucher checks; 4 designates laser checks, and 5 designates laser voucher checks. If you are using multipart laser check forms, you need to specify the number of additional copies that should be printed.

Fig. 3.19.

The Type of Checks screen.

If you are using regular checks such as those shown in figures 3.16 and 3.18, press 1. (Chapter 1, "Getting Started with Quicken," describes in more detail Quicken's various check form options.)

After you verify that the check form alignment is correct, set the Print to field correctly, and enter the Print postdated checks through date, you are ready to print your checks. You can print them by pressing Enter while the cursor is on the Print postdated checks through field or by using the shortcut key combination, Ctrl-Enter, while the cursor is on any field of the Print Checks screen. Quicken then asks you for the number of the next check to print as shown in figure 3.20.

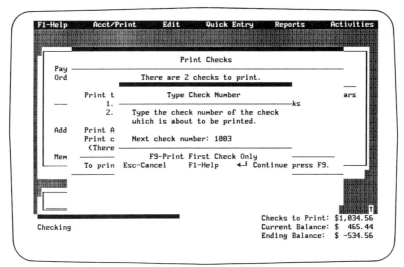

Fig. 3.20.

The Type Check Number screen.

Quicken displays the number of the next check. If the number Quicken displays is the same as the number that appears in the upper-left hand corner of the next check form, press Enter to print the checks. If the number Quicken displays is not correct, type the correct check number and then press Enter to print the checks. You can use the + and − keys to change the number.

After Quicken finishes printing the check, the program asks you if the check(s) printed correctly. Figure 3.21 shows the screen that Quicken uses to ask the question.

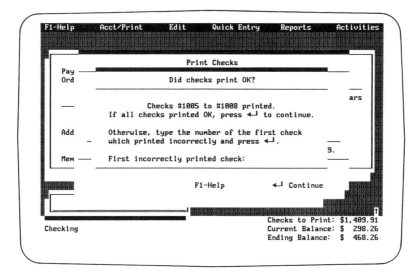

Fig. 3.21.

Quicken asks whether the checks printed correctly.

If each of your checks printed correctly, press Return. If one or more of your checks printed incorrectly—perhaps the alignment is not right or maybe the check forms jammed in the printer half way through printing—enter the number of the first check that printed incorrectly. Quicken then returns you to the Print Checks screen, and you repeat each of the print checks steps to reprint the checks that printed incorrectly.

CPA Tip: Write "VOID" in large letters across the face of checks that Quicken incorrectly prints. This precaution prevents you and anyone else from later signing and cashing the checks.

Exporting and Importing Files

The final two options on the Acct/Print menu are **Export** and **Import**. The **Export** option enables you to take the transactions in the register for the current account and create an ASCII file from those transactions. You then can use the ASCII file in another software program. Word processing and spreadsheet applications, for example, commonly enable you to use ASCII files. To execute an export operation, select **Export** from the Acct/Print menu. Quicken displays the Export Transactions screen shown in figure 3.22.

Fig. 3.22.

The Export Transactions screen.

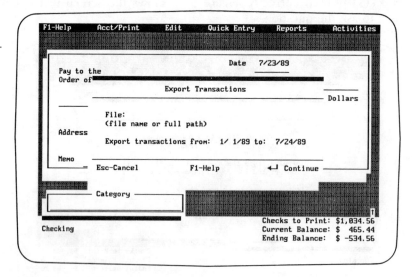

To complete the screen, enter the DOS file name you want Quicken to use to name the new ASCII file in the File field. You also can include a path name. For example, figure 3.22 shows the Export Transactions screen filled to create an ASCII file named QREG on drive C of your hard drive in the WORD directory. The Export Transactions from and to date fields enable you to specify only a certain range of dates as a basis for exporting transactions. The following list is the actual ASCII file information Quicken writes out to record the check to Big National Bank used in figures earlier in the chapter:

```
D7/24/89
T-1,000.00
N*****
PBig National Bank
L[Savings]
^
```

The first line, beginning with D, shows the transaction date. The second line begins with T and shows the transaction amount as − 1000.00. The third line shows the transaction number set to asterisks because the check has yet to be printed. The fourth line begins with P and shows the payee. The fifth line begins with L and shows the Category field entry. The sixth line shows only a caret, ^, that designates the end of a transaction.

The **Import** option enables you to retrieve files stored in the Quicken export format and store the files in a Quicken register. You can take an ASCII file created as part of an export operation, like QREG in figure 3.22, and import the file back into the Quicken register. Figure 3.23 shows the Import Transactions screen filled to import data from the ASCII file QREG. If you happen to be importing an ASCII file created using the Quicken **Export** option, set the Include items which are transfers (Y/N) field to Y. If an item is a transfer, therefore, the file is not only recorded in the current register, but also in whatever other register money is being transferred to or from.

Fig. 3.23.

*The Import
Transactions
screen.*

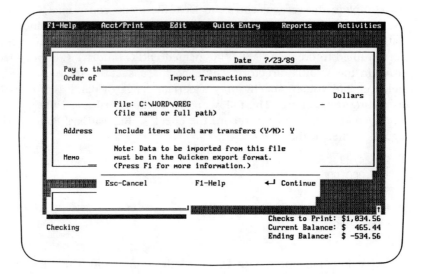

```
  F1-Help      Acct/Print      Edit      Quick Entry      Reports      Activities

                                        Date    7/23/89
     Pay to th
     Order of                      Import Transactions

                                                                   Dollars
                      File: C:\WORD\QREG                           —
                      (file name or full path)

     Address          Include items which are transfers (Y/N): Y

                      Note: Data to be imported from this file
     Memo             must be in the Quicken export format.
                      (Press F1 for more information.)


              Esc-Cancel              F1-Help           ↵ Continue



                                                Checks to Print: $1,034.56
     Checking                                   Current Balance: $  465.44
                                                Ending Balance:  $ -534.56
```

Chapter Summary

This chapter describes the basics of using Quicken's major timesaving feature—the Write/Print Checks feature. These basics include the components of the Write Checks screen; how to use the screen to record and
postdate checks; and how to review, edit, and print checks. The next
chapter describes the three Write Checks options not included in this
chapter: Edit, Quick Entry, and Activities.

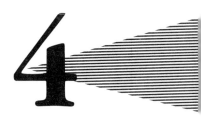

Using the Write Checks
Menu Options

$\mathbf{T}$he basic features of the Write/Print Checks option described in the preceding chapter make printing checks with Quicken fast and easy. Check writing can become even faster and easier if you use three additional Write Checks menu options:

1. **Edit**
2. **Quick Entry**
3. **Activities**

This chapter describes how you can use each of these three options. (The one Write Checks menu option not yet discussed, **Reports**, accesses the same menu as the **Reports** option on the Main menu and is described in Chapter 11.)

Using the Edit Menu—F3

The Edit menu, shown in figure 4.1, provides you with eight options, each of which is described in detail in the following paragraphs.

Fig. 4.1.

The Edit menu.

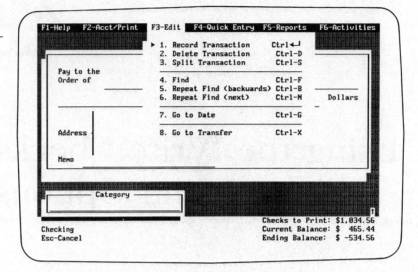

Recording Transactions

Equivalent to Ctrl-Enter and F10, the **Record Transaction** option records checks in the register and on the disk specified as the data directory. (You set the data directory for an account group by using the **Select/Set Up Account Group** option on the Account Group Activities menu. All of the Account Group Activities options, including **Select/Set Up Account Group**, are described in Chapter 2.)

Deleting Transactions

The **Delete Transaction** option on the Edit menu removes the check displayed on the Write Checks screen from the register and the data directory. You also can use the **Delete transaction** option to erase the information in the Write Checks screen's fields if you have begun filling the fields but have not yet recorded the check. When you delete a transaction using the menu option or the shortcut key combination (Ctrl-D), Quicken asks you to confirm that you want to delete the transaction (see fig. 4.2).

To delete the check, select the first option, **Delete transaction**. To change your mind, select the second option, **Do not delete**, or press Esc.

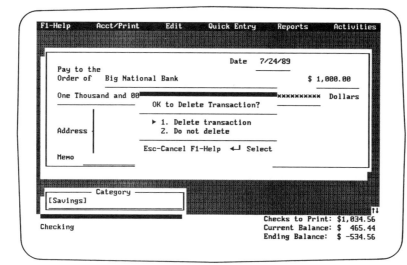

Fig. 4.2.

The OK to Delete Transaction? prompt.

Using Split Transactions

The **Split Transaction** option, the third choice on the Edit menu, provides additional Category fields so that you can use more than one category on a check or have more space to describe and document a check. You access the Split Transaction screen, shown in figure 4.3, by selecting **Split Transaction** or by using the shortcut key combination, Ctrl-S.

```
 F1-Help      Acct/Print      Edit      Quick Entry      Reports      Activities

       ┌─────────────────────────────────────────────────────────┐
       │                                     Date    7/23/89       │
       │  Pay to the                                               │
       │  Order of    Seattle Power Company           $ 60.37      │
       │                                                           │
       ├───────────────────────────────────────────────────────────┤
       │                      Split Transaction                    │
       │                                                           │
       │              Category          │   Description   │  Amount │
       │  1:Utilities:Electric/Wash     │                 │  34.56  │
       │  2:Utilities:Electric/Oregon   │                 │  25.81  │
       │  3:                            │                 │         │
       │  4:                            │                 │         │
       │  5:                            │                 │         │
       │  6:                            │                 │         │
       │                                                           │
       │         Enter categories, descriptions, and amounts       │
       │  Esc-Cancel    Ctrl-D Delete   F9-Recalc Transaction Total   Ctrl◄┘ Done │
       └─────────────────────────────────────────────────────────┘
                                                                56
  Checking                              Current Balance: $  465.44
                                        Ending Balance:  $ -534.56
```

Fig. 4.3.

The Split Transaction screen enables you to use multiple categories.

You fill one, two, or three fields when using the **Split Transaction** option: Category, Description, or Amount. These fields are described in the following paragraphs.

Using the Category Field

The Category field on the Split Transaction screen is used in the same way as the Category field on the Write Checks screen. You can use the field to enter categories, subcategories, classes, and subclasses. The Split Transaction screen has 30 lines available for categories. Just as with the Category field on the Write Checks screen, if you enter a category that has not been defined, you also can add the category to the Category List; if you enter a class that has not been defined, you can add that class to the Class List.

Note: Remember that Quicken provides predefined home and business categories. The home category has descriptions for most general household expenses, and the business category has general business income and expense categories. These categories are accessed by pressing Ctrl-C from the Write/Print Checks or Register menus.

If you decide to use these fields, you should be aware that, when you use checks with vouchers, Quicken prints the first 15 lines of the split transaction information on the voucher. The feature usually works to your benefit because it enables you to provide additional detail about why you are writing a check. If you use vouchers, however, payees see these descriptions just as they see the memo description you write on the face of the check.

Using the Description Field

The description field provides a 27-character space you can use to further describe a transaction or the reasons you selected a certain category, subcategory, class, or subclass.

Using the Amount Field

You use the Amount field in two slightly different ways depending on whether you select **Split Transaction** before or after you enter the amount on the Write Checks screen.

If you select **Split Transaction** before you enter anything in the Amount field on the Write Checks screen, Quicken adds each of the amounts you enter together. Quicken then takes the total of these amounts and enters that total in the Amount field on the Write Checks screen. When you have several invoices to pay with one check, therefore, you only have to enter the invoice amounts on the Split Transaction screen. Quicken then calculates and enters the total check amount for you.

CPA Tip: If you use check forms with vouchers, putting the individual invoices and invoice amounts on the Split Transaction Screen means that Quicken prints this information on the voucher. Vendors then can record your payments correctly, and you no longer have to spend time trying to explain what invoice(s) a check pays.

If you select **Split Transaction** after you enter the amount on the Write Checks screen, Quicken pulls the amount entered on the Write Checks screen into the Amount field on the Split Transaction screen. If you then enter a figure into the first Amount field, Quicken calculates the difference between the Write Checks screen amount and the amount you entered in the first Amount field on the Split Transaction screen and puts this difference in the second Amount field.

Quicken continues to use the next unused Amount field to balance the amount you enter on the Write Checks screen with the amounts entered on the Split Transaction screen. If you use all 30 of the available Amount fields, however, Quicken has no unused field to make the Write Checks screen amount equal the total Split Transaction amounts. In that case, manually adjust the Write Checks screen amount or one of the Split Transaction screen amounts. You also can press F9 to total the split transaction amounts to insert that total in the Amount field on the Write Checks screen.

Using Find

The **Find** option on the Edit menu enables you to search through the checks you created with the Write Checks screen but have not yet printed. When you select **Find** or use the shortcut key combination (Ctrl-F), Quicken displays the Transaction to Find screen shown in figure 4.4.

Fig. 4.4.

The Transaction to Find screen.

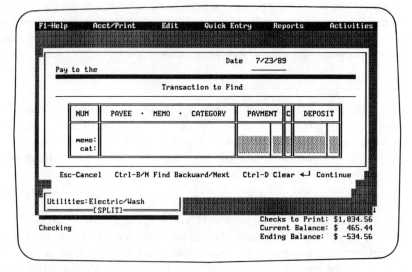

When you enter the payment amount in the PAYMENT column, Quicken searches through the checks for one with a payment amount equal to the amount you entered on the Transaction to Find screen. The variable you enter is called a search argument. If Quicken finds a check that matches your search argument, the program displays the check on the Write Checks screen. If Quicken does not find a check that matches your search argument, the program displays the message no matching items found.

You also can use the NUM, PAYEE, MEMO, and CATEGORY fields as search arguments. You can use these fields to search for an exact match or for a key-word match.

In exact matches, Quicken searches for the exact words that you type. For example, if you enter *mortgage* in the MEMO field, Quicken looks for checks with *mortgage* in that field. Because the case of the letters does not matter, *Mortgage*, *MORTGAGE*, and *mortgage* are all exact matches from Quicken's perspective. If the MEMO field is *May mortgage*, however, Quicken does not find the check.

Key-word matches come in handy because they enable you to search based on a field including or excluding certain letters, characters, or series of characters. Key-word matches use three special characters: periods, question marks, and tildes (~). Periods act as wild card indicators that can represent any character, group of characters, or even no character. The question mark can represent any one character. The tilde character identifies a word, character, or group of characters you want to exclude from your search.

Note: Although the C and DEPOSIT fields are displayed on the Write Checks screen, do not use them as search arguments. These fields are used for the register and, accordingly, are discussed in Chapters 5 and 6.

You can search by using more than one exact match or key-word argument. Figure 4.5, for example, shows the Transaction to Find screen filled to search for checks using *big national* in the PAYEE field and *mortgage* in the MEMO field.

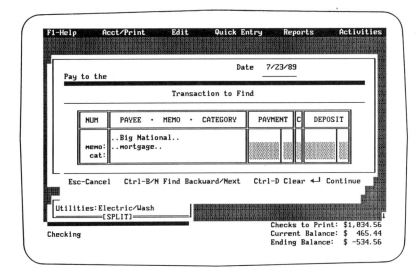

Fig. 4.5.

The completed Transaction to Find screen.

If you use more than one match test, Quicken locates only those checks that meet both match tests. With the Transaction to Find screen shown in figure 4.5, **Find** does not locate checks with the phrase *big national* in the PAYEE field unless the word *mortgage* also is in the MEMO field and vice versa.

After you fill the Transaction to Find screen and press Enter, Quicken asks you which direction you want to search (see fig. 4.6).

You have two options, **Find backwards** and **Find next**. **Find backwards** uses the shortcut key combination Ctrl-B and looks through checks with dates earlier than the date of the check currently shown on the Write Checks screen. **Find next** searches through checks with dates later than the date of the check shown on-screen and uses the shortcut key combination Ctrl-N.

Fig. 4.6.

*Quicken asks
which direction
to search.*

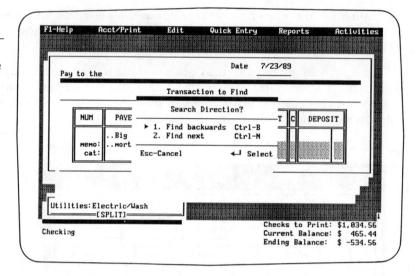

Using Repeat Find Previous
and Repeat Find Next

The **Repeat find previous** and **Repeat find next** options repeat the Find operation already specified on the Transaction to Find screen. These two menu options basically enable you to skip the **Find** option's Transaction to Find screen and jump to the spot where you specify the search direction. This procedure enables you to locate two checks made out to the same payee. For example, if you enter 30 checks and one appears to be familiar, you can use the **Repeat find** functions to locate all the checks and then delete the duplicate check.

Using Go To Date

By using the **Go to Date** option or shortcut key combination Ctrl-G, you can find transactions using the date. Specify the date you want to use as the basis for your search on the Go to Date screen, shown in figure 4.7.

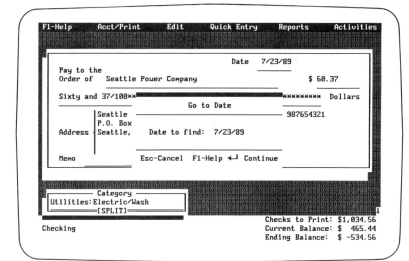

F1-Help   Acct/Print   Edit   Quick Entry   Reports   Activities

```
                                        Date    7/23/89
      Pay to the
      Order of    Seattle Power Company                $ 60.37

      Sixty and 37/100**▬▬▬▬▬▬▬▬▬▬▬▬▬▬       *********** Dollars
                                  Go to Date
                  |Seattle                          — 987654321
                  |P.O. Box
      Address ────|Seattle,     Date to find:  7/23/89

      Memo                       Esc-Cancel  F1-Help  ↵ Continue


      ─────── Category ───────
     |Utilities:Electric/Wash |
      ───────[SPLIT]──────────                Checks to Print: $1,034.56
      Checking                                Current Balance: $   465.44
                                              Ending Balance:  $  -534.56
```

Fig. 4.7.

Quicken also can search using a date.

Quicken initially displays the current system date on the Go to Date screen. You can change the date by typing the date you want over this default date. You also can use the + and − keys to move the date forward or backward one day at a time.

After you set the date you want, Quicken finds and displays the first check with the date you entered. If the program finds no check with the date you entered, the check with the date closest to the date you entered is displayed.

Because Quicken arranges the checks by the check date, you do not need to specify a search direction for the **Go to Date** option. By comparing the date on the currently displayed check to the date you enter, Quicken determines which direction it needs to search. If the date you want to search for is before the date on the current check, Quicken looks through the previous checks. If the date you want to search for is greater than the date on the current check, Quicken looks through the following checks.

Using Go To Transfer

You can select the **Go to Transfer** option (Ctrl-X) if you want to go to the transfer transaction related to the currently displayed check. To use **Go to Transfer**, the transfer must have been set up under the Select/Set Up Account menu. If you entered the transfer account [savings] in the Category field, recorded the check, and then executed the **Go to Trans-**

VERSION 3.0

fer option, Quicken displays the Savings register with the corresponding transaction—a deposit to savings—showing. Pressing Ctrl-X again returns you to the original check register.

Using the Quick Entry Menu

The Quick Entry menu, shown in figure 4.8, provides six options that enable you to store frequently used checks, define categories and classes, and group frequently used transactions.

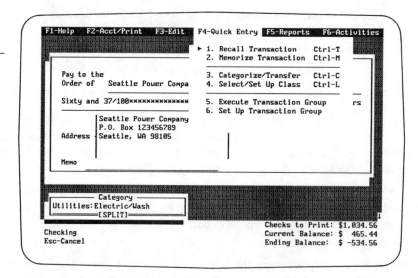

Fig. 4.8.

*The Quick
Entry menu.*

The following paragraphs describe how you can use these six options. The discussion follows the order in which you are most likely to use these options, not the order shown on the menu.

Memorizing Transactions

The **Memorize Transaction** option (Ctrl-M) is the second option on the Quick Entry menu. **Memorize Transaction** takes the fields shown on the Write Checks screen and saves the information in a file called the Memorized Transactions List. The beauty of the Memorized Transactions List is that, by saving the Write Checks screen information for checks you repeatedly write, you do not need to rewrite the checks from scratch. You can retrieve the check information from the Memorized Transactions List and use that information to fill out the Write Checks screen.

To memorize a transaction such as the one shown in figure 4.9, select **Memorize Transaction** from the Quick Entry menu while the check information you want to save is shown on the Write Checks screen.

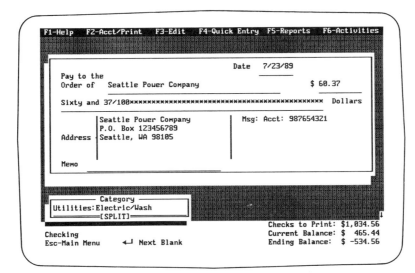

Fig. 4.9.

You may want to memorize the monthly utility check.

Quicken displays a message telling you that the information marked on the Write Checks screen is about to be memorized (see fig. 4.10). Quicken highlights and memorizes every piece of information on the Write Checks screen except the date.

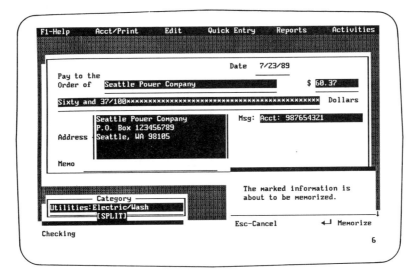

Fig. 4.10.

Quicken highlights information about to be memorized.

To memorize the transaction, press Enter. The value of this newly mem-orized transaction is demonstrated in the next section.

Recalling Transactions

With the **Recall Transaction** option, you can fill the Write Checks screen with memorized transactions. Suppose that you have memorized the check shown in figure 4.9 to pay your monthly utility bill to Seattle Power Company.

When you need to pay Seattle Power Company again, select the **Recall Transaction** option from the Quick Entry menu or press the shortcut key combination Ctrl-T. Either approach displays the Memorized Transactions List shown in figure 4.11. This Memorized Transactions List shows only the check to Seattle Power because this check is the only one memorized. Your Memorized Transactions List, however, includes all the transactions you have memorized. Typical transactions you may want to memorize are your auto loan, utilities, bank card payments, phone, and mortgage payments.

Fig. 4.11.

The Memorized Transactions List screen.

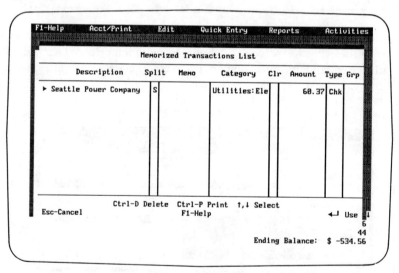

Figure 4.11 shows the information saved as part of using the **Memorize Transaction** option. Of the seven fields shown on-screen, you may recog-nize several as fields that you filled on the Write Checks screen. These fields include the payee name shown in the Description column; the memo shown in the Memo column; any category, subcategory, class, or subclass in the Category column, and the check amount shown in the Amount column.

If you split a check transaction, the Split column also shows an S. Quicken places the abbreviation Chk in the Type field to identify the transaction as a check. The Clr column shows whether you have marked the transaction as cleared using the **Register** option—described in more detail in Chapter 8, "Reconciling Your Bank Account." The Grp column identifies whether the memorized transaction is actually part of a group of transactions. (Transaction groups are described later in this chapter.)

To select a memorized transaction, use the up- and down-arrow keys to move the selection triangle at the left of the description field until it is next to the transaction you want to recall. Press Enter, and Quicken fills the Write Checks screen fields with the information from the memorized transaction. You can edit any of the fields. To record the check, press Enter.

CPA Tip: Consider each of the checks you now regularly write as candidates for the Memorized Transactions List: rent, mortgage, utility, loan payments, and so on. Memorized transactions save you valuable time that you can use to tap Quicken's other financial management tools such as the categories and reports.

Using the Categorize/Transfer Option

With the **Categorize/Transfer** option (Ctrl-C), you can create or retrieve a category. Figure 4.12 shows the Category and Transfer List screen. If you want to retrieve a category or an account name for a transfer, select the category or account you want to use by moving the selection triangle to the left of the category you want to use and pressing Enter. Quicken retrieves the category or account name from the list and puts it in the Category field.

You also can use the Category and Transfer List screen to create categories. To create a category, select the first line of the Category and Transfer List. Quicken displays the Set Up Category screen shown in figure. 4.13.

You may recognize the screen as the same one Quicken displays when you define a new category as part of filling the Write Checks screen Category field.

Fig. 4.12.

The Category and Transfer List screen.

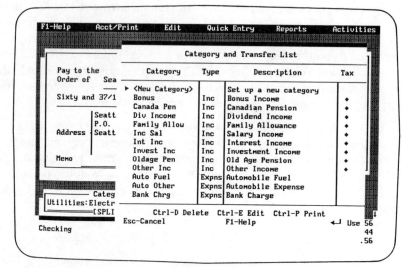

Fig. 4.13.

The Set Up Category screen.

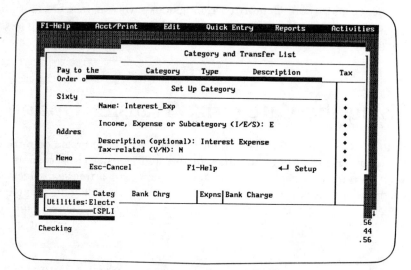

To define a new category, enter the name you want to use for the category in the name field, identify the type of category by entering an I, E, or S in the income, expense or subcategory field, type a description, and mark the category as tax-related using a Y or N.

You also can use the PgUp, PgDn, Home, and End keys to move quickly through long lists of categories. PgUp displays the preceding page of categories in the list; PgDn displays the next page of categories in the list; Home displays the first page of categories, and End displays the last page of categories.

To delete a category, select the category and press Ctrl-D. Quicken warns you that it is about to permanently delete the category (see fig. 4.14). When you press Enter, Quicken deletes the category.

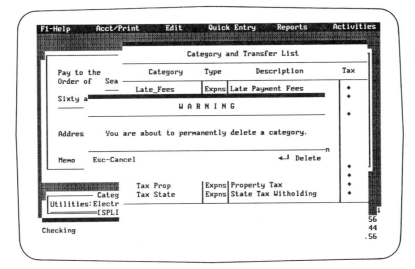

Fig. 4.14.

Quicken warns you when a category is about to be deleted.

Selecting and Setting Up a Class

You use the fourth option on the Quick Entry menu, **Select/Set Up Class**, to select, add, edit, and delete classes. (Chapter 7, "Using Categories and Classes," describes the reasons you may want to use the classes and provides some examples of approaches you may want to take.) If you select **Select/Set Up Class**, Quicken displays the Class List screen shown in figure 4.15.

To select a class, use the arrow keys to move the selection triangle next to the class you want to select and press Enter.

To add a class to the list, select the ‹New Class› line on the list by using the up- and down-arrow keys to position the selection triangle and press Enter. Quicken displays the Set Up Class screen, shown in figure 4.16, on which you enter a class name and description.

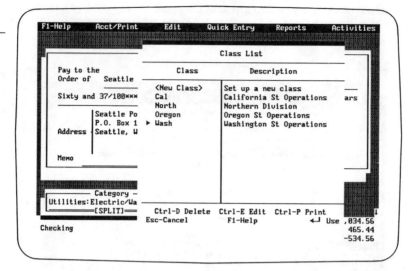

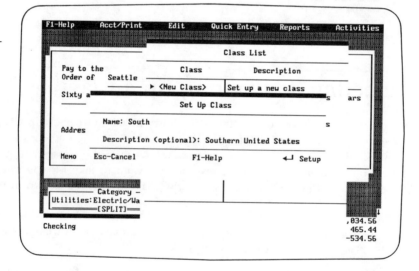

To edit a class on the list, select the class you want to modify and press Ctrl-E. Quicken displays the Edit Class screen, shown in figure 4.17, that you can use to modify the class name or description.

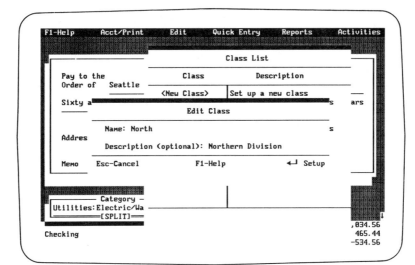

Fig. 4.17.

The Edit Class screen.

To delete a class on the list, select the class you want to delete and press Ctrl-D. Quicken alerts you that you are about to delete a class with the message shown in figure 4.18.

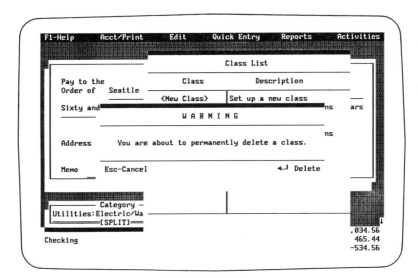

Fig. 4.18.

Quicken warns you when a class is about to be deleted.

To complete the deletion, press Enter. To cancel the deletion, press Esc.

Setting Up Transaction Groups

Transaction groups are collections of memorized transactions. These groups are another time-saving technique Quicken provides to make your bill paying and check writing even easier. With transaction groups, you can recall several memorized transactions at the same time.

The first step in using a transaction group is to set up the group by selecting the **Set Up Transaction Group** option on the Quick Entry menu. Figure 4.19 shows the Select Transaction Group to Set Up/Change screen that appears after you choose this option.

Fig. 4.19.

The Select Transaction Group to Set Up/Change screen.

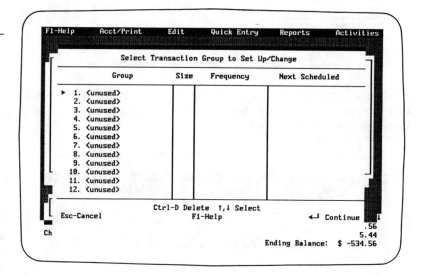

The Select Transaction Group screen contains four fields: Group, Size, Frequency, and Next Scheduled. The Group field describes the number and name of the group. The Size field gives the number of memorized transactions in the group. The Frequency field identifies how often you use the transaction group. The Next Scheduled field shows the next scheduled date the transaction group should be used to create a group of check transactions. Until you complete the set-up process, the Group fields are all labeled unused, and the other three fields are blank (see fig. 4.19).

The first step is to choose the transaction group you want to set up or change by using the up- and down-arrow keys to move the selection triangle and pressing Enter. Figure 4.20 shows the Describe Group screen you use to define the fields of a transaction group. Name, Frequency, and Next Scheduled date are the same fields that appear on the Select Transaction Group to Set Up/Change screen.

Identify the transfer group by using a descriptive name such as Beginning of the Month, End of the Month, Utilities, and so on. You have up to 20 characters to describe the name. Set the frequency by typing the number of one of the nine settings shown in figure 4.20: None, Weekly, Every two weeks, Twice a month, Every four weeks, Monthly, Quarterly, Twice a year, or Annually. If you set the frequency as something other than none, you also must set the next scheduled date. Quicken provides nine groups and eight frequencies, enough space to set up a group for all eight frequencies and still have an extra group.

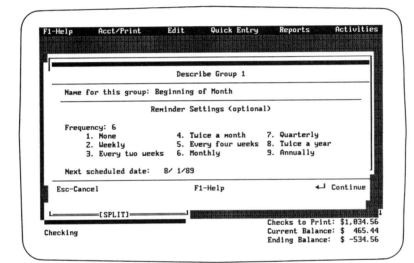

Fig. 4.20.

The Describe Group 1 screen.

Figure 4.20 shows the Describe Group screen filled out to set up the first group for a series of monthly bills that you pay at the beginning of the month. Using the next scheduled date shown in the figure as 8/1/89, Quicken reminds you of this scheduled date just as it reminds you of post-dated checks.

After you complete the Describe Group screen, press Enter. Quicken displays the Assign Transactions screen shown in figure 4.21.

Use the up- and down-arrow keys to move the selection triangle to the transaction that you want included in a group. When a memorized transaction is marked, press the space bar to assign that transaction to a group. You can tell when a transaction has been assigned, because the last column on the Assign Transaction screen, Grp, shows the group number. Figure 4.21 shows three memorized transactions. Two are selected for

Fig. 4.21.

The Assign Transactions to Group 1 screen.

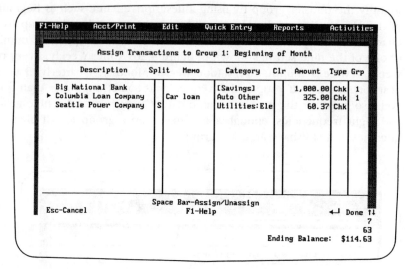

transaction group 1: the transfer payment to Big National and the car loan payment to Columbia Loan Company. When you assign transactions to a group, press Enter.

If you want to change or modify a transaction group, use the **Set Up Transaction Group** option again and select the previously set up transaction group. Access the Describe Group and Assign Transactions screens shown in figures 4.20 and 4.21 and make the required changes. Then press Enter to continue.

Executing Transaction Groups

The **Execute Transaction Group** option creates checks for each of the memorized transactions in the transaction group. This option is roughly equivalent to simultaneously recalling the memorized transactions that constitute a transaction group.

The **Execute Transaction Group** option also takes the date in the Next scheduled date field for the transaction group and moves the date forward, using whatever frequency you specified, to set the new date.

Figure 4.22 shows the Select Transaction Group to Execute screen. The Write Checks screen no longer appears. The Register screen is behind the Select Transaction Group to Execute screen. (Chapters 5 and 6 describe the Quicken account register.)

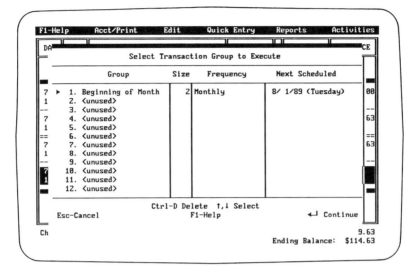

Fig. 4.22.

The Select Transaction Group to Execute screen.

To select a group, move the selection triangle to the group you want to execute and press Enter. Quicken prompts you for the transaction date—the date that appears on the checks—as shown in figure 4.23.

Fig. 4.23.

The Transaction Group Date screen.

If you need to edit the date Quicken displays, do so. You can use the + and − keys to change the date one day at a time. Press Enter when the transaction date is correct. Quicken then adds the memorized transactions as checks to the account register, saves the transaction, and displays the message shown in figure 4.24.

Fig. 4.24.

The Transaction Group Entered screen.

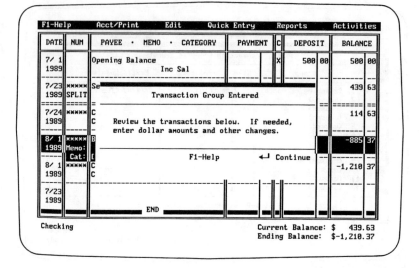

You can review and edit the checks by using the Register screen—where you are after you finish executing the transaction group—or the Write Checks screen. To return to the Write Checks screen, press Esc. Return to the Main menu and select the **Write Print Checks** option. If the checks created differ from what you need, edit the checks that need changes.

Using the Activities Menu

The Write Checks Activities menu has five options, as shown in figure 4.25.

Register accesses the Register screen and menu options—just as the **Register** option on Quicken's Main menu does. The register is described in Chapters 5 and 6.

Reconcile accesses the Reconciliation screen and options just as the **Reconcile** option on Quicken's Main menu does. Reconciling is described in Chapter 8.

Order Supplies accesses the Print Supply Order Form screen, shown in figure 4.26. You print this three-page order form and then use the form to purchase supplies such as check forms and envelopes from Intuit, the manufacturer of Quicken. The order form is not shown here, but it mirrors the order form that Intuit provides in the Quicken packaging.

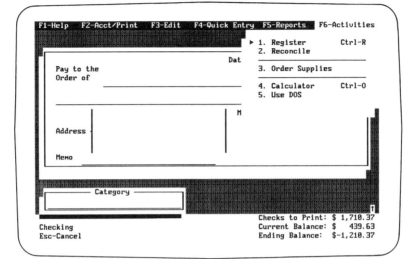

Fig. 4.25.

The Activities menu.

```
F1-Help  F2-Acct/Print  F3-Edit  F4-Quick Entry  F5-Reports  F6-Activities
                                            ▶ 1. Register        Ctrl-R
                                              2. Reconcile
                                   Dat     ───────────────────
   Pay to the                                3. Order Supplies
   Order of           ──────────────────── ───────────────────
                                             4. Calculator       Ctrl-O
                      ──────────────────     5. Use DOS
                      │                   M
   Address            │
                      │
   Memo               ────────────────────

        ───── Category ─────

                                       Checks to Print: $ 1,718.37
   Checking                            Current Balance: $   439.63
   Esc-Cancel                          Ending Balance:  $-1,210.37
```

Fig. 4.26.

The Print Supply Order form.

```
F1-Help    Acct/Print    Edit    Quick Entry    Reports    Activities
                               Date   7/23/89
   Pay t
   Orde             Print Supply Order Form
                                                          ollars
   ───        Print to: 1
                  1. Report Printer        3. HP LJetII-Checks
                  2. Alt Report Printer    4. Disk
   Addr
              For additional information about Quicken Supplies,
              call Intuit at (800) 624-8742 between 8:30 AM and
   Memo       4:30 PM Pacific time.

                      Position paper in printer
              Esc-Cancel            F1-Help          ↵ Continue

                                       Checks to Print: $ 1,718.37
   Checking                            Current Balance: $   439.63
                                       Ending Balance:  $-1,210.37
```

Calculator accesses the on-line, 10-key calculator that Quicken provides. Figure 4.27 shows the on-line calculator. Chapter 1, "Getting Started with Quicken," describes the on-line calculator.

Fig. 4.27.

The on-line calculator.

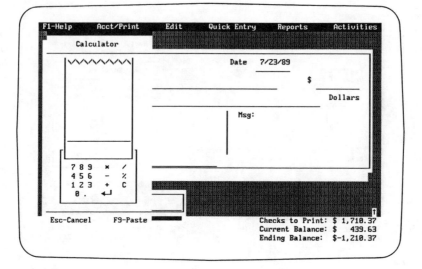

Use **DOS** calls up DOS and displays the DOS prompt:

```
To return to Quicken, type EXIT.

Microsoft® MS-DOS® Version 3.30
            ©Copyright Microsoft Corp 1981-1987


C:\QUICKEN3›
```

This feature is handy when you want to execute DOS commands before leaving Quicken. For example, you may want to format a disk to make a backup copy of an account. To return from DOS to Quicken, type *EXIT* at the C> prompt.

Chapter Summary

This chapter described the details of using the three sets of Write Checks menu options that are not covered in the preceding chapter: the Edit, Quick Entry, and Activities menus. The options on these three menus should make using the Write Checks screen even easier and faster.

5

Using the Register

Your checkbook, or check register, represents the most fundamental financial tool you use. You probably agree that your check register largely summarizes your financial life. Money flows into the account in the form of wages for a household or sales collections for a business and money flows out of the account to pay for your expenses.

Moving your check register to Quicken provides two major benefits. First, Quicken does the arithmetic of deducting withdrawals and adding deposits—a trivial contribution until you remember the last time an error in your arithmetic caused you to bounce a check. Second, Quicken records each of your checking account transactions in the check register so that you can use Quicken's Reports feature to summarize and extract information from the register—information that helps you to better plan and control your finances.

This chapter describes the basics of using Quicken's register. These basics include the following:

1. Completing the Register screen

2. Recording register transactions

3. Reviewing and editing register transactions

4. Using the Acct/Print menu options

Chapter 6, "Using the Register Menu Options," describes how you can use three additional menu options—**Edit**, **Quick Entry**, and **Activities**—to make using the check register even easier. Chapter 10, "Accounting for Other Assets and Liabilities," describes how you also can use the **Register** option to keep track of assets besides cash and liabilities like credit cards and bank loans.

Getting To Know the Register Screen

You select the **Register** option on Quicken's Main menu to access the Register screen. You use the Register screen, shown in figure 5.1, to record most of the checking account transactions—manual checks, deposits, interest, bank fees, and so on—that affect your checking account.

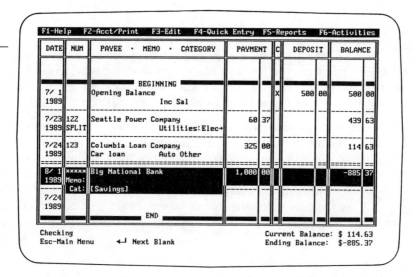

Fig. 5.1.

The Register screen.

The only transaction you do not record using the **Register** option is a check you record and print using the **Write/Print Checks** option. (Chapters 3 and 4 describe in detail the **Write/Print Checks** Main menu option.) After collecting the information, Quicken records the transaction in the register and updates the account balance. The fields you fill to record a transaction on the Register screen are described next.

The Register screen can be broken down into roughly three parts: the menu bar at the top of the screen, the actual check register, and the information bar at the bottom of the screen.

The menu bar shows the function keys you can use on the Register screen to access menus of options. F1 accesses help. F2 accesses the Acct/Print menu. F5 accesses the same menu as does the **Reports** option on Quicken's Main menu and is described in Chapter 11, "Using Quicken's Reports." F3, F4, and F6 access the Edit, Quick Entry, and Activities menus described in Chapter 6, "Using the Register Menu Options."

The second part of the Register screen is the actual check register you use to record account transactions. The steps for completing the register are described in the next section, "Completing the Register Screen."

The third part of the Register screen is the information bar at the bottom of the screen. This bar shows several interesting pieces of information including the bank account name (checking), information on what the Esc and Enter keys do, and the ending and current balances in the account. The ending balance, $ − 885.37 in figure 5.1, incorporates all the transactions for the account including post-dated transactions. If you enter post-dated transactions, however, Quicken also displays the current balance, $114.63 in figure 5.1, which is the account balance at the current date. (Quicken determines the current date by looking at the system date.)

Completing the Register Screen

Completing the Register screen means filling nine fields: DATE, NUM, PAYEE, MEMO, CATEGORY, PAYMENT, C (an abbreviation for cleared), DEPOSIT, and BALANCE. You already know most of what you need to do because the process for completing the Register screen parallels the process for manually recording a checking account transaction in your register. Like Quicken's Write Checks screen, however, the Register screen makes the whole process easier. The fields you fill in to complete the Register screen are described in the following sections.

Using the DATE Field

The DATE field is the check date in a month/day/year format. The first time you use Quicken, the program fills the DATE field with the system date. After you record your first transaction using the Register screen, Quicken fills the DATE field with the last date you used. To edit the date, you have two choices. First, you can move to the part of the date—month, day, or year—you want to change and type over what already is showing on-screen. Second, you can use the + and − keys to change the date one day at a time. Each time you press the + key, Quicken moves the date ahead one day. Each time you press the − key, Quicken moves the date back one day. When you finish editing the date, press Enter or Tab, and Quicken moves the cursor to the NUM field.

CPA Tip: Businesses and individuals often receive discounts for paying bills early. Consider early payment in setting the check date. Not taking early payment discounts is an extremely expensive way to borrow money from the vendor. Suppose that a vendor normally requires payment within 30 days but allows a 2 percent discount for payments received within 10 days. If you pay within 30 rather than ten days, you essentially pay the vendor a 2 percent interest charge for paying 20 days later. Because one year contains roughly 18, 20-day periods, the 2 percent for 20 days equals approximately 36 percent annually.

Although you may need to "borrow" this money, you probably can find a much cheaper lender. As a rough rule of thumb, if a vendor gives you a 1 percent discount for paying 20 days early, you are borrowing money from him at about an 18 percent annual interest rate if you do not pay early. A 3 percent discount works out to a whopping 54 percent a year.

Using the NUM Field

You enter the number of the checks you write manually into the NUM field. You also might enter the receipt numbers for deposits you make. If you use the Write/Print Checks screen, however, this field takes on special significance. Checks you recorded on the Write/Print Checks screen but have not printed, show asterisks as their numbers. Figure 5.1, for example, shows the check number of the check to Big National Bank as ***** because the check was recorded on the Write Checks screen but has not been printed. Quicken determines which checks the program should print by looking for those with asterisks in the NUM field. After a check is printed, the field shows the check number.

If you do not want a check to print as part of the **Print Checks** option on the Write Checks screen, use the Register screen to delete the asterisks from the NUM field for the checks that you do not want to print. When you do want the check to print, replace the asterisks. If you want to reprint a check, change the NUM field to asterisks.

Using the PAYEE Field

For checks, the PAYEE field is where you enter the name of the person or business the check pays. For other transactions, you enter a description of the transaction. Payroll deposits might be described as "payroll check." Bank service charges might be described as "checking account fees."

Interest might be described as "October interest income." Type into the field the name or description you want to appear on the transaction. You have space for up to 31 characters.

Using the PAYMENT Field

The PAYMENT field shows the amount of the withdrawals from the account. Depending on the transactions you experience, this field might include checks, automatic payments made from your account, transfers from the account, and bank service fees. You can use up to 10 characters to input the amount. Quicken enables you to enter only numbers. In the PAYMENT field, you can enter any amount up to $9,999,999.99.

CPA Tip: Consider the monthly service fees a bank charges in choosing a bank and in keeping minimum balances. Most banks charge monthly service fees of about $5. Some banks waive the $5 fee if you keep a balance of $200 at all times in your account. The $5 a month translates into $60 a year. Because $60 in fee savings equals $60 in interest, the interest rate the bank pays people who keep their minimum balance at $200 is $60/$200 or 30 percent. The return is even better than that for most people because the interest income gets taxed, but the fee savings do not. Probably no other $200 investment in the world is risk-free and pays 30 percent interest.

Using the Cleared Field

The C field shows if a transaction has been recorded by the bank. You use this field as part of reconciling, or explaining the difference between your check register account balance and the balance the bank shows on your monthly statement. To mark a transaction as cleared, enter an asterisk in the C field. (Quicken allows only an asterisk in this field.) During the reconciliation process, Quicken changes the asterisk to an "X." Chapter 8, "Reconciling Your Account," describes the bank account reconciliation process.

Using the DEPOSIT Field

The DEPOSIT field shows the amount of the increases in the account. Depending on your situation, your increases might include payroll checks, interest income, and transfers from savings accounts. As with the PAY-MENT field, Quicken enables you to enter only numbers and the amount can be as large as $9,999,999.99.

Using the MEMO Field

MEMO is the sixth field you fill on the Register screen. Using this field is optional, but MEMO can be useful to describe the reasons for a transaction. You can use up to 31 characters to describes a transaction.

Using the CATEGORY Field

You use the CATEGORY field to describe the category into which a transaction falls, such as utilities expense, interest expense, or entertainment. You also can use the CATEGORY field to describe the class into which a transaction falls. (Categories and classes are described in Chapter 7.) Use Ctrl-C to access the existing categories as provided by Quicken or those you have previously added.

To use the CATEGORY field to describe a category, enter the name or select from the Category List the name you used to define the category. Figure 5.2 shows a check to the Seattle Power Company filled with the category, subcategory, and class combination, Utilities:Electric/Wash.

Fig. 5.2.

The Seattle Power Company check uses categories.

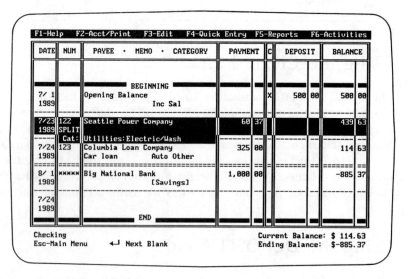

To use subcategories, enter the category name or select a previously established category from the Category List. Then, enter a colon followed by the subcategory name. Figure 5.2 shows the category/subcategory combination Utilities:Electric.

To use classes, enter a slash followed by the class name. Using the Quick Entry menu (F4) from the Register menu accesses the previously established classes. You also can access these classes by using the Ctrl-L shortcut key combination. Figure 5.2 shows the class name Wash used to further define the check to Seattle Power.

You even can use subclasses: follow the class name with a colon and then the subclass name. Figure 5.3 shows a subclass following the class.

```
 F1-Help   F2-Acct/Print   F3-Edit   F4-Quick Entry  F5-Reports   F6-Activities
┌────┬────┬─────────────────────────────┬───────┬──┬────────┬────────┐
│DATE│ NUM│ PAYEE  ·  MEMO  ·  CATEGORY  │PAYMENT│C │ DEPOSIT│ BALANCE│
├────┼────┼─────────────────────────────┼───────┼──┼────────┼────────┤
│    │    │ ═══════ BEGINNING ═══════    │       │  │        │        │
│7/ 1│    │Opening Balance              │       │x │ 500 00 │ 500 00 │
│1989│    │              Inc Sal        │       │  │        │        │
├────┼────┼─────────────────────────────┼───────┼──┼────────┼────────┤
│7/23│122 │Seattle Power Company        │ 60 37 │  │        │ 439 63 │
│1989│SPLIT│                            │       │  │        │        │
│    │Cat:│Utilities:Electric/Wash:West │       │  │        │        │
│7/24│123 │Columbia Loan Company        │325 00 │  │        │ 114 63 │
│1989│    │Car loan          Auto Other │       │  │        │        │
├────┼────┼─────────────────────────────┼───────┼──┼────────┼────────┤
│8/ 1│xxxxx│Big National Bank           │1,000 00│ │        │-885 37 │
│1989│    │              [Savings]      │       │  │        │        │
├────┼────┼─────────────────────────────┼───────┼──┼────────┼────────┤
│7/24│    │                             │       │  │        │        │
│1989│    │ ═══════ END ═══════         │       │  │        │        │
└────┴────┴─────────────────────────────┴───────┴──┴────────┴────────┘
 Checking                               Current Balance: $ 114.63
 Esc-Main Menu    ↵ Next Blank          Ending Balance:  $-885.37
```

Fig. 5.3.

The subclass West follows the class.

If you enter a category that Quicken does not recognize because you have not used the category before, Quicken alerts you that the category cannot be found and provides you with the two options shown in figure 5.4.

The first option enables you to add the new category to the Category list. If you select this option, another screen appears on which you enter the income, expense, or subcategory code, an optional 25-character description, and the tax-related flag as shown in figure 5.5.

The second option enables you to select an already used category from the Category and Transfer List shown in figure 5.6.

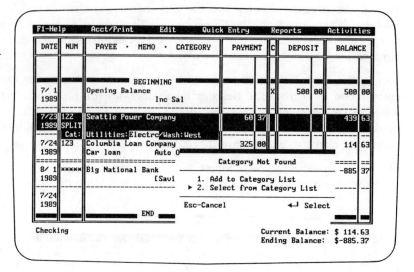

Fig. 5.4.

The Category Not Found screen.

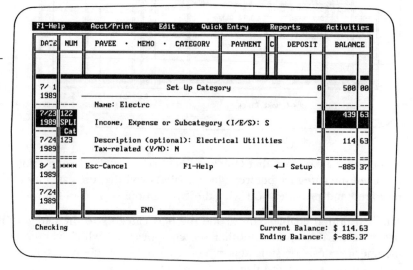

Fig. 5.5.

The Set Up Category screen.

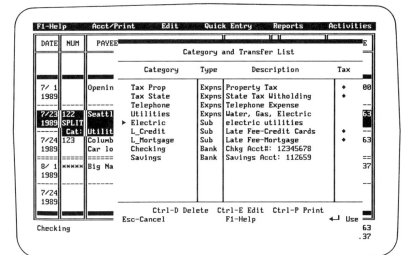

Fig. 5.6.

The Category and Transfer List screen.

Notice that Quicken highlights the predefined category Electric. Quicken tries to find the place in the Category List that most closely matches the undefined category you enter in the MEMO field. The match is not always perfect, but is usually close. If you use a class that Quicken does not recognize, Quicken provides you with the two options shown in figure 5.7.

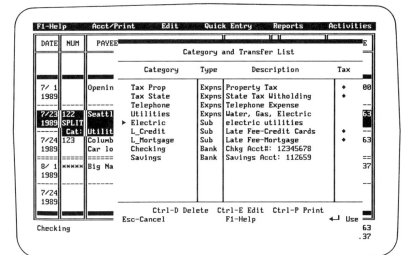

Fig. 5.7.

The Class Not Found screen.

The first option enables you to add the new class to the Class List. If you select this option, the Set Up Class screen appears on which you enter the class description as shown in figure 5.8.

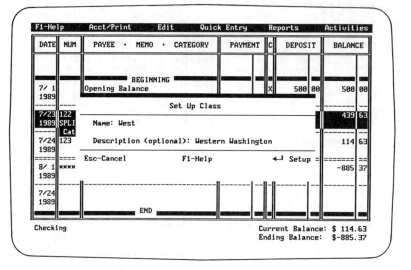

Fig. 5.8.

The Set Up Class screen.

The second option enables you to select an already used class from the Class List shown in figure 5.9.

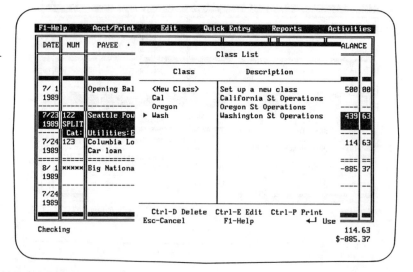

Fig. 5.9.

The Class List screen.

Chapter 7, "Using Categories and Classes," describes in detail how to use classes to add another dimension to your record keeping.

If you have problems with the MEMO field—for example, Quicken keeps expecting you to use a category, but you decide you do not want to use categories—you probably set the required categories flag on the Other Settings screen to yes. (**Other Settings** is accessed from the Change Settings menu.) If you do not want categories required, return to that menu and enter *N* for no. Chapter 2 describes each of the Change Settings menu options.

Using the BALANCE Field

Quicken calculates the BALANCE field when you record a transaction. If the balance is too large for a positive or negative number to display, Quicken displays asterisks in the BALANCE field. Quicken shows negative numbers as having a minus sign. For example, figure 5.1 shows the balance after the payment to Big National Mortgage as $-885.37. If you have a color monitor, Quicken also displays negative amounts in a different color to distinguish the negative balance. For example, with the **Navy/Azure** color setting, negative balances show in red.

Using the CATEGORY Field
To Record Transfers

You also can use the CATEGORY field to record transfers from one account to another. Suppose that you are recording a check for deposit to your savings account. The check obviously is not an expense—it is a transfer of funds from one account to another. You can identify such transfers by entering the account name in brackets as shown in figure 5.10.

If you record a transfer, Quicken records the transfer in the registers for both accounts. In the transaction shown in figure 5.10, a payment of $1000 is recorded for the checking account and, at the same time, a deposit of $1000 is recorded for the savings account. Figure 5.11 shows the register for the savings account with the $1,000 deposit. You may access the register receiving the transfer by using the Ctrl-X key combination to toggle between the two registers.

Fig. 5.10.

Transfers can be recorded in the CATEGORY field.

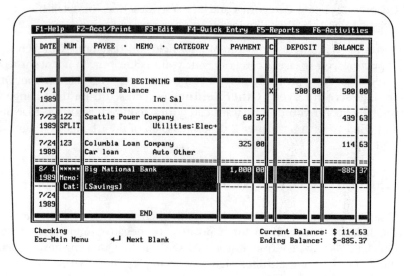

Fig. 5.11.

Transfers record a corresponding transaction.

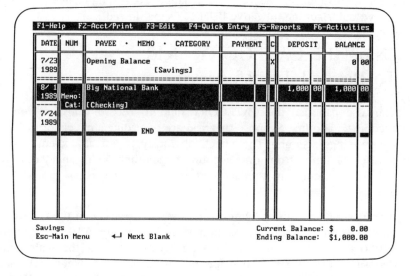

Recording the Transaction

You can record a transaction in several ways after you fill in the fields. If the cursor is on the last field, MEMO, you can press Enter. Quicken displays a prompt, asking you to confirm that you want to record the transaction, and, if you select **Record transaction**, the transaction is recorded (see fig. 5.12).

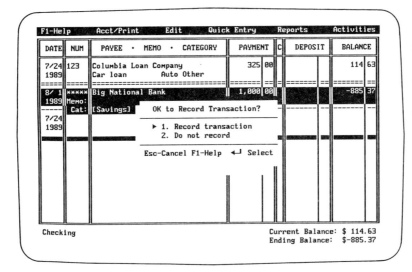

Fig. 5.12.

The OK to Record Transaction prompt.

You can record the transaction while the cursor is on any screen field by pressing Ctrl-Enter or F10. You also can select **Record transaction** from the Edit menu on the Register screen described in the next chapter.

Whatever method you choose to record a transaction, you briefly see a flashing message in the lower, left-hand corner of the screen that says, RECORDING. (If you use a very fast computer, you hardly can read the message; it appears and disappears so fast.) When Quicken finishes recording the transaction, your computer beeps and an empty row is added to the bottom of the register with the cursor positioned at the empty DATE field. (Because Quicken arranges checking account transactions by date, if you enter transactions in an order that differs from the order of their dates, Quicken also rearranges the transactions.)

Reviewing and Editing Transactions

You can review and edit transactions using the **Register** option from the Main menu at any time. Use the arrow keys to move from row to row and the Tab and Shift-Tab keys to move forward and backward among fields within a row. You also can use PgUp and PgDn to move through pages of transactions on the Register screen, Home to move to the first transaction in the register, and End to move to the last transaction in the register. To edit a transaction, move to the transaction you want to change, edit the fields, and re-record the transaction using Ctrl-Enter, F10, the **Record Transaction** option on the Edit menu, or by pressing Enter while the cursor is on the CATEGORY field.

Using the Acct/Print Menu

The Acct/Print menu (accessed by pressing F2) has six options as shown in figure 5.13.

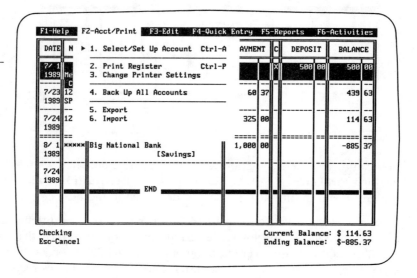

Fig. 5.13.

The Acct/Print menu.

The **Select/Set Up Account** option is the same as the Main menu option, **Select Account** described in Chapter 2. The **Print Register** option prints the current register. The **Change Printer Settings** option operates the corresponding option on the Change Settings menu accessed from Quicken's Main menu. The **Back Up All Accounts** option is the same as the **Back Up Accounts** option on the Account Group Activities menu (also accessed from the Change Settings menu). The **Export** option creates an ASCII file from transactions in the register. The **Import** option retrieves transactions stored in an ASCII file and records the transactions in the register. Only the second, fifth, and sixth options are described in this chapter because the other options are described in Chapter 2, "Selecting Accounts and Changing Settings."

Using the Print Register Option

The **Print Register** option (Ctrl-P), displays a screen you use to print the check register. Before you select this option, reload your regular paper if you have been printing check forms.

The Print Register screen, shown in figure 5.14, provides six fields to control the printing of your checks. These six fields are described in the following paragraphs.

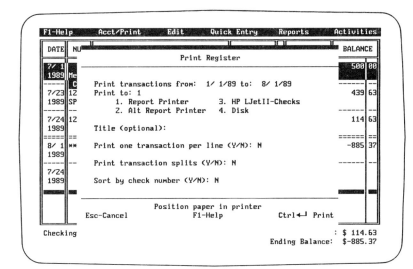

Fig. 5.14.

The Print Register screen.

Using the Print Transactions
from and to Date Fields

Because Quicken arranges transactions by date, the Print transactions from and to date fields enable you to print only the portion of the register you need. The print transaction from date usually is the date you last printed the check register and the print transaction to date usually is the current date.

CPA Tip: As part of good internal control, you always want to have a printed copy of all the transactions in your check register. Chapter 9, "Protecting Your System," describes the importance of and the reasons for internal controls. You should keep a printed record of the money that has been deposited into and withdrawn out of your account—and your check register records these transactions.

Using the Print to Field

The Print to field, which you answer by typing 1, 2, 3, or 4, selects the printer you want to use to print the register or enables you to print to the disk you specified as your data directory. (Chapter 2 describes where and how you set up the data directory.) If you used printer names on the printer set up options, you see those names in this field.

If you select 4, Quicken prints an ASCII file. (ASCII files are standardized text files that you can use to retrieve your Quicken register into a word processing program such as WordPerfect or Word.) To create an ASCII file, Quicken requests three pieces of information: file name, lines per page, and width. Enter the name you want Quicken to use for the ASCII file in the File field on the Print To Disk screen. If you want to use a data directory different from the Quicken data directory, QUICKEN3, you also can specify a path name. (See your DOS user's manual for information on path names.) Set the number of register lines Quicken prints between page breaks in the Lines per page field. If you are using 11-inch paper, the page length usually is 66 lines. If you address page length considerations elsewhere—such as in the word processing program you are going to import the data into, you can set this field to 0. Set the number of characters including blanks that Quicken prints on a line in the Width field. If you are using 8 1/2-inch paper, the characters per line usually is 80. Figure 5.15 shows the completed Print To Disk screen.

Using the Title Field

The Title field on the Print Register screen enables you to put a header such as "June Check Register" on top of each page of the printed register. If you leave this field blank, Quicken uses Register as the report title.

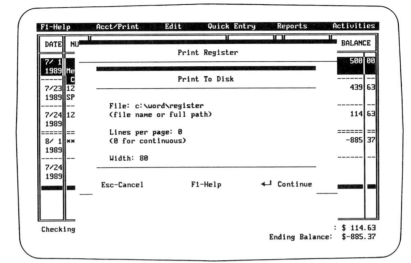

Fig. 5.15.

The completed Print To Disk screen.

Using the Print One Transaction Per Line Field

The Print one transaction per line field tells Quicken you want to print the register in a compact format. Quicken prints each transaction on one line and abbreviates some of the fields. Figure 5.16 shows the check register printed to give you a hard copy record of the register shown in figure 5.1. In figure 5.16, the Print one transaction per line field is set to N. Figure 5.17 shows the same register with the Print one transaction per line field set to Y.

Using the Print Transaction Splits Field

If you split transactions, you can have the additional category fields used to split the transaction also printed on the register. To do so, type *Y* in the Print transaction splits field. Split transactions are described in the next chapter.

Fig. 5.16.

The printed register with One transaction per line set to No.

```
                                Check Register
Checking
7/24/89                                                          Page 1

Date  Num    Transaction                  Payment  C  Deposit   Balance
----  -----  ---------------------------- --------  -  --------  --------
7/ 1         Opening Balance                       X   500.00    500.00
1989 memo:
        cat:Inc Sal

7/23 122     Seattle Power Company          60.37                439.63
1989 SPLIT
        cat:Utilities:Electric/Wash

7/24 123     Columbia Loan Company         325.00                114.63
1989 memo: Car loan
        cat:Auto Other

8/ 1 *****   Big National Bank           1,000.00               -885.37
1989 memo:
        cat:[Savings]
```

Fig. 5.17.

The printed register with One transaction per line set to Yes.

```
                                Check Register
Checking
7/24/89                                                          Page 1

Date     Num      Payee            Memo       Category    Pmt/Dep     C  Balance
-------  -----    ---------------- ---------  ----------  ----------  -  ----------
7/ 1/89           Opening Balance             Inc Sal        500.00   X   500.00
7/23/89 122   S   Seattle Power Com           Utilities:    -60.37        439.63
7/24/89 123       Columbia Loan Com Car loan  Auto Other   -325.00        114.63
8/ 1/89 *****     Big National Bank           [Savings]  -1,000.00       -885.37
```

Using the Sort by Check Number Field

Unless you use the Sort by check number field to specify otherwise, Quicken arranges transactions in the register by the transaction dates. If you set this field to Y, however, Quicken arranges transactions first by the check numbers and second by the transaction dates. (The transaction date only gets used for arranging those transactions that do not have a check number because the NUM field is blank.)

Exporting and Importing Files

The final two options on the Acct/Print menu are **Export** and **Import**. **Export** enables you to take transactions in the current register and create an ASCII file from those transactions. You then can use this ASCII file in another software program. Word processing and spreadsheet applications, for example, commonly enable you to retrieve and use information in ASCII files. To execute an export operation, select that option from the Acct/Print menu. Quicken displays the Export Transactions screen shown in figure 5.18.

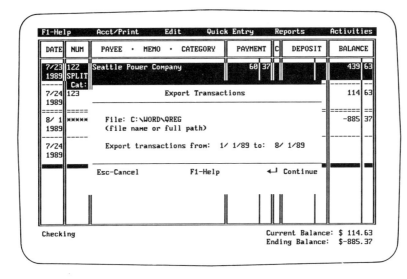

Fig. 5.18.

The Export Transactions screen.

To complete the screen, in the File field enter the DOS file name you want Quicken to use to name the new ASCII file. You also can specify a path name so that Quicken creates the ASCII file in the directory or subdirectory where you want the file located. Figure 5.18, for example, shows the Export Transactions screen filled to create an ASCII file named QREG on the hard drive in the WORD directory. The Export transactions from and to date fields enable you to specify only a certain range of dates as a basis for exporting transactions. The following list is the actual ASCII file information that Quicken writes out to record the check to Big National Bank used in figures earlier in the chapter:

```
D8/ 1/89
T-1,000.00
N*****
PBig National Bank
L[Savings]
```

The first line, which begins with D, shows the transaction date. The second line begins with T and shows the transaction amount as −1,000.00. The third line shows the transaction number. The fourth line begins with P and shows the payee. The fifth line begins with L and shows the CATEGORY field entry. The sixth line shows only a caret, ^, which designates the end of the transaction.

With this break down of register transactions—one field on a line—using the register in word processing and spreadsheet programs is easy.

Note: The **Export** option does not produce the same ASCII file as the **Print To Disk** option described earlier in the chapter. **Export** creates an ASCII file with each transaction field on one line. **Print To Disk** creates an ASCII text file that looks like a printed check register.

The **Import** option enables you to retrieve ASCII files stored in the Quicken export format and store the transactions listed in the register. You can, for example, take the ASCII file created as part of an export operation and import the file back into the register. Figure 5.19 shows the Import Transactions screen filled to import data from the ASCII file QREG. If you import an ASCII file created with the **Export** option, set the Include items which are transfers field to Y. If an item shows as a transfer, therefore, the transaction is not recorded in only the current register, but also in whatever other register money is being transferred to or from. If you previously have established passwords, Quicken does not enable you to import data without entering the proper password.

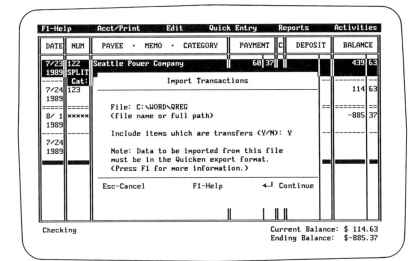

Fig. 5.19.

The Import Transactions screen.

Chapter Summary

This chapter described the basics of using Quicken's register— the central repository of all your checking account information. These basics include the components of the Register screen, how to use the register to record checking account transactions, how to review and edit transactions, and how to print the register. The next chapter, "Using the Register Menu Options," describes three additional register options—**Edit**, **Quick Entry**, and **Activities**.

Using the Register Menu Options

Chapter 5 described the basic steps for using the register; Chapter 6 describes three additional sets of menu options you can select while working with your register. These options can help you perform various functions. For example, these menus can help you search through your register for specific transactions or save and re-use information you record repeatedly in your check register. This chapter discusses the following three menus:

1. Edit (F3)

2. Quick Entry (F4)

3. Activities (F5)

This chapter describes each of these three menus and how you can use them.

Using the Edit Menu

The Edit menu, shown in figure 6.1, provides you with nine options.

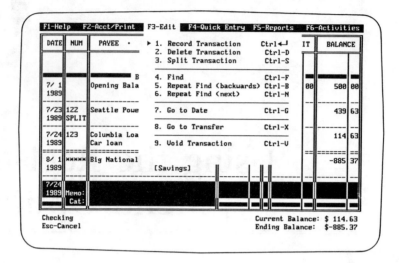

Fig. 6.1.

The Edit menu.

Recording a Transaction

Record Transaction is the same as pressing Ctrl-Enter or F10. Selecting **Record Transaction** records the transaction in the register and the data directory. You set the data directory for an account group using the **Select/Set Up Account Group** option on the Account Group Activities menu. All of the Account Group Activities menu options, including **Select/Set Up Bank Account Group**, are described in Chapter 2.

Deleting a Transaction

Selecting **Delete Transaction** (Ctrl-D) from the Edit menu removes the selected transaction from the register and the data directory. You also can use **Delete Transaction** to erase the Register screen's fields if you have not yet recorded the transaction. After you select **Delete Transaction**, Quicken asks you to confirm that you want to delete the transaction by displaying the message shown in figure 6.2.

To delete the transaction, select the first option, **Delete transaction**. To change your mind, select the second option, **Do not delete**, or press Esc.

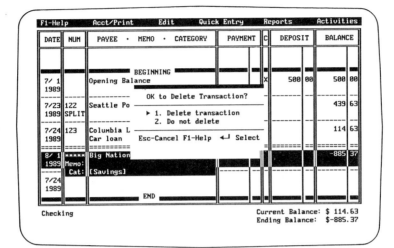

Fig. 6.2.

*The OK to
Delete
Transaction?
prompt.*

Splitting a Transaction

Selecting **Split Transaction** (Ctrl-S) from the Edit menu provides additional Category fields so that you can use more than one category for a transaction or further describe a transaction. Selecting this option accesses the Split Transaction screen, shown in figure 6.3.

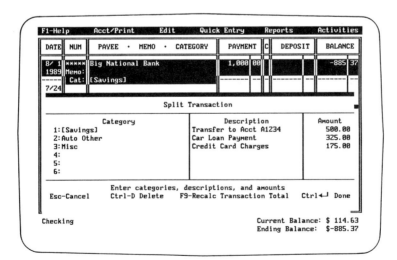

Fig. 6.3.

*The Split
Transaction
screen.*

You fill one, two, or three fields when you use the Split Transaction screen: Category, Description, or Amount. These fields are described in the following paragraphs.

Using the Category Field

The Category field on the Split Transaction screen is used like the Category field on the Register screen. You can enter categories, subcategories, classes, and subclasses. You also can use the field to record transfers. Thirty lines are available on the Split Transaction screen for descriptions or for categories. As with the Category field on the Register screen, Quicken enables you to add a category or class if it has not been defined.

If you decide to use these fields, Quicken identifies a transaction as split on the Register screen by printing SPLIT below the transaction number, as shown in figure 6.4.

Fig. 6.4.

Quicken identifies split transactions.

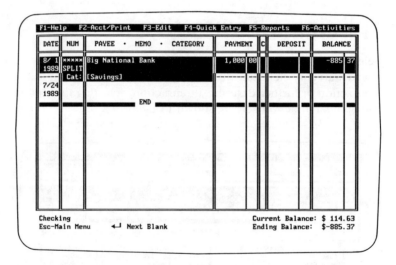

Using the Description Field

The Description field provides a 27-character space you can use to further describe a transaction or to explain why you selected a category, subcategory, class, or subclass.

Using the Amount Field

You use the Amount field in two ways, depending on whether you select **Split Transaction** before or after you enter the payment or deposit amount on the Register screen.

If you select **Split Transaction** before you enter a figure into the Amount field, Quicken adds each of the amounts you enter into the Amount fields on the Split Transaction screen together. Quicken then takes the total of these amounts and puts that total in the Payment or the Deposit field on the Register screen. If the total of the split transaction amounts is negative, Quicken places the amount into the Payment field; if the total is positive, Quicken places the amount into the Deposit field.

If you select **Split Transaction** after you enter the payment or deposit amount on the Register screen, Quicken pulls the amount entered onto the Split Transaction screen into the first amount field. When you enter the register amount as a payment, Quicken pulls the amount onto the Split Transaction screen as a negative number; when you enter the amount as a deposit, Quicken pulls the amount onto the screen as a positive number. If you then enter a number in the first Amount field on the Split Transaction screen, Quicken calculates the difference between the Register screen amount and the amount you have entered, and places this difference in the second Amount field on the Split Transaction screen.

Quicken continues to use the next, unused Amount field on the Split Transaction screen to balance the amount you entered on the Register screen with the amounts you entered on the Split Transaction screen. If you use all 30 of the Split Transaction Amount fields, however, Quicken has nowhere to make the Register screen amount equal the total Split Transaction amounts. You must adjust manually the Register screen amount or one of the Split Transaction screen amounts. You also can press F9 to total the Amount fields on the Split Transaction screen and to insert that total into the Amount field on the Register screen.

After making your changes on the Split Transaction screen, you are prompted to record the transaction. Press 1 to record the transaction; press 2 not to record the transaction.

If you split transactions, you may want to see the extra Memo fields and amounts on the Register screen. The register has a Print Split Transactions setting that you set to Y for Yes or N for No. Because the default is N, you want to set the switch to Y when you select the **Print Register** option (see Chapter 5, "Using the Register").

Using the Find Option

Select **Find** (Ctrl-F) from the Edit menu to search through the transactions you recorded in the register. Quicken displays the Transaction to Find screen shown in figure 6.5.

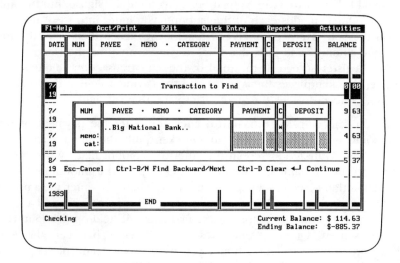

If you enter an amount in the PAYMENT column on the Transaction to Find screen, Quicken searches through the transactions in the register for an amount equal to the one you entered. The amount you are looking for is called a *search argument.* If you enter an amount in the DEPOSIT column on the Transaction to Find screen, Quicken searches the register transactions for an amount equal to the one you entered. If Quicken finds a transaction that matches your search argument, the transaction is highlighted on the Register screen. If Quicken does not find a transaction that matches your search argument, the program displays the message, No matching items found.

You also can use the PAYEE, MEMO, NUM, and C fields as search arguments. You can search with these fields by using an exact or a key-word match.

Quicken searches for an exact match to what you type. If you enter an asterisk in the C field, for example, Quicken searches for those transactions that you marked as cleared with an asterisk. If you enter *Walt Lumens* in the PAYEE field, Quicken searches for transactions with the Payee description field exactly equal to Walt Lumens. Quicken does not recognize case; WALT LUMENS, walt lumens, and wALT lUMENS are all exact matches from Quicken's perspective. If the PAYEE field is *Walter Lumens*, *W. Lumens*, or *Mr. Walt Lumens*, however, Quicken does not find the transaction.

Key-word matches enable you to search a field that includes or excludes certain letters, characters, or series of characters. Key-word matches use three characters: the period, question mark, and tilde (˜). Periods are wildcard indicators that can represent any character, a group of characters, or even no characters. The question mark represents any character. The tilde identifies a word, character, or characters you want to exclude from your search. Table 6.1 summarizes what various search arguments do and do not find.

Table 6.1
Summary of Search Arguments Using Special Characters*

Argument	What It Finds	What It Does Not Find
..interest	interest car loan interest mortgage interest mortgage interest	car loan interest expense mortgage expense war loan
interest..	interest interest expense	car loan car loan interest mortgage expense mortgage interest war loan
..interest..	interest car loan interest interest expense mortgage interest	car loan mortgage expense war loan
˜..interest	car loan interest expense mortgage expense war loan	interest car loan interest mortgage interest
˜interest..	car loan car loan interest mortgage expense mortgage interest war loan	interest interest expense

Table 6.1—*continued*

Argument	What It Finds	What It Does Not Find
~..interest..	car loan mortgage expense war loan	car loan interest interest interest expense mortgage interest
?ar loan	car loan war loan	car loan interest interest interest expense mortgage expense mortgage interest
~?ar loan	interest car loan interest interest interest expense mortgage expense mortgage interest	car loan war loan

* If the list of memo descriptions searched contains the following: car loan, car loan interest, interest, interest expense, mortgage expense, mortgage interest, and war loan.

You can search with more than one exact match or key-word argument. Figure 6.5 shows the Transaction to Find screen filled so that you search for transactions that use the phrase "big national bank" in the PAYEE field and that are marked as cleared with an asterisk (*).

If you use more than one match test, the **Find** operation locates any transactions that meet all match tests. With the Transaction to Find screen shown in figure 6.5, for example, **Find** does not locate transactions with the phrase "big national bank" used in the PAYEE field unless the asterisk character also is used in the C field. **Find** also does not locate transactions with the asterisk character used in the C field unless the phrase "big national bank" also is used in the PAYEE field.

After you fill the Transaction to Find screen and press Enter, Quicken asks which direction you want to search by displaying the screen shown in figure 6.6.

You have two options: **Find backwards** and **Find next**. **Find backwards** (Ctrl-B) looks through transactions with dates earlier than the transaction currently selected on the Register screen. **Find next** (Ctrl-N) looks through transactions with dates later than the date of the transaction currently selected on the Register screen.

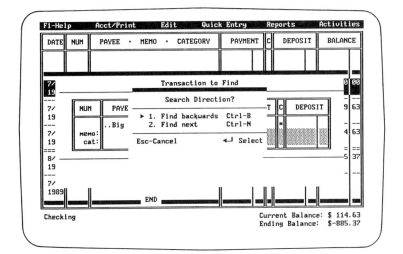

Fig. 6.6.

*The Search
Direction
screen.*

Using the Repeat Find (Backwards) and Repeat Find (Next) Options

The **Repeat Find (backwards)** and **Repeat Find (next)** options on the Edit menu repeat the Find operation already specified on the Transaction to Find screen.

Using the Go to Date Option

You may have wondered about the absence of a date field on the Transaction to Find screen. You use the **Go to Date** option (Ctrl-G) on the Edit menu to look for a transaction or account balance for a specific date. Specify the date you want to use as the basis for your search on the Go to Date screen, shown in figure 6.7.

Quicken initially displays the current system date as the Go to Date. You can change the date by typing the date you want over the default date. You also can use the + and − keys to move the date forward or backward one day at a time.

After you set the date you want, Quicken finds and displays the first transaction with the date you entered. If no transaction has the date you entered, the transaction with the date closest to the date you entered is displayed.

```
┌────────────────────────────────────────────────────────────────┐
│ F1-Help      Acct/Print      Edit      Quick Entry    Reports    Activities │
│ ┌──────┬─────┬──────────────────────────────┬─────────┬─┬─────────┬─────────┐ │
│ │ DATE │ NUM │ PAYEE · MEMO · CATEGORY      │ PAYMENT │C│ DEPOSIT │ BALANCE │ │
│ │      │     │                              │         │ │         │         │ │
│ │      │     │      ══ BEGINNING ══         │         │ │         │         │ │
│ │ 7/ 1 │     │ Opening Balance              │        │X│ 500 00 │ 500 00 │ │
│ │ 1989 │Memo:│                              │         │ │         │         │ │
│ │──────│Cat: │ Inc Sal ┌── Go to Date ──┐   │         │ │─────── ─ │─────── │ │
│ │ 7/23 │ 122 │ Seattle P                    │         │ │         │ 439 63 │ │
│ │ 1989 │SPLIT│         │                 │   │         │ │         │         │ │
│ │──────│─────│──────── Date to find: 7/24/89│         │ │─────── ─ │─────── │ │
│ │ 7/24 │ 123 │ Columbia│                 │   │         │ │         │ 114 63 │ │
│ │ 1989 │     │ Car loan└─────────────────┘   │         │ │         │         │ │
│ │══════│═════│═════════ Esc-Cancel F1-Help ↵ Continue ══│═│═══════ ═ │═══════ │ │
│ │ 8/ 1 │xxxxx│ Big Natio                    │         │ │         │ -885 37 │ │
│ │ 1989 │SPLIT│                              │         │ │         │         │ │
│ │──────│─────│──────────────────────────────│         │ │─────── ─ │─────── │ │
│ │ 7/24 │     │                              │         │ │         │         │ │
│ │ 1989 │     │        ══ END ══             │         │ │         │         │ │
│ └──────┴─────┴──────────────────────────────┴─────────┴─┴─────────┴─────────┘ │
│  Checking                         Current Balance: $ 114.63                   │
│                                   Ending Balance:  $-885.37                   │
└────────────────────────────────────────────────────────────────┘
```

Fig. 6.7.

The Go to Date screen.

Because Quicken arranges transactions in the register by date, you do not need to specify a search direction for the **Go to Date** option. By comparing the date on the currently selected transaction to the Go to Date, Quicken determines which direction it needs to search. If the Go to Date is earlier than the date on the selected transaction, Quicken looks through the previous transactions; if the Go to Date is later than the date on the selected transaction, Quicken looks through the next transactions.

Using the Go to Transfer Option

If the currently selected transaction is a transfer transaction, you can use the **Go to Transfer** option on the Edit menu to display the register with the corresponding transaction. For example, figure 6.8 shows that the Big National Bank check is selected. By looking at the CATEGORY field, which displays [Savings], you can see that this is a transfer transaction.

You must have set up the bank account receiving the transfer through the Select Account menu. The name of the account to which the transfer is taking place is shown in the CATEGORY field with brackets around the name. For example, [Savings] identifies the transaction as a transfer.

If you select **Go to Transfer** (Ctrl-X) from the Edit menu, Quicken displays the savings account register with the corresponding transaction selected. Figure 6.9 shows the corresponding transaction in the savings register.

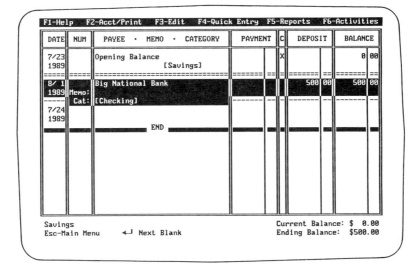

Fig. 6.8.

The Big National Bank check is part of a transfer.

Fig. 6.9.

The corresponding transaction.

You may notice that the transaction shows up in the first account as a payment—because it reduces that account balance, and in the second account as a deposit—because it increases that account balance. If you use the **Go to Transfer** option on a split transaction, Quicken asks you to identify the category you want to go to (see fig. 6.10). With a split transaction, you can make transfers to more than one account. If you try to change a split transaction from one of the other registers, Quicken tells you that the transaction was created through a transfer, and you must return to the original transaction to make changes.

Fig. 6.10.

For split transactions, you need to choose the transfer operation.

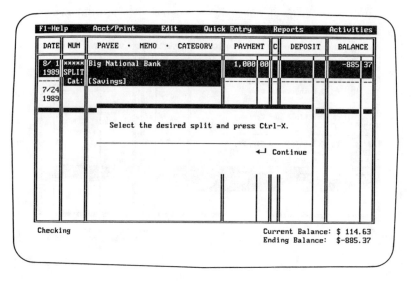

Voiding a Transaction

The **Void Transaction** option is the final option on the Edit menu. If you select **Void Transaction**, Quicken inserts VOID, before the payee name, changes the payment or deposit amounts to zero, and sets the cleared flag to X. Figure 6.11 shows the now voided check to Big National Bank.

Fig. 6.11.

A voided transaction.

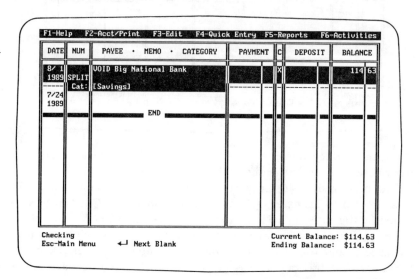

If you void a transaction that is part of a transfer from one account to another, voiding any part of the transaction also voids the other parts of the transaction—those recorded in the other registers. Figure 6.12 shows the other part of the Big National Check that also is voided.

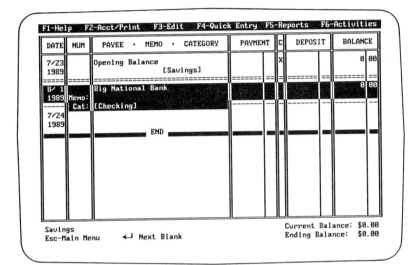

Fig. 6.12.

The corresponding transfer transaction also is voided.

CPA Tip: **Void Transaction** enables you to keep track of voided transactions in your check register along side actual transactions. You can keep an audit trail of voided and stop-payment checks. Use **Void Transaction** to perform this sort of record keeping. Chapter 9, "Protecting Your System," talks more about internal controls and audit trails.

Using the Quick Entry Menu

The Quick Entry menu, shown in figure 6.13, provides six options that enable you to define categories and store and group frequently used transactions.

The following paragraphs describe how you can use these six options; the options are described in the order of those most frequently used, not in the order in which they appear on the menu.

Fig. 6.13.

*The Quick
Entry menu.*

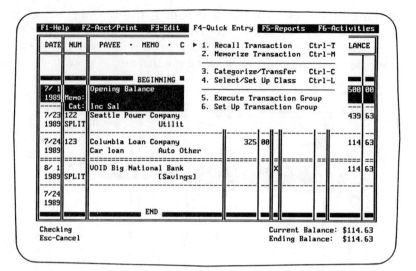

Memorizing a Transaction

Selecting **Memorize Transaction** (Ctrl-M) from the Quick Entry menu
retrieves the fields shown for the selected transaction on the Register
screen and saves the information in a file called the Memorized Transactions List. This list saves the information for transactions you repeatedly
record, so that you are not forced to start from scratch every time you
record the same transaction. You can retrieve the information from the
Memorized Transactions List and use this information to record payments
or deposits in the register.

To have Quicken memorize a transaction, such as the one shown in figure
6.14, select **Memorize Transaction** from the Quick Entry menu when
the transaction information you want to save is highlighted on the Register screen.

Quicken displays a message telling you that the information highlighted
on the Register screen is about to be memorized (see fig. 6.15).

To finish the memorize operation, press Enter. The value of this memorized transaction is demonstrated in the next section.

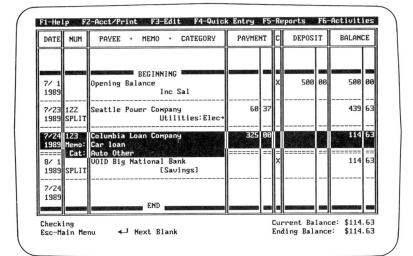

Fig. 6.14.

You can memorize the monthly car payment.

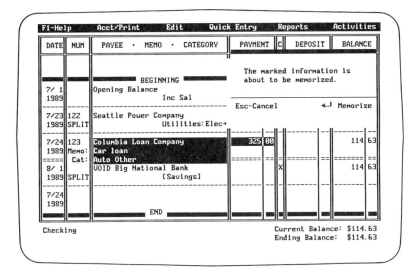

Fig. 6.15.

Quicken tells you that the marked information is about to be memorized.

Recalling a Transaction

Selecting **Recall Transaction** (Ctrl-T) enables you to fill a row in the register with memorized transactions. Suppose that you have Quicken memorize the payment shown in figure 6.14 to record your monthly car payment.

When you need to record the payment in the following month, select **Recall Transaction** from the Quick Entry menu. The Memorized Transactions List is displayed as shown in figure 6.16. Only the car loan payment is shown because this transaction is the only one that has been memorized.

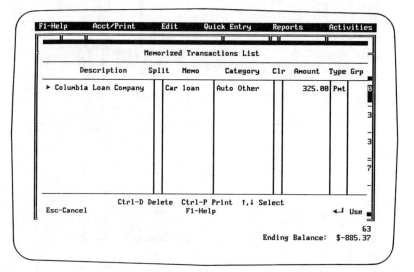

Fig. 6.16.

The Memorized Transactions List.

Figure 6.16 shows the information saved as part of the **Memorize Transaction** operation. Seven fields are shown on-screen, all of which you may have filled to record a register transaction.

The payee name is in the Description column; the memo is in the Memo column; the category name is in the Category column, and the check amount is in the Amount column. If you split a check transaction, an S appears in the Split column. Quicken also places the abbreviation Pmt in the Type field to identify the transaction as a payment, Dep in the Type field to identify the transaction as a deposit, or Chk in the Type field to identify the transaction as a check. The Clr column shows whether you have marked the transaction as cleared (see Chapter 8, "Reconciling Your Bank Account"). The Grp column identifies whether the memorized transaction is part of a group of transactions.

To select a memorized transaction, use the ↑ and ↓ keys to move the selection triangle to the left of the description field. Press Enter, and Quicken fills the next empty row in the register with the information from the memorized transaction. You then can edit any field. To record the check, press Ctrl-Enter. Figure 6.17 shows the transaction created from the Memorized Transactions List.

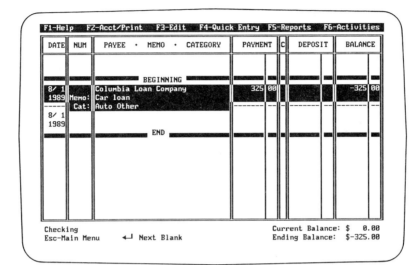

Fig. 6.17.

The recalled transaction.

Deleting Memorized Transactions

You also use the **Recall Transaction** option to delete memorized transactions from the Memorized Transactions List.

To delete a transaction from the list, select the transaction and press Ctrl-D. Quicken reminds you that you are about to delete a memorized transaction.

CPA Tip: Consider each of the transactions you now regularly record as candidates for the Memorized Transactions List: rent, house payment, utility payment, school loans, payroll deposits, bank service fees, and so on. Using the **Memorized Transaction** option saves you time that you can use to tap Quicken's other financial management tools (categories and reports, for example).

Using the Categorize/Transfer Option

The **Categorize/Transfer** option (Ctrl-C) enables you to create or retrieve a category. Figure 6.18 shows the Category and Transfer List screen. If you want to retrieve a category or an account name for a transfer, select the category or account you want to use by moving the selection triangle to the left of the one you want to use and press Enter. Quicken retrieves the category or account name from the list and places it in the CATEGORY field on the Register screen. (If you selected **Split transaction**, the account name appears in the highlighted Category field on the Split Transaction screen.)

Fig. 6.18.

The Category and Transfer List screen.

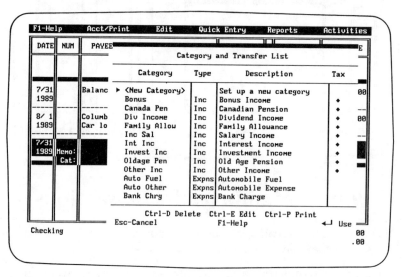

You also can use the Category and Transfer List screen to create categories. Select the first line of the Category and Transfer List, ‹New Category›. Quicken displays the Set Up Category screen shown in figure 6.19.

The Set Up Category screen is filled to define a new category for computer repair expenses; the same screen is displayed when you define a new category from the CATEGORY field on the Register screen. To define a new category, enter the name you want to use, identify the type of category by entering an I, E, or S in the Income, Expense, or Subcategory field, type a description, and mark the category as tax-related by using a Y or N. (Categories marked as tax-related appear on the special report, Personal Tax Summary, described in Chapter 11.)

CPA Tip: Review last year's tax return to help you identify tax-deductible expenses. On your Form 1040 (Federal Individual Tax Return), Schedule A lists deductible itemized expenses including medical bills, personal interest, contributions, moving expenses, investments, and so on. Call your CPA if you have specific questions when trying to identify a potential tax-deductible expense.

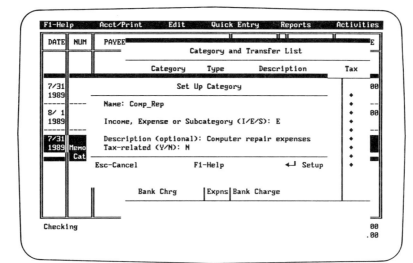

Fig. 6.19.

The Set Up Category screen.

Selecting and Setting Up a Class

Use the fourth option on the Quick Entry menu, **Select/Set Up Class**, to select, add, edit, and delete classes. (Chapter 7, "Using Categories and Classes," describes the reasons you may want to use classes and provides some examples of approaches you may want to take.) If you select **Select/ Set Up Class**, Quicken displays the Class List screen shown in figure 6.20.

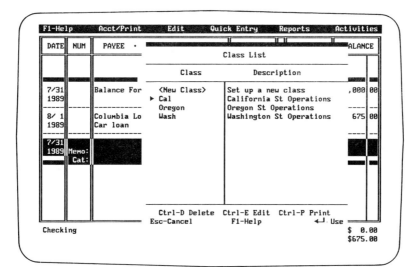

Fig. 6.20.

The Class List screen.

To select a class, use the arrow keys to move the selection triangle to the class you want and press Enter.

To add a class to the list, select the ‹New Class› line on the list with the selection triangle and press Enter. Quicken displays the Set Up Class screen, shown in figure 6.21, on which you can enter a class name and description.

Fig. 6.21.

The Set Up Class screen.

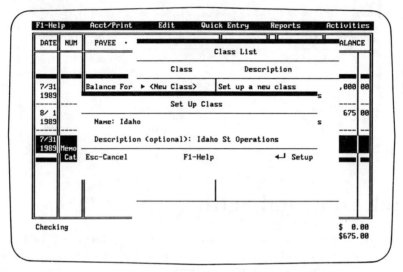

To edit a class on the list, select the class you want to modify and press Ctrl-E. Quicken displays the Edit Class screen, shown in figure 6.22, that you can use to modify the class name or description.

Fig. 6.22.

The Edit Class screen.

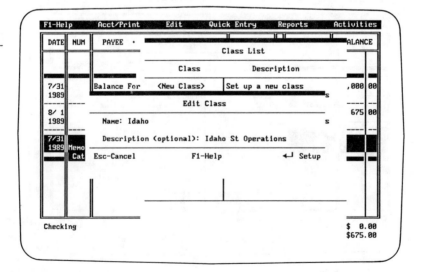

To delete a class on the list, select the class you want to delete and press Ctrl-D. Quicken alerts you that a class is about to be deleted (see fig. 6.23).

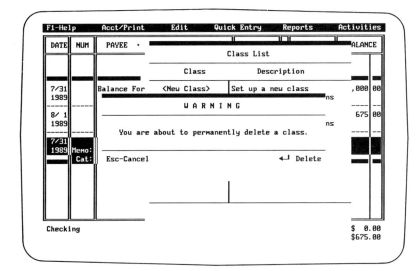

Fig. 6.23.

Quicken warns you when you are about to delete a class.

To complete the deletion, press Enter. To cancel the deletion, press Esc.

Setting Up a Transaction Group

Transaction groups are collections of memorized transactions that function as time-saving devices to make record keeping easier. You probably want to use transaction groups because they enable you to recall several memorized transactions at the same time.

The first step in using a transaction group is to set up a group by selecting **Set Up Transaction Group** from the Quick Entry menu. The Select Transaction Group to Set Up/Change screen is displayed as shown in figure 6.24.

Four fields are on the Select Transaction Group screen: Group, Size, Frequency, and Next Scheduled. The Group field describes the number and name of the group. The Size field indicates the number of memorized transactions in a group. The Frequency field identifies how often you use a transaction group. The Next Scheduled group shows the next scheduled date that the transaction group should be used to create a group of check

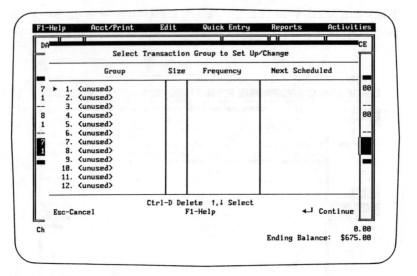

Fig. 6.24.

The Select Transaction Group to Set Up/Change screen.

```
F1-Help      Acct/Print      Edit      Quick Entry      Reports      Activities
DA                                                                           CE
                  Select Transaction Group to Set Up/Change

             Group          Size     Frequency       Next Scheduled
 7  ▶  1. <unused>                                                          00
 1     2. <unused>
--     3. <unused>
 8     4. <unused>                                                          00
 1     5. <unused>
--     6. <unused>                                                          --
 7     7. <unused>
 1     8. <unused>
       9. <unused>
      10. <unused>
      11. <unused>
      12. <unused>

                        Ctrl-D Delete  ↑,↓ Select
     Esc-Cancel              F1-Help                    ↵ Continue
 Ch                                                            0.00
                                              Ending Balance: $675.00
```

transactions. Until you complete the set-up process, the groups are labeled as unused, and the other three fields are blank as shown in figure 6.24.

Choose the transaction group you want to set up or change by using the ↑ and ↓ keys to move the selection triangle and pressing Enter. Figure 6.25 shows the Describe Group screen you use to define aspects of a transaction group: the name, frequency, and next scheduled date. These fields also appear on the Select Transaction Group to Set Up/Change screen.

You can use a maximum of 20 characters to describe the name. Set the frequency using one of the nine settings shown in figure 6.25: None, Weekly, Every two weeks, Twice a month, Every four weeks, Monthly, Quarterly, Twice a year, or Annually. Select the frequency you want by typing the number that corresponds with the desired frequency. Quicken provides nine groups and eight frequencies, which gives you enough space to set up a group for each of the eight frequencies and still have an extra group. If you set the frequency to something other than None, you also must set the next scheduled date.

Figure 6.25 shows the Describe Group screen filled out to set up the first group for a series of monthly transactions recorded at the beginning of every month. Quicken reminds you of the next scheduled date—in this example, 8/1/89.

After you complete the Describe Group screen, press Enter to display the Assign Transactions screen shown in figure 6.26. Use the ↑ and ↓ keys to move the selection triangle to the transaction that should be included in a

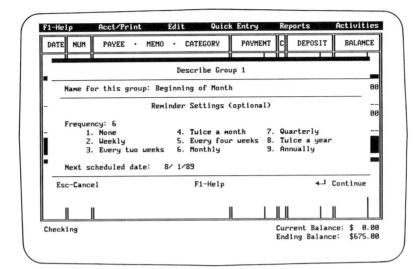

Fig. 6.25.

The Describe Group screen.

group. The list of transactions appearing on the Assign Transaction screen are those transactions you previously memorized. When a memorized transaction is marked, press the space bar to assign that transaction to a group. You can tell when a transaction has been assigned to a group, because the last column on the Assign Transactions screen, Grp, displays the group number.

Figure 6.26 shows two memorized transactions selected for Transaction Group 2: the transfer to savings and the monthly car payment. After you assign transactions to a transaction group, press Enter.

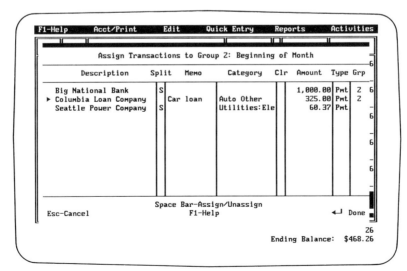

Fig. 6.26.

The Assign Transactions screen.

If you want to change or modify a transaction group, use the **Set Up Transaction Group** option on the Quick Entry menu again and select the previously set up transaction group. You access the Describe Group and Assign Transactions screens as shown in figures 6.25 and 6.26. Make the required changes on the appropriate screen and press Enter to continue to the next screen.

Executing a Transaction Group

Selecting **Execute Transaction Group** creates transactions for each of the memorized transactions in the group. This option is roughly equivalent to simultaneously recalling the memorized transactions that constitute a transaction group.

The **Execute Transaction Group** operation also moves the next scheduled date for the Transaction group forward, using whatever frequency you specified. The Select Transaction Group to Execute screen is shown in figure 6.27.

Fig. 6.27.

The Select Transaction Group to Execute screen.

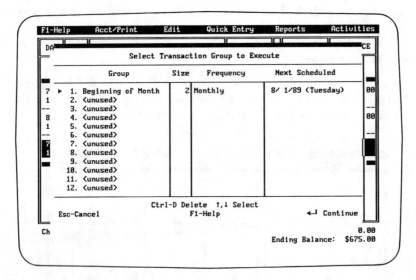

```
 F1-Help      Acct/Print      Edit      Quick Entry      Reports      Activities
 DA                                                                          CE
                       Select Transaction Group to Execute

              Group           Size    Frequency       Next Scheduled
 7   ▶  1. Beginning of Month    2  Monthly         8/ 1/89 (Tuesday)    00
 1      2. <unused>
 --     3. <unused>
 8      4. <unused>                                                      00
 1      5. <unused>
 --     6. <unused>                                                      --
 7      7. <unused>
 1      8. <unused>
        9. <unused>
       10. <unused>
       11. <unused>
       12. <unused>
                      Ctrl-D Delete   ↑,↓ Select
    Esc-Cancel             F1-Help                      ↵ Continue
 Ch                                                        0.00
                                          Ending Balance:  $675.00
```

To select a group, move the selection triangle to the appropriate group and press Enter. Quicken prompts you for the Transaction Group Date as shown in figure 6.28.

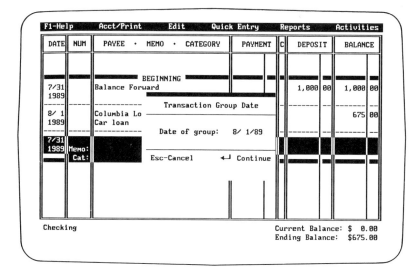

Fig. 6.28.

The Transaction Group Date screen.

Edit the default date, if necessary, by using the + and − keys to change the date one day at a time. Press Enter when the transaction date is correct. Quicken records the memorized transactions to the register, saves the transactions, and displays the message shown in figure 6.29.

Fig. 6.29.

The Transaction Group Entered screen.

You can review and edit the transactions by using the Register screen.

Using the Activities Menu

The register Activities menu has five options as shown in figure 6.30.

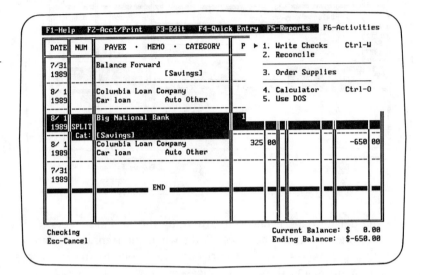

The **Write Checks** option (Ctrl-W) accesses the Write Checks screen like the **Write/Print Checks** option on Quicken's Main menu does. The **Write/Print Checks** option is described in Chapters 3 and 4.

The **Reconcile** option accesses the Reconciliation screen and options as does the **Reconcile** option on the Main menu (see Chapter 8).

The **Order Supplies** option displays the Print Supply Order Form screen, shown in figure 6.31, that you print and then use as a three-page order form for purchasing supplies. These forms can be used to order check forms and envelopes from Intuit (the manufacturer of Quicken). Although the actual order form is not shown here, the form is similar to the order form that Intuit provides in the Quicken packaging.

The fourth Activities menu option, **Calculator** (Ctrl-O), accesses the on-line, 10-key calculator. Figure 6.32 shows the calculator. If you want to use the calculator, see Chapter 1, "Getting Started with Quicken," which describes the steps for using this helpful feature.

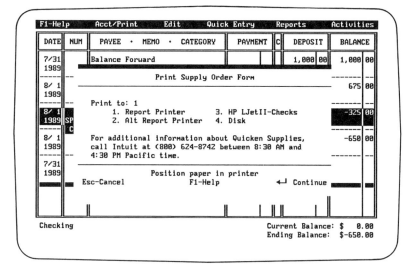

Fig. 6.31.

The Print Supply Order Form screen.

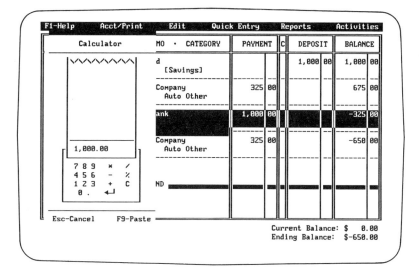

Fig. 6.32.

The on-line calculator.

The **Use DOS** option calls DOS and displays the DOS prompt, as follows:

```
To return to Quicken, type EXIT.

Microsoft® MS-DOS® Version 3.30
            ©Copyright Microsoft Corp 1981-1987

C:\QUICKEN3›
```

This feature is handy when you want to execute DOS commands before leaving Quicken. For example, you may want to format a disk to make a backup copy of a bank account.

Chapter Summary

This chapter described the details of using the three register menus not covered in the preceding chapter. The Edit, Quick Entry, and Activities menus provide the capability to search through your register for specific transactions and to save and re-use transaction information you repeatedly record.

Maintaining
Your Accounts

Includes

Using Categories and Classes

Reconciling Your Bank Account

Protecting Your System

Using Categories and Classes

Your current check register represents a wealth of information about your personal or business finances. If you could somehow summarize the information your check register contains, keeping track of tax deductions, the amounts spent for various items, and the types of money that flow into and out of the account would be easy. Quicken's categories and classes provide the tools you need to do all of this.

This chapter describes categories and classes, tells why and when you should use them, shows the predefined categories Quicken provides for business and personal use, describes the steps for using predefined categories and the steps for adding, deleting, and editing your own categories and classes.

Working with Categories

Categories enable you to group the payments that flow out of your account and the deposits that flow into your account. You may find that the deposits into your account stem from two sources: earned wages from a full-time job and profits from a part-time business. You also may find that your payments stem from four expenditures: rent, food, transportation, and your part-time business expenses. By grouping each payment from and deposit into your account, Quicken easily adds up the totals for each type of payment and deposit. You then can see exactly how much each category contributes to your cash flow. You may find, for example, that your cash flows into and out of your account look like those summarized in Table 7.1.

Table 7.1
Personal Cash Flows

Deposits	
Wages from job	$15,400
Business profits	4,300
Total Deposits	19,700
Withdrawals	
Housing	6,000
Food	3,000
Transportation	3,000
Business Expenses	500
Total Withdrawals	12,500
Cash Flows	7,200

Why Use Categories?

Is the information shown in table 7.1 valuable? Categorizing your income and outgo is the first step in beginning to manage your personal or business finances.

When you use Quicken for personal use, categories enable you to do the following:

1. Track and tally income tax deductions for individual retirement accounts, mortgage interest deductions, or charitable contributions

2. Break checking account deposits and payments down into groups of similar transactions so that you can summarize your personal income and outgo

3. Budget income and outgo and compare budgeted amounts with actual amounts

If you want to use Quicken for a business, the predefined categories enable you to prepare most of the reports you need for managing your business finances. These reports include the following:

1. A report that resembles and performs most of the arithmetic required to complete your federal income tax form, Schedule C. (The Schedule C form reports the profits or losses from a business or profession.)

2. Income and cash flow statements on a monthly and annual basis that enable you to understand your cash flows and measure your business profits or losses

3. Employee payroll checks and reports

If any of the reasons listed above look like benefits you want to enjoy as part of using Quicken, you want to use Quicken's categories. How involved or complicated your use of the categories becomes depends on what your goals are.

Building a List of Categories

Your needs determine the various categories you want to use to group similar payments or deposits. Three basic rules apply when building a list of categories.

First, if you want to use categories for tallying and tracking income tax deductions, you need a category for each deduction. If you use the individual retirement account deduction, the mortgage interest deduction, and the state and local taxes deduction, you need categories for each of these. The following list shows the itemized deductions you may want to track to more easily prepare your personal income tax return. The list is based on the federal income tax form, Schedule A.

Sample personal tax deduction categories

Medical and dental*
Medical and dental—other*
State and local income taxes
Real estate taxes
Other taxes including personal property taxes
Deductible home mortgage interest paid to financial institutions
Deductible home mortgage interest paid to individuals
Deductible points
Deductible investment interest
Contributions by cash or check
Contributions other than by cash or check
Casualty or theft losses**
Moving expenses**
Unreimbursed employee expenses
Other miscellaneous expenses

* The first medical expense category includes prescription medicines and drugs, insulin, doctors, dentists, nurses, hospitals, and medical insurance premiums. The second includes items like hearing aids, dentures, eyeglasses, transportation, and lodging.

** This itemized deduction must be supported by an additional tax form. Therefore, you also want to consider setting up the individual amounts that need to be reported on that form as categories.

The following list shows the income and deduction categories you may want to use to prepare your business income tax return. (The list is based on the federal income tax form, Schedule C.)

Income categories

>   Gross receipts or sales
>   Sales returns and allowances
>   Cost of goods sold*
>   Other income

Deduction categories

>   Advertising
>   Bad debts from sales or services
>   Bank service charges
>   Car and truck expenses
>   Commissions
>   Depletion
>   Depreciation**
>   Dues and publications
>   Employee benefit programs
>   Freight
>   Insurance
>   Interest—mortgage
>   Interest—other
>   Laundry and cleaning
>   Legal and professional services
>   Office expense
>   Pension and profit-sharing plans
>   Rent on business property
>   Repairs
>   Supplies
>   Taxes
>   Travel
>   Meals and entertainment
>   Utilities and telephone
>   Wages
>   Wages—job credit
>   Other deductions

* The cost of goods sold needs to be calculated or verified using part III of Schedule C.

** This deduction amount must be supported by an additional tax form; consider setting up the individual amounts reported on that form as categories.

Second, if you want to use categories to summarize your cash inflows and outflows, you need a category for each income or expense account you want to use in your summaries. For example, if you want to account for your work expenses and your spouse's work expenses, you need categories for both.

Third, if you want to use categories to budget (so that you later can compare what you budgeted and what you actually spent), you need a category for each comparison you want to make. If you want to budget entertainment expenses and clothing expenses, you need categories for both.

By applying these three rules, you should be able to build a list of the categories you want to use. As an aid in creating your own list, figure 7.1 shows the Category List that Quicken provides for personal accounts. Figure 7.2 shows the Category List Quicken provides for business accounts.

```
                        Category and Transfer List
QDATA                                                          Page 1
7/13/89

                                          Tax
        Category          Description     Rel  Type   Budget Amount
     ---------------   ------------------- --- -----  -------------
     Bonus             Bonus Income         *   Inc
     Canada Pen        Canadian Pension     *   Inc
     Div Income        Dividend Income      *   Inc
     Family Allow      Family Allowance     *   Inc
     Inc Sal           Salary Income        *   Inc
     Int Inc           Interest Income      *   Inc
     Invest Inc        Investment Income    *   Inc
     Oldage Pen        Old Age Pension      *   Inc
     Other Inc         Other Income         *   Inc
     Auto Fuel         Automobile Fuel          Expns
     Auto Other        Automobile Expense       Expns
     Bank Chrg         Bank Charge              Expns
     Canada Pension    Canadian Pension Plan    Expns
     Charity           Charitable Donations *   Expns
     Childcare         Childcare Expense        Expns
     Christmas         Christmas Expenses       Expns
     Clothing          Clothing                 Expns
     Dining            Dining Out               Expns
     Dues              Dues                     Expns
     Education         Education                Expns
     Enter.            Entertainment            Expns
     FICA              Social Security Tax  *   Expns
     Gifts             Gift Expenses            Expns
     Groceries         Groceries                Expns
     Home Rpair        Home Repair & Maint.     Expns
     Household         Household Misc. Exp      Expns
     Housing           Housing                  Expns
     Insurance         Insurance                Expns
     Int Exp           Interest Expense     *   Expns
     Invest Exp        Investment Expense   *   Expns
     Medical           Medical & Dental     *   Expns
     Misc              Miscellaneous            Expns
     Mort Int          Mortgage Interest Exp *  Expns
     Mort Prin         Mortgage Principal       Expns
     Other Exp         Other Expenses           Expns
     Recreation        Recreation Expense       Expns
     RRSP              Reg Retirement Sav Plan  Expns
     Subscriptions     Subscriptions            Expns
     Tax Fed           Federal Tax Withholding * Expns
     Tax Other         Misc. Taxes          *   Expns
     Tax Prop          Property Tax         *   Expns
     Tax State         State Tax Witholding *   Expns
     Telephone         Telephone Expense        Expns
     Utilities         Water, Gas, Electric     Expns
     Checking          Chkg Acct#: 12345678     Bank
```

Fig. 7.1.

Quicken's sample category list for personal use.

Fig. 7.2.

Quicken's sample category list for business use.

```
                            Category and Transfer List
QBUSINSS                                                              Page 1
7/13/89

                                              Tax
        Category            Description       Rel   Type   Budget Amount
     ---------------   ------------------------  ---   -----   -------------
      Gr Sales          Gross Sales             *    Inc
      Other Inc         Other Income            *    Inc
      Rent Income       Rent Income             *    Inc
      Ads               Advertising             *    Expns
      Bank Chrg         Bank Charge             *    Expns
      Canada Pension    Canadian Pension Plan        Expns
      Car               Car & Truck             *    Expns
      Commission        Commissions             *    Expns
      Enter.            Entertainment           *    Expns
      Freight           Freight                 *    Expns
      Insurance         Insurance               *    Expns
      Int Paid          Interest Paid           *    Expns
      L&P Fees          Legal & Prof. Fees      *    Expns
      Late Fees         Late Payment Fees       *    Expns
      Misc              Miscellaneous Expense        Expns
      Mort Int          Mortgage Interest       *    Expns
      Office            Office Expenses         *    Expns
      Other Exp         Other Expenses          *    Expns
      Rent Paid         Rent Paid               *    Expns
      Repairs           Repairs                 *    Expns
      Returns           Returns & Allowances    *    Expns
      Supplies          Supplies                *    Expns
      Taxes             Taxes                   *    Expns
      Travel            Travel Expenses         *    Expns
      Utilities         Utilities & Phone       *    Expns
      Wages             Wages & Job Credits     *    Expns
      Checking          Chkg Acct#: 1234567          Bank
```

After you complete your list, review the categories for any redundancies produced by two of the rules calling for the same category. For example, for personal use of Quicken, you may add a category to budget for monthly individual retirement account (IRA) payments. You also may add a category to tally IRA payments because they represent potential tax deductions. Because both categories are the same, you can cross one off your list.

Sometimes, however, overlapping or redundant categories are not as easy to spot. A tax deduction you need to calculate may be only a portion of a budgeting category, or a budgeting amount you need to calculate may be only a portion of a tax-deduction category. You need to use categories that are smaller than the tax-deduction amount or the budgeting amount so that you can add up the individual categories that make up a tax-deduction, accounting amount, or budgeted amount.

Categories act as building blocks you use to calculate the amounts you really want to know. For example, you may use the following categories to calculate the tax-deduction amounts and the budgeted amounts shown in table 7.2:

Mortgage interest
Mortgage principal
Mortgage late-payment fees
Credit card late-payment fees
Property taxes

Table 7.2
Personal Budget and Tax Amounts

Amounts	Categories Used
Late fees (a budgeted amt.)	Mortgage late-payment fees Credit card late-payment fees
Housing (a budgeted amt.)	Mortgage principal Mortgage interest Property taxes
Mortgage interest (deduction)	Mortgage interest Mortgage late-payment fees
Property taxes (deduction)	Property taxes

Using Subcategories

If you want to use categories as building blocks to calculate other budgeted or tax-deduction amounts, you need to know about subcategories. Suppose that taking the first row of the data from table 7.2, you create two building block categories to track late payment fees on your mortgage and credit cards, L_Mortgage and L_Credit. If you also set up a category for late fees, Late_Fees, you can assign mortgage late-payment fees to the category-subcategory combination, Late_Fees and L_Mortgage. You also can assign credit card late-payment fees to the category-subcategory combination, Late_Fees and L_Credit. On your reports, the totals for L_Mortgage and L_Credit as well as Late_Fees will show. Figure 7.3 shows an example of a report that illustrates the effect of all this.

Within Quicken, you cannot produce reports comparing the actual amounts spent for a subcategory with a budgeted amount, because Quicken only enables you to enter a budgeted amount for the category, not the subcategory. If you set up the category, Late_Fees and the two subcategories, L_Mortgage and L_Credit, the budgeted amount Quicken shows on the budget reports is for Late_Fees.

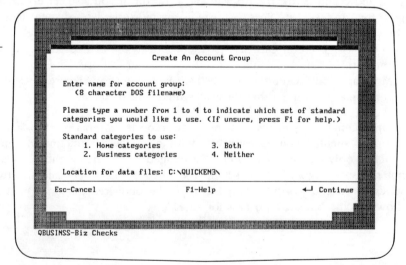

Fig. 7.3.

Using subcategories.

```
                    Showing Subcategories on Report
                       7/ 1/89 Through 7/31/89
Checking                                                          Page 1
7/15/89
                                             7/ 1/89-
                    Category Description      7/31/89
                    --------------------   ------------
INFLOWS
  Salary Income                               2,000.00
                                            ------------
TOTAL INFLOWS                                 2,000.00

OUTFLOWS
  Automobile Expense                            178.12
  Entertainment                                  34.56
  Federal Tax Witholding                        245.21
  Groceries                                     453.90
  Home Repair & Maint.                          125.00
  Housing                                       650.00
  Interest Expense                               32.46
  Late Payment Fees:
    Late Fee-Credit Cards          23.45
    Late Fee-Mortgage              50.00
                                 ----------
    Total Late Payment Fees                      73.45
  Reg Retirement Sav Plan                        50.00
  Water, Gas, Electric                           54.32
                                            ------------
TOTAL OUTFLOWS                                1,897.02

                                            ------------
OVERALL TOTAL                                   102.98
                                            ============
```

Setting Up Categories

When you create account groups, you have the option, on the Create An Account Group screen, of using the predefined home or business categories as the foundation of your own category list (see fig. 7.4).

Fig. 7.4.

The Create An Account Group screen.

```
                    Create An Account Group

  Enter name for account group:
     (8 character DOS filename)

  Please type a number from 1 to 4 to indicate which set of standard
  categories you would like to use. (If unsure, press F1 for help.)

  Standard categories to use:
     1. Home categories          3. Both
     2. Business categories       4. Neither

  Location for data files: C:\QUICKEN3\

  Esc-Cancel                      F1-Help              ↵ Continue

QBUSINSS-Biz Checks
```

If you specified that the home categories should be used, you already have set up the categories shown in figure 7.1. If you specified that the business categories should be used, you already have set up the categories shown in figure 7.2. Even if you elected to use one of the sample category lists, however, you may need to modify the category list. The next paragraphs describe adding, editing, and deleting categories.

Adding Categories

The easiest place to add categories is from the Register screen. Access the Register screen by selecting **Register** from the Main menu. From the Register screen, press F4 to access the Quick Entry menu shown in figure 7.5.

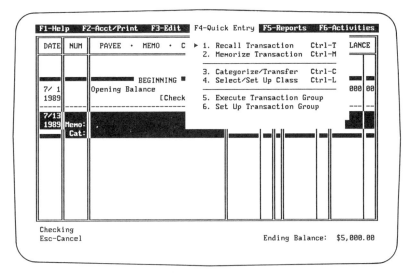

Fig. 7.5.

The Quick Entry menu.

To add a category, select **Categorize/Transfer** or use the shortcut key combination Ctrl-C. After you select **Categorize/Transfer**, the Category and Transfer List screen appears as shown in figure 7.6.

To add a category, select the first item on the list, ‹New Category›. Quicken then displays the Set Up Category screen, shown in figure 7.7.

Fig. 7.6.

The Category and Transfer List screen.

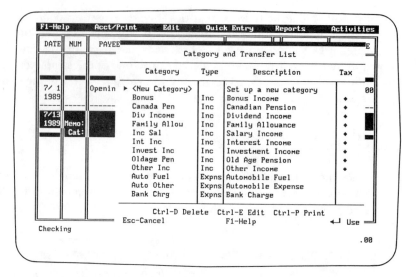

Fig. 7.7.

The Set Up Category screen.

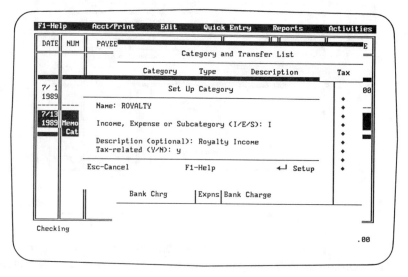

Type the category name you want to use in the Name field. The Income, Expense, or Subcategory field tells Quicken whether a category should appear in the income or expense section of a report or if the category is a subcategory. You do not need to tell Quicken whether a subcategory is an income or expense figure because the program knows by looking at the subcategory's category. You can use up to 25 characters to describe the category. The Tax-related field determines whether or not the tax reports include the category. You use this field to mark those categories for which you need totals for preparing your personal income tax returns.

Note: You should have plenty of room for as many categories as you want to add. The maximum number depends on your available memory, the length of your category names and descriptions, and on the other information stored in memory. You should have room for about 150 categories with 320K of memory and over 1,000 categories with 512K of memory.

Deleting Categories

Deleting categories is even easier than adding categories. On the Category and Transfer List screen, you need to highlight the category you want to delete with the selection triangle and press Ctrl-D. Quicken alerts you that a category is about to be deleted (see fig. 7.8). Press Enter, and Quicken deletes the category. If you do not want to delete the category, press Esc.

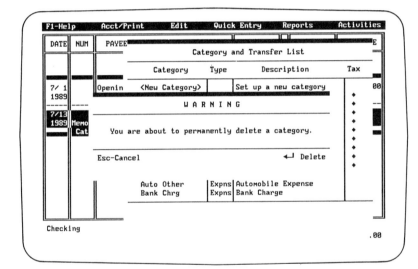

Fig. 7.8.

Quicken warns you that a category is about to be deleted.

After you delete a category, you cannot use the category unless you add it again. If you already have used the deleted category to describe transactions, you need to return to the register and change the invalid category used to current, valid categories. (Chapter 5 and 6 describe how to use the register.)

Editing Categories

The steps for editing a category parallel those for deleting one. First, you select the category you want to edit with the selection triangle and press Ctrl-E. Quicken displays the Edit Category screen shown in figure 7.9.

Fig. 7.9.

The Edit Category screen.

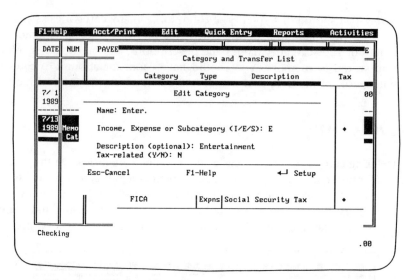

```
 F1-Help      Acct/Print      Edit      Quick Entry      Reports      Activities
 DATE  NUM    PAYEE                                                           E
                              Category and Transfer List

                       Category      Type       Description        Tax
 7/ 1                         Edit Category                            00
 1989
 --------  ----  Name: Enter.

 7/13           Income, Expense or Subcategory (I/E/S): E                •
 1989 Memo
      Cat      Description (optional): Entertainment
               Tax-related (Y/N): N

               Esc-Cancel              F1-Help              ↵ Setup

                       FICA           Expns Social Security Tax        •

 Checking
                                                                    .00
```

You can change any of the four fields you defined when adding a category: Name; Income, Expense, or Subcategory; Description, and Tax-related. To make changes, edit the fields that you want modified and press Enter.

Recording Categories for Transactions

Chapters 3 and 5 describe in detail how to use the Write/Print Checks menu and the register to record the categories for transactions. Both options include the Category field on the data-entry screen. To record a category, you enter the category name in the field. For example, to record a transaction category as SALES, you enter *SALES* in the Category field on-screen. If you use subcategories, enter the primary income or expense category first, a colon, and then the subcategory. If you further categorized sales by your two product lines, GUNS and BUTTER, you record gun sales by entering *SALES:GUNS* in the Category field. If you have more then one subcategory, you also separate the subcategories from each other with colons. Chapter 3, "Writing and Printing Checks," and Chapter 5, "Using the Register," describe and demonstrate the mechanics of recording categories.

Working with Classes

Classes are an extension of categories that enable you to add a second dimension to the income and expense summaries that categories provide. Personal users of Quicken probably do not need this second dimension. The examples in this section, therefore, focus on business applications.

Why Use Classes?

If you need or want to group revenues and expenses by more than just the type of transaction—what categories do—you can classify them some other way. Figure 7.10 illustrates sample classes that various businesses might apply: by job or project, by revenue producers, by geography, and by functional company areas.

```
F1-Help    Acct/Print      Edit      Quick Entry      Reports      Activities

 DATE  NUM    PAYEE  ·                                            ALANCE
                                         Class List
 8/31       Balance For                                           823 26
 1989                           Class            Description
 8/31       Balance Adj   <New Class>      Set up a new class     808 26
 1989                    ▶ Cal             California St Operations
                           Idaho           Idaho St Operations
 9/ 1       September M     Oregon          Oregon St Operations   696 26
 1989                       Wash            Washington St Operations
 10/ 1      October mor                                           583 26
 1989

 11/ 1      November mo                                           468 26
 1989

 7/25
 1989  Memo:
       Cat:          Ctrl-D Delete  Ctrl-E Edit  Ctrl-P Print
                     Esc-Cancel       F1-Help          ↵ Use
    Checking                                              $298.26
                                                          $468.26
```

Fig. 7.10.

Examples of businesses and classes that might be useful.

Selecting and Setting Up Classes

To create and work with classes, use the **Select/Set Up Class** option on the Quick Entry menu (see fig. 7.11).

After you select **Select/Set Up Class**, Quicken displays the Class List screen shown in figure 7.12.

Fig. 7.11.

*The **Select/Set Up Class** option.*

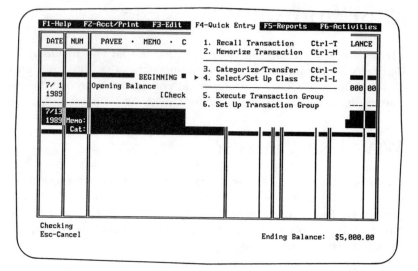

Fig. 7.12.

The Class List screen.

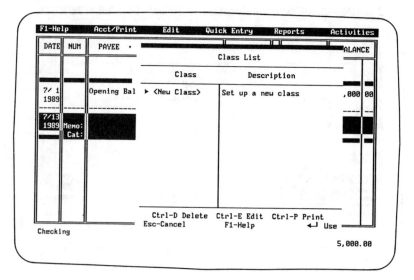

Adding a Class

To add a class, select the ‹New Class› item on the list and press Enter. Quicken displays the Set Up Class screen that you use to define and describe a class. If you were setting up classes to track your business revenues and expenses by state, you would complete the screen as shown in figure 7.13.

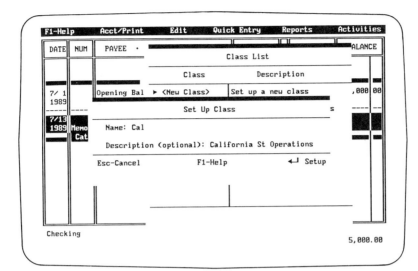

Fig. 7.13.

The Set Up Class screen.

Deleting a Class

To delete a class, press Ctrl-D while the class you want to delete is selected on the Class List. Quicken warns you, as shown in figure 7.14, that a class is about to be deleted. Press Enter to complete the deletion or Esc to cancel the deletion.

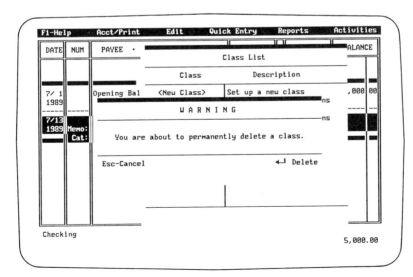

Fig. 7.14.

Quicken warns you that a class is about to be deleted.

Editing a Class

To edit a class, press Ctrl-E while the class you want to change is selected on the Class List screen. Quicken displays the Edit Class screen, shown in figure 7.15 that you use to make the changes you want.

Fig. 7.15.

The Edit Class screen.

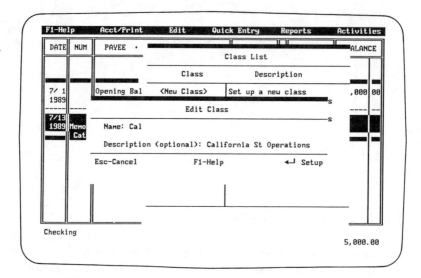

Using Subclasses

If you use classes to add another dimension to your reporting and recording, you also need to know about subclasses. Subclasses are classes within classes. If you were to use a geographical scheme in creating classes, your classes might be states. Within each state, you might choose to use subclasses corresponding to portions of the state. For example, Washington State, a class, might have the subclasses Eastern Washington and Western Washington. California, another class, might have the subclasses Northern California (excluding the Bay Area), Bay Area, Southern California (excluding Los Angeles County), and Los Angeles County.

Recording Classes for Transactions

To record a class, you enter a slash followed by the class name in the Category field after any category or subcategory names. For example, if you want to record the income category, SALES, and the California class,

CAL, for a transaction, you enter *SALES/CAL* in the Category field on the data screen.

If you use subclasses, enter the primary class, a colon, and then the subclass. For example, if the class, CAL, had the subclass, NORTH, you might record sales for Northern California by entering *SALES/CAL:NORTH* in the Category field.

If you have more then one subclass—classes within classes within classes—you also separate the subclasses from each other with colons. Chapters 3 and 5 describe and demonstrate the mechanics of recording classes.

Chapter Summary

This chapter described the preparation necessary to begin using Quicken's categories and classes. This chapter defined categories and classes, described when you should use them, showed the predefined categories Quicken provides, told you how to use predefined categories, and detailed the steps for adding and deleting categories and classes.

Reconciling Your
Bank Account

Regularly reconciling your bank account is one of the most important steps you can take to protect your cash and the accuracy and reliability of your banking records. Reconciling is a method of catching errors you might have made when writing checks or recording transactions in your check register. Reconciling also enables you to discover unauthorized or fraudulent transactions in your account (see Chapter 9, "Protecting Your System").

Chapter 8 reviews the reconciliation process and describes the steps for reconciling your accounts in Quicken, printing and using the reconciliation reports Quicken creates, and correcting and catching reconciliation errors.

Reviewing the Reconciliation Process

Reconciling your bank account is not difficult. You probably already understand the mechanics of the reconciliation process. For those readers who are a bit rusty with the process, however, the next few paragraphs briefly describe how reconciliation works.

To reconcile a bank account, you perform three basic steps:

1. Review the bank statement for new transactions and errors.

2. Review which transactions have not been recorded or cleared by the bank and adjust the register balance accordingly.

3. Verify that the adjusted check register balance equals the bank balance.

Note: If you still find the process confusing, examine your monthly bank statement. The back or your current bank statement probably explains the whole process step-by-step.

Reviewing the Bank Statement for New Transactions and Errors

The first step in reconciling your account is to review the bank statement. You first should find any new transactions that the bank recorded and which you now need to record. These transactions might include bank service fees, overdraft charges, and interest income. You need to record these transactions in your register before proceeding further with the reconciliation.

For each transaction, confirm that the checking account transaction recorded in your register and on your bank statement are the same amount. If you find a transaction not recorded in both places for the same amount, review the discrepancy and identify which transaction is incorrect.

CPA Tip: Carefully review each canceled check for authenticity. If a check forger successfully draws a check on your account, you can discover the forgery by reviewing canceled checks. As Chapter 9 outlines, you need to find such forgeries if you hope to ever recover the money.

Adjusting the Check Register Balance

The second step is to recalculate the check register balance by using only those transactions that have cleared the bank. By adding back any checks that have not cleared (usually called outstanding checks) and also any deposits (usually called deposits in transit), you calculate an adjusted check register balance that should agree with the bank's statement balance.

Note: You also can reconcile the account by adjusting the bank statement balance instead of the check register balance. This second approach means that you add back to the bank statement balance the transactions that have not cleared the bank. (Often, bank statement reconciliation instructions direct you to adjust the bank statement balance.) Essentially, however, both approaches use the following formula:

> Check Register Balance
> + Outstanding Checks
> − Deposits in Transit
> _____
> Bank Statement Balance

If you are adjusting the bank statement balance instead of the check register balance, you use a slightly different form of the same formula:

> Bank Statement Balance
> + Deposits in Transit
> − Outstanding Checks
> _____
> Check Register Balance

Either way, you are totaling the uncleared transactions and then confirming that the total represents the difference between the two accounts.

Verifying that Balances Correspond

The final step is a quick one; you verify that the adjusted check register balance agrees with the bank statement balance. If you have correctly performed steps one and two in the reconciliation process, the two amounts should equal. If the two amounts differ, you must repeat steps one and two until you locate and correct the error.

Reconciling Your Account with Quicken

Quicken makes reconciling your bank account easier by automating the steps and doing the arithmetic. To reconcile your account, select **Reconcile** from the Activities menu on the Write Checks or Register screens. Quicken then displays the screen shown in figure 8.1.

Fig. 8.1.

The Reconcile Register with Bank Statement screen.

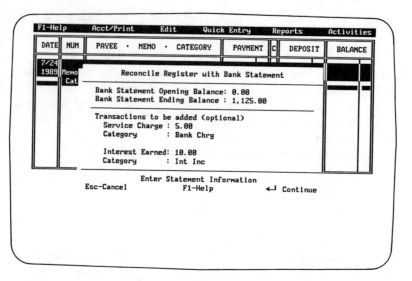

```
 F1-Help      Acct/Print      Edit      Quick Entry      Reports      Activities
┌──────┬─────┬──────────────────────────────────┬─────────┬─┬─────────┬──────────┐
│ DATE │ NUM │ PAYEE  ·  MEMO  ·  CATEGORY       │ PAYMENT │C│ DEPOSIT │ BALANCE  │
├──────┼─────┼──────────────────────────────────┴─────────┴─┴─────────┴──────────┤
│ 7/24 │     │                                                                    │
│ 1989 │Memo │      Reconcile Register with Bank Statement                        │
│      │Cat  │                                                                    │
│      │     │   Bank Statement Opening Balance: 0.00                             │
│      │     │   Bank Statement Ending Balance : 1,125.00                         │
│      │     │                                                                    │
│      │     │   Transactions to be added (optional)                              │
│      │     │     Service Charge : 5.00                                          │
│      │     │     Category       : Bank Chrg                                     │
│      │     │                                                                    │
│      │     │     Interest Earned: 10.00                                         │
│      │     │     Category       : Int Inc                                       │
│      │     │                                                                    │
│      │     │              Enter Statement Information                           │
│      │     │   Esc-Cancel              F1-Help           ↵ Continue             │
└──────┴─────┴────────────────────────────────────────────────────────────────────┘
```

You fill six fields on the Reconcile Register with Bank Statement screen: opening balance, ending balance, service charge, service charge's category, interest earned, and the interest earned category.

In the Bank Statement Opening Balance field, type the bank statement balance shown at the start of the period your statement covers if the balance is different than the one shown. In the Bank Statement Ending Balance field, type the bank statement balance shown at the end of the period your bank statement covers. If you have not recorded monthly service fees or interest earnings and the appropriate categories, record those amounts in the Service Charge, service charge Category, Interest Earned, and interest earned Category fields. Figure 8.1 shows the completed Reconcile Register screen assuming that the opening bank statement balance is 0; the ending balance is $1,125, and you had not previously recorded $5 of service charges nor $10 of interest.

Press Enter to access the Transaction List screen that shows each checking account transaction (see fig. 8.2). If you want to view the checking account transactions as they appear in the register, you can press F9 to redisplay the same information in an abbreviated form of the standard register. Figure 8.3 shows an example transactions shown as they appear in the register.

Both screens show transaction information at the top of the screen. At the bottom of either screen, summary information is displayed. This information includes the number and dollar amount of the check and deposit transactions you marked as cleared, the cleared transaction total, the ending balance, and the difference between the two. You finish the reconciliation when the difference shown equals zero.

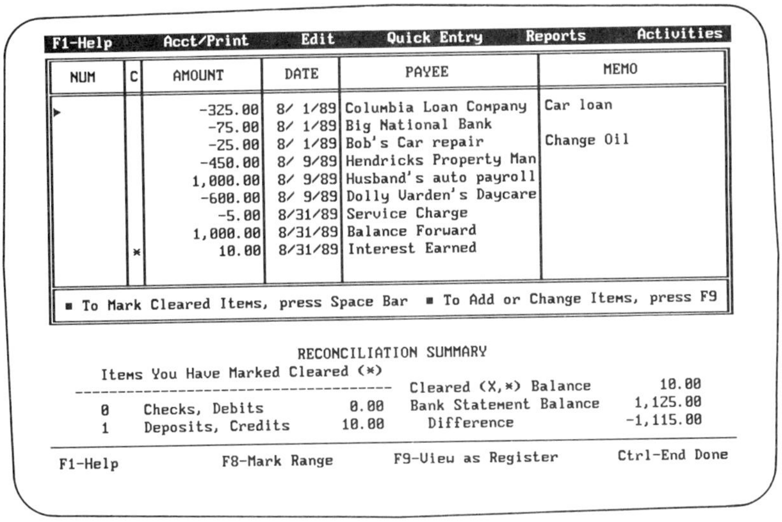

Fig. 8.2.

Checking account transactions shown in a list.

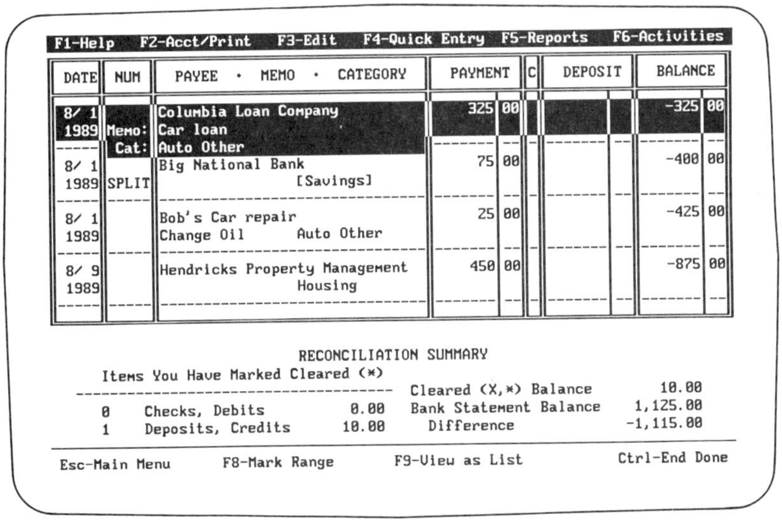

Fig. 8.3.

Checking account transactions shown in the register.

Working on the Abbreviated Check List and Check Register Screens

You can stay on the abbreviated check list screen showing the checking account transactions (see fig. 8.2). On this screen, you can mark items only as cleared. To mark one item as cleared, use the up- and down-arrow keys to move the selection triangle to the left of the transaction you want to mark. When the triangle is in place, press the space bar. Quicken enters an asterisk in the cleared column. To mark a range of transactions as cleared, press F8. Quicken displays the Mark Range of Check Numbers as Cleared screen (see fig. 8.4). You use this screen to specify that all the transactions with check numbers within the indicated range should be marked as cleared.

Fig. 8.4.

Marking a range of transactions as cleared.

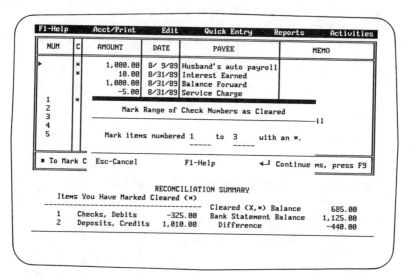

You also probably want to edit or add checking account transactions. You can do this with the abbreviated check register screen shown in figure 8.3. To access the screen, press F9.

This screen works similarly to the regular register and includes all the function key options that the regular Register screen does. If you are not comfortable with the function key options available from the Register screen—Account, Edit, Quick Entry, Reports, and Activities—you may want to refer back to Chapters 5 and 6 for a description of the register and its menu options.

To mark a transaction as cleared on this screen, type an asterisk in the cleared column of the register. The cleared column is identified by C. You also can use F8 to mark a range of transactions as cleared.

When you finish marking all the cleared transactions and entering any new ones, the cleared balance should equal the bank statement balance. Figure 8.5 shows an example of this.

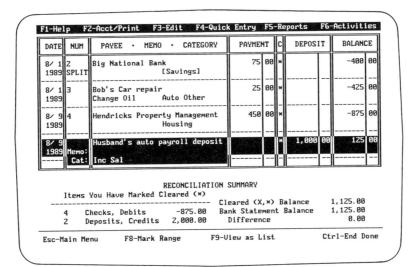

Fig. 8.5.

You are finished when the cleared and bank statement balances agree.

When you finish reconciling, press Ctrl-End to tell Quicken that you are done. You now are ready to print the reconciliation report.

Note: If you understand double-entry bookkeeping, you probably recognize that Quicken uses the labels *Debit* and *Credit* incorrectly from your perspective. Do not be confused by this. The screen uses the terms from the bank's perspective to further help people who do not understand double-entry bookkeeping.

Printing Reconciliation Reports

When you press Ctrl-End to tell Quicken that you are finished, Quicken changes each asterisk in the C field to an X, and asks if you want to print a reconciliation report (see fig. 8.6).

If you answer Y for yes, Quicken displays the Print Reconciliation Report screen, shown in figure 8.7. This screen enables you to specify where you want the report printed, the reconciliation date you want to appear on the report, the report title, and whether you want a full or summary report.

You answer the Print to field by pressing 1 for printer 1, 2 for printer 2, 3 for printer 3, or 4 for disk. If you used printer names on the Change Printer Settings screen, you see those printer names on the Print Reconciliation Report screen. Figure 8.7 shows, for example, that your third printer is HP LJetII-Checks.

Fig. 8.6.

*Quicken
congratulates
you when your
account
balances.*

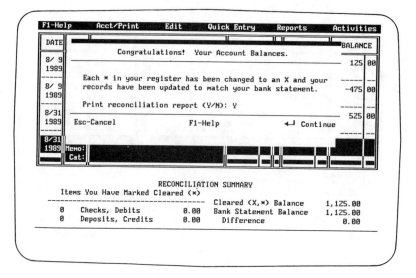

Fig. 8.7.

*The Print
Reconciliation
Report screen.*

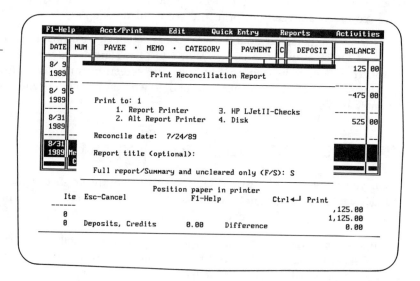

To print an ASCII file, press 4 to print to disk. ASCII files are standardized text files you create so that you can retrieve the reconciliation report file into a word processing program such as WordPerfect or Microsoft Word. If you press 4, Quicken requests three pieces of information: the file name, the number of lines per page, and the width. In the File field, enter the name you want Quicken to use for the created ASCII file. If you want to use a data directory different than QUICKEN3, you also can specify a path name. In the Lines per page field, set the number of report lines between page breaks. If you use 11-inch paper, for example, the page length usually is 66 lines. In the Width field, set the number of characters including blanks that Quicken prints on a line. If you use 8 1/2-inch paper, for example, a line contains 80 characters. Figure 8.8 shows the completed Print To Disk screen with the file specified as PRNT_TXT.

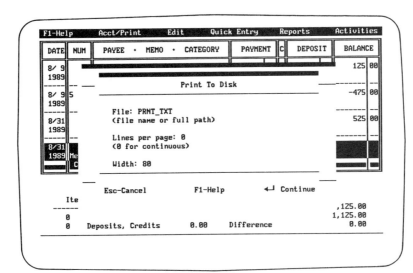

Fig. 8.8.

The Print To Disk screen.

The reconciliation date is the date that appears on the reconciliation report. You probably want to use the date you actually perform the reconciliation on or the end of the month for which you are reconciling.

The Report title field on the Print Reconciliation Report screen enables you to enter your own heading as a title on the reconciliation report.

Answer the Full report/Summary and uncleared only field with an F for Full or S for Summary. This field enables you to choose how much detail shows on your reconciliation report. The default is Summary, because Full includes all the detail on every transaction you mark as cleared.

The printed reconciliation report includes three distinct components: the Reconciliation Summary shown in figure 8.9, the Cleared Transaction Detail shown in figure 8.10, and the Uncleared Transaction Detail shown in figures 8.11 and 8.12. (If you select Summary, only the first and third parts of the reconciliation report print.)

The Reconciliation Summary report, shown in figure 8.9, essentially restates the Reconciliation Summary shown at the bottom of the abbreviated check register screen. The Reconciliation Summary has two sections:

1. Bank statement—cleared transactions

2. Your records—uncleared transactions

Fig. 8.9.

The printed reconciliation summary report.

```
                                    August Reconciliation
Checking                                                              Page 1
7/24/89
                                   RECONCILIATION SUMMARY


   BANK STATEMENT -- CLEARED TRANSACTIONS:

      Previous Balance:                                         0.00
                                                           --------------
         Checks and Payments:            4 Items             -875.00
         Deposits and Other Credits:     2 Items            2,000.00
                                                           --------------
      Ending Balance of Bank Statement:                     1,125.00

   YOUR RECORDS -- UNCLEARED TRANSACTIONS:


      Cleared Balance:                                       1,125.00
                                                           --------------
         Checks and Payments:            1 Item              -600.00
         Deposits and Other Credits:     0 Items                0.00
                                                           --------------

      Register Balance as of  8/31/89:                        525.00
                                                           --------------
         Checks and Payments:            0 Items                0.00
         Deposits and Other Credits:     0 Items                0.00
                                                           --------------

      Register Ending Balance:                                 525.00
```

The first section calculates the ending balance according to the bank statement by subtracting the cleared checks and adding the cleared deposits from the beginning bank balance. The second section calculates the ending register balance by subtracting the outstanding checks and adding the deposits in transit from the ending bank balance.

The Cleared Transaction Detail report, shown in figure 8.10, shows each of the cleared checks and payment transactions and each of the cleared deposits and other credit transactions you marked with an asterisk as part of the most recent reconciliation. The report does not include transactions you marked as cleared in some prior reconciliation.

The Cleared Transaction Detail report includes most of the information related to a transaction, including the transaction date, the check or transaction number, the payee name or transaction description, any memo description, and the amount. Checks and payments are displayed as nega-

```
                          August Reconciliation                          Page 2
 Checking
 7/24/89                 CLEARED TRANSACTION DETAIL


    Date    Num        Payee           Memo          Category    Clr    Amount
 --------  -----  ----------------  ----------------  ----------------  ---  ------------

 Cleared Checks and Payments

   8/ 1/89 1      Columbia Loan Co Car loan          Auto Other    X       -325.00
   8/ 1/89 2      Big National Ban                   [Savings]     X        -75.00
   8/ 1/89 3      Bob's Car repair Change Oil        Auto Other    X        -25.00
   8/ 9/89 4      Hendricks Proper                   Housing       X       -450.00
                                                                        ------------
 Total Cleared Checks and Payments                    4 Items           -875.00


 Cleared Deposits and Other Credits

   8/ 9/89        Husband's auto p                   Inc Sal       X      1,000.00
   8/31/89        Balance Forward                    [Savings]     X      1,000.00
                                                                        ------------
 Total Cleared Deposits and Other Credits             2 Items          2,000.00

                                                                        ============
 Total Cleared Transactions                           6 Items          1,125.00
```

Fig. 8.10.

The cleared transaction detail report.

tive amounts because they decrease the account balance. Deposits are displayed as positive amounts because they increase the account balance. Because of space constraints, some of the Payee, Memo, and Category field entries are truncated on the right. The total amount and number of cleared transactions on the Cleared Transaction Detail report support the data shown in the first section of the Reconciliation Summary.

The Uncleared Transaction Detail report, shown in figures 8.11 and 8.12, is identical to the Cleared Transaction report except that the still uncleared transactions for your checking account are summarized. The report is broken down into transactions dated prior to the reconciliation date and transactions dated subsequent to the reconciliation date.

Like the Cleared Transaction Detail report, the Uncleared Transaction Detail report includes most of the information related to a transaction including the transaction date, the check or transaction number, the payee name or transaction description, any memo description, and the amount. Checks and payments are shown as negative amounts because they decrease the account balance. Deposits are shown as positive amounts because they increase the account balance. The total amount and total number of cleared transactions on the Uncleared Transaction Detail report support the data shown in the second section of the Reconciliation Summary.

Fig. 8.11.

Uncleared transactions dated prior to the reconciliation date.

```
                          August Reconcilation
Checking                                                       Page 3
7/24/89
              UNCLEARED TRANSACTION DETAIL UP TO   8/31/89

  Date    Num      Payee          Memo         Category    Clr    Amount
-------- ----- ---------------- --------------- ---------------- --- ------------

Uncleared Checks and Payments
  8/ 9/89 5    Dolly Varden's D              Childcare            -600.00
                                                           ------------
Total Uncleared Checks and Payments             1 Item           -600.00

Uncleared Deposits and Other Credits

                                                           ------------
Total Uncleared Deposits and Other Credits      0 Items             0.00

                                                           ============
Total Uncleared Transactions                    1 Item           -600.00
```

Fig. 8.12.

Uncleared transactions dated subsequent to the reconciliation date.

```
                          August Reconcilation
Checking                                                       Page 4
7/24/89
              UNCLEARED TRANSACTION DETAIL AFTER   8/31/89

  Date    Num      Payee          Memo         Category    Clr    Amount
-------- ----- ---------------- --------------- ---------------- --- ------------

Uncleared Checks and Payments
                                                           ------------
Total Uncleared Checks and Payments             0 Items             0.00

Uncleared Deposits and Other Credits
                                                           ------------
Total Uncleared Deposits and Other Credits      0 Items             0.00

                                                           ============
Total Uncleared Transactions                    0 Items             0.00
```

Creating Balance Adjustment Transactions

VERSION 3.0

If you cannot reconcile your account—the difference amount shown on the Reconciliation Summary equals something other than zero, you may want to make a balance adjustment. A balance adjustment means that Quicken creates a transaction that forces the difference amount to equal zero. You can make a balance adjustment by pressing Esc on the Register screen before you have reduced the difference between the cleared balance and the bank statement balance to zero. Quicken then displays the Reconciliation is Not Complete screen, shown in figure 8.13.

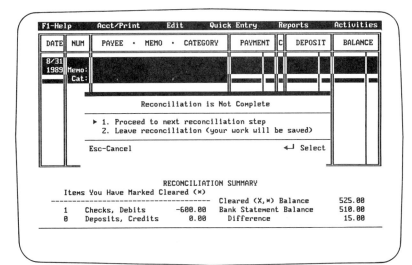

Fig. 8.13.

The Reconciliation is Not Complete screen.

The Reconciliation is Not Complete screen identifies two alternatives: **Proceed to next reconciliation step**, and **Leave reconciliation (your work will be saved)**. If you select the second alternative, Quicken returns you to the Main menu.

If you select the first alternative, Quicken displays the screen shown in figure 8.14. This screen informs you of the magnitude of the problem and possible causes. Press Enter to continue. Quicken alerts you that the difference still exists and asks you if you want a balance adjustment.

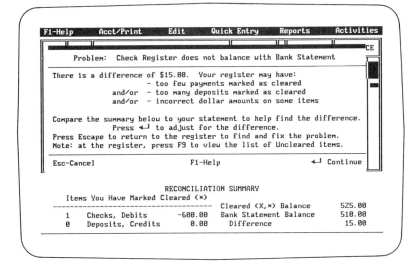

Fig. 8.14.

Quicken alerts you when the register does not balance.

Press Enter if you want to make a balance adjustment. Quicken displays the Adding Balance Adjustment Entry screen shown in figure 8.15 that alerts you that the adjustment is about to be made and suggests that you reconsider your decision. To make the adjustment, press Y for Yes. You also can categorize your adjustment transaction by entering a category name in the optional Category field. If you do not want to make the adjustment, press N for No. If you want to leave the screen and return to the abbreviated register screen, press Esc.

Fig. 8.15.

The Adding Balance Adjustment Entry screen.

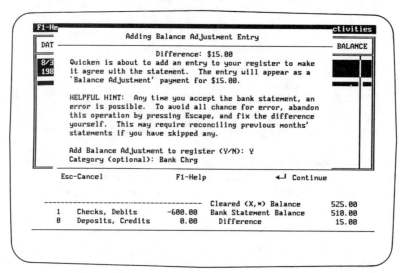

Quicken next tells you that the register has been adjusted to agree with the bank statement balance and displays a screen you can use to print the reconciliation report, as shown in figure 8.16.

Fig. 8.16.

The Register Adjusted to Agree With Statement screen.

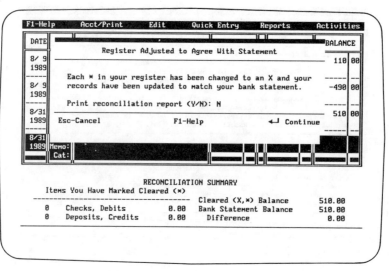

The Balance Adjustment transaction created by Quicken is shown in figure 8.17.

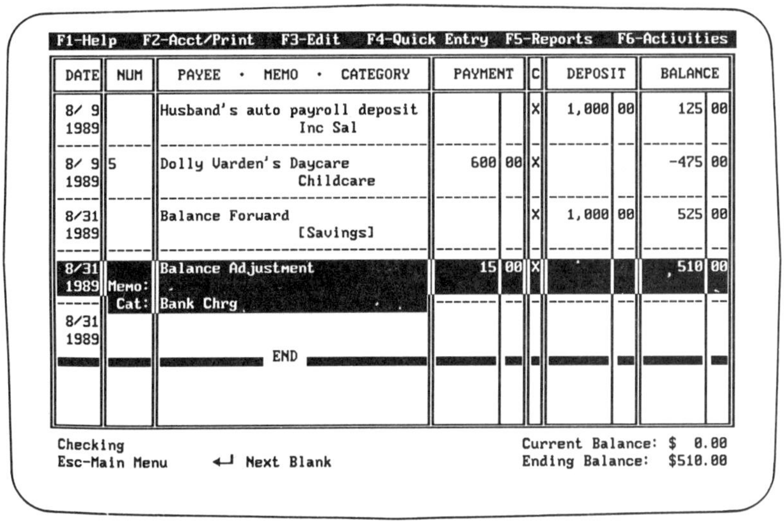

F1-Help	F2-Acct/Print	F3-Edit	F4-Quick Entry	F5-Reports	F6-Activities

DATE	NUM	PAYEE · MEMO · CATEGORY	PAYMENT	C	DEPOSIT	BALANCE
8/ 9 1989		Husband's auto payroll deposit Inc Sal		X	1,000 00	125 00
8/ 9 1989	5	Dolly Varden's Daycare Childcare	600 00	X		-475 00
8/31 1989		Balance Forward [Savings]		X	1,000 00	525 00
8/31 1989	Memo: Cat:	Balance Adjustment Bank Chrg	15 00	X		510 00
8/31 1989		END				

Checking
Esc-Main Menu   ↵ Next Blank

Current Balance: $ 0.00
Ending Balance: $510.00

Fig. 8.17.

The balance adjustment transaction in the register.

CPA Tip: Although Quicken provides the adjustment feature, you probably should not use the feature because it camouflages errors in your register, so that you are unsure where the error occurs. Your difference amount equals something other than zero because you are missing some transaction in your register or because you incorrectly marked a transaction as cleared. The difference also can be because someone has forged checks or embezzled from your account. If you cannot reconcile your account, make sure that the previous month's reconciliation resulted in a difference equal to zero. If the previous month's reconciliation shows a difference other than zero, correctly reconcile that month and perhaps the months prior to that before you can get the current month's difference to be displayed as zero.

Catching Common Errors

You easily can make several errors when recording transactions in your checking account; these errors may make reconciling your account difficult and even impossible. Because it sometimes is helpful not just to look for errors, but to look for certain kinds of errors, the next few paragraphs identify some common errors and tricks for catching those errors.

Transposing Numbers

Transposing numbers is a frequent error in recording any financial transaction. People accidentally transpose two of the numbers in an amount. If the difference is divisible by 9, a transposition error is likely. For example, you may write a check for $32.67 and record the check as $23.67 or $32.76. This appears to be an obvious error, but is surprisingly easy to make and sometimes very difficult to catch. When you review each transaction, you see all the correct numbers; however, they are arranged in a slightly different order.

When searching for transposed numbers you can focus on the decimal places of the transaction where the transposition error may have occurred. Table 8.1 summarizes by amounts where the transposition error might have occurred:

Table 8.1
Possible Locations of Transposition Errors

Error Amount	Decimal Places of Transposition
$.09 to $.72	In cents. For example, $.12 vs. $.21 or $1.19 vs. $1.91.
$.90 to $7.20	Between first dollar decimal position to left of decimal place and first cents decimal position to right of decimal place. For example, $32.56 vs. $35.26 or$2004.56 vs. $2005.46.
$9.00 to $72.00	Between first and second dollar decimal positions to the left of decimal place. For example, $1423 vs. 1432 or $281 vs. $218.
$90 to $720	Between second and third dollar decimal positions to left of decimal place. For example, $1,297 vs. $1,927 or $1,124 vs. $1,214.

Forgetting to Record Transactions

The most common mistake many people make is forgetting to record transactions. In a personal checking account, these omissions often include decreases in the account—for example, automated teller machine withdrawals—and increases in the account such as interest income. In a business checking account, manual checks seem to be a common culprit; you tear out a blank check for a purchasing trip and forget to record the check later.

If the amounts differ as a result of one transaction, identifying the missing transaction can be as easy as finding a transaction on the bank statement that equals the difference. You also should check the sequence of checks to see if any are missing.

Entering Payments as Deposits or Deposits as Payments

Another error is to enter a payment transaction as a deposit transaction or a deposit transaction as a payment transaction. Until you find this error, it can be particularly frustrating. If you look at your register, you see that every transaction is recorded, and every number is correct.

An easy way to find such an error is to divide your error in half and see if the result equals some transaction amount. If it does, you may have recorded that transaction incorrectly. For example, suppose that you currently have a difference of $1,234.56 between the register and the bank statement balances. If you divide $1,234.56 by 2, you get an amount of $617.28. If you see a $617.28 transaction in your register, verify that you recorded that transaction in the correct column. If you recorded the $617.28 as a deposit when you should have recorded it as a payment, or if you recorded it as a payment when it should have been a deposit, the difference will equal twice the transaction amount, or $1,234.56.

Offsetting Errors

You may have more than one error in your account, and these errors may partially offset each other. Suppose that you forgot to record an automated teller machine withdrawal of $40, for example, and made a transposition error where you recorded a deposit as $216 instead of the correct amount of $261. The difference equals $10, which is the combined effect of both transactions and can be calculated as

$$-\$40 + (\$261 - \$216)$$

Despite the fact that the difference seems small, you actually have two rather large errors in the account.

When offsetting errors, remember that finding one of the errors some-times makes it seem as though you are getting farther away from your goal of a zero difference. Do not get discouraged if one minute you are $10 away from completing the reconciliation, and the next minute, you are $50 away from completing the reconciliation. Clearly, you are making progress if you are finding errors—even if the difference is getting bigger.

Chapter Summary

This chapter described how to reconcile your account with Quicken. This chapter described the Reconciliation screen, menu options, and reports that you can use to simplify the process of reconciling your bank accounts. The **Reconcile** option helps you turn what used to be an unpleasant financial chore into a quick and easy task.

9

Protecting Your System

By this point, you have installed the Quicken software on your computer, set up your bank accounts, fine-tuned the system settings, and defined any of the categories you want to use. Now, it is up to you to protect your system and your money.

First, you should know how Quicken can help you protect yourself from forgery and embezzlement. This issue is very important, particularly for small businesses. The U.S. Commerce Department estimates that employee theft annually costs American businesses about $40 billion.

Second, you should know about internal controls—ways you can minimize human errors within the Quicken system. Internal controls protect the accuracy and reliability of your data files and the cash you have in your bank accounts.

Forgery and Embezzlement

Forgery is fraudulently marking or altering any writing that changes the legal liability of another person. When someone signs your name to one of your checks or endorses a check made payable to you, that person has committed forgery. Forgery also occurs when somebody alters a check that you wrote.

Embezzlement is fraudulently appropriating property or money owned by someone else. In a home or small-business accounting system, an embezzler usually is an insider—an employee, partner, friend, or family member —who intercepts incoming deposits to or makes unauthorized withdrawals from a bank account. The steps you can take to prevent either crime are not difficult. Providing your system with protection is not an accusation of guilt; ensuring that embezzlement and forgery are made more difficult or almost impossible is a wise investment of money and time.

Preventing Forgery

Typically, a professional forger finds out when the bank mails you your monthly statements. He intercepts one of your monthly bank statements, which provides him with samples of your signature, information about your average balances, and when you make deposits and withdrawals. The forger is ready to go into action; he can order preprinted checks from a printer just as you would, or he can steal blank check forms from you. If he follows the latter course of action, the forms usually are taken from the back of your checkbook or from an unused set of blank checks, so that you do not notice their disappearance as quickly.

Unfortunately, you may not discover the forged checks until they clear your account or until you reconcile your bank account.

You should know a few things about forgery. First, your bank is responsible for paying only on checks with genuine signatures. The bank should use the signature card that you signed when you opened your account to judge the authenticity of the signature on your checks. The bank, therefore, cannot deduct from your account amounts stemming from forged checks. If the bank initially deducts money based on forged checks, the amounts must be added back to your account later. In certain cases, however, you are responsible for the money involved with forged checks.

You can make mistakes that will cause you to bear the cost of a forgery. One mistake is to be careless and sloppy, or *negligent*, in managing your checking account. For example, you may own a business that uses a check-signing machine easily available to anyone within the company, including a check forger. Another example of negligence is to routinely leave your checkbook on the dashboard of your red convertible. The courts are responsible for determining whether such behavior represents negligence; if the court determines that your conduct falls short of the care a reasonable person would exercise, the bank may not have to pay for the forger's unauthorized transactions.

Another mistake that may leave you liable for forgery losses is failure to review monthly statements and canceled checks. You should examine these items closely for any forged signatures, and you must report the forgeries promptly. If you do not—generally, you have one year—your bank is not obligated to add back to your account the amounts stolen by the check forger.

If you do not examine your monthly statements and canceled checks within fourteen days of receiving them, you lose your right to force the bank to add back to your account additional amounts stolen by the same check forger. If a forger writes ten checks for $50 on your account, for example, and you look at your bank statement a month late, the bank must add back the first forged $50 check, but is not liable for the nine other checks that followed.

CPA Tip: Never let someone occasionally sign checks for you. If you are out of town, for example, do not let an employee or neighbor use your checkbook to pay urgent bills for you. If that person signs a check for you and you do not report the signature as a forgery to the bank within fourteen days and if that person forges checks at a later date without your knowledge, the bank probably will not be responsible for payment on these forgeries.

At the very least, check forgery wastes your time and the bank's time. If you are not careful, forgery can cost you all the money you have. Following are some useful precautions that you may take to avoid this catastrophe:

1. Treat your blank checks as would treat cash. Do not leave check forms in places easily accessible to others. Better yet, lock your checks up or at least put them away in a desk drawer or cabinet, so that they are not easy to find. (This rule also goes for the box of Quicken computer checks.)

2. Use Quicken to keep your check register up-to-date. This precaution enables you to notify the bank immediately to stop payment on checks that have not been recorded in your check register, but are missing from your pad or box of blank checks.

3. Watch for your monthly bank statement and canceled checks. If they do not arrive at the usual time of the month, call the bank to find out whether the statements are late that month. You want to make sure that your statement has not been intercepted by a forger who will use your canceled checks to practice your signature.

4. Review the canceled checks you receive with your bank statement and verify that you or one of the other signers on the checking account wrote the checks. Also verify that none of the checks were altered.

5. Reconcile the balance shown in your check register with the balance shown on the monthly bank statement as soon as possible. The reconciling process does not take very long. For more information on reconciling your account, see Chapter 8.

6. Be sure to write "VOID" in large letters across the face of checks you will not use. If you have old blank check forms you no longer need—your name or address has changed or you have closed the account, for example—destroy the check forms.

7. Fill in all the blanks, particularly the payee and amount fields, on a check form to prevent a forger from altering a check you actually wrote and signed. If you have set the alignment correctly on your printer, Quicken completely fills out each of the required check form fields. For those checks that you manually write, however, do not leave space on the payee line for a forger to include a second payee, and do not leave space on one of the amount fields so that $5.00 can be changed to $500.00 (see figs. 9.1 and 9.2). The first figure is a perfect example of a check so poorly filled out that it almost invites forgery. The second figure shows how a check written like the one shown in figure 9.1 can be modified by a forger.

Fig. 9.1.

A good example of a bad way to write a check.

Fig. 9.2.

How your check may be altered by the forger.

8. Avoid using a signature that consists of a wavy line with a couple of dashes or dots, or a printed signature. These types of signatures are copied easily by a skilled forger.

Preventing Embezzlement

Embezzlement is more of an issue for business users of Quicken than for home use. Accordingly, the next few paragraphs focus on the business aspects of the problem.

Generally, embezzlement is a risk any time you have others working with business assets (cash, inventory, or equipment, for example), or with a business's financial records.

Because embezzlement takes so many different forms, the process cannot be generalized. You should take precautions against embezzlement, even if you have no suspicions that this crime may be a risk for you. When you fail to erect barriers to forgery, you become an appealing target. Often the embezzler is the least likely person to be expected of such a crime.

You can take certain precautions to minimize or even eliminate the opportunities for embezzlement in a small business.

Keeping Complete Financial Records

In many small-business embezzlement cases, messy or incomplete financial records are involved. If the accounting records are a mess, locating certain transactions is usually difficult or impossible, especially fraudulent ones.

By using Quicken, you keep complete financial records for most parts of your business. If there are other areas where you are not using Quicken, however, such as in billing and collecting from customers, be especially diligent and careful.

Segregating Duties

Try to separate physical custody of an asset, such as cash or accounts receivable, from the records for the asset. If one employee keeps the company checking account records using Quicken, for example, another employee should sign all the checks and collect all the cash. If another employee keeps track of the amounts customers owe and how much they pay on their bills, someone else should count and deposit the incoming cash. In these examples, the person who keeps the records indirectly double-checks the work of the person with physical custody of the asset, and the person with physical custody of the asset indirectly checks the work of the person keeping the records.

Checking Employee Backgrounds

Before hiring anyone, check his or her background and references carefully. Be sure to carefully check the background of those you rely on for important parts of your business, such as counting cash and accounting.

Embezzlement tends to be a habit with some people. In many cases, you find that an embezzler has stolen from his or her previous employer.

Requiring Vacations

Even if you follow the three precautions described previously, a clever embezzler still can steal from you, but embezzling becomes difficult. Usually such schemes require a lot of on-going effort and maintenance on the part of the embezzler. You should require people to take vacations. By following this precaution, you can take over or reassign their duties, and the embezzlement scheme crumbles or becomes obvious to others. If an embezzler skims a portion of the incoming cash daily, for example, when he is on vacation, you will notice that the cash deposits increase. If an embezzler writes checks for more than the actual amount and pockets the difference, during his vacation you might notice that cash expenses decrease.

Using Internal Controls

Internal controls are rules and procedures that protect your business assets and the accuracy and reliability of accounting records. Within Quicken, you can use two internal controls to further protect your system: leave a paper audit trail and retain your documents.

Creating Paper Trails

One of the most important internal control procedures you can use is to make sure that you create paper evidence that accurately describes and documents each transaction. The capability to produce this paper evidence is one of Quicken's greatest strengths—a strength that you should take advantage of as much as possible.

Obviously, you record every check you write and every deposit you make in the check register. But you also should record individual cash withdrawals from automated teller machines, bank service fees, and monthly interest expenses. Entering these transactions provides you with solid descriptions of each transaction that affects your cash flow.

The extensive reporting that Quicken offers provides you with another important piece of the paper trail for transactions. As an audit trail, the check register links the individual checking account transactions to the summary reports. For example, suppose that you notice a balance in some expense category that is much larger than you expected. Using the Reports feature, you can look through the check register for the specific transactions that affected the expense category.

Using computer-based accounting systems, including Quicken, probably uses and generates more paper than any manual system. From an internal control perspective, this fact is comforting. The clean, easy-to-read, and well-organized information produced by Quicken makes reviewing transactions, checking account balances, and researching suspicious income or expense conditions much easier. As a result, you are more likely to find any errors or omissions in your checking account records.

Retaining Documents

After looking at all the paper a computer-based accounting system can generate (check forms, registers, and other special reports), you may wonder how long you need to keep this paperwork.

Table 9.1 provides guidelines on the length of time you should keep canceled checks, check registers, and any of the other special reports generated by Quicken. These guidelines are based on statutory and regulatory requirements and statutes of limitations. If you have more questions about other personal or business financial records and documents, talk to your tax advisor or attorney.

Table 9.1
Document Storage Guidelines

Reports and Forms	1 year	3 years	7 years	Permanent
Check register				X
Backup files	X			
Canceled checks				X
Category lists				X
Monthly personal income expense statements		X		
Yearly personal income/ expense statements			X	
Other personal reports	X			
Monthly business income/ expense statements		X		
Yearly business income/ expense statements			X	
Other business reports	X			

Note: In addition to practicing the procedures described in this chapter, you can use a simple device called a surge protector to protect your equipment from electrical surges that can damage the fragile electronic components. Talk to your local computer supplier to see which type of surge protector is best for your system.

Chapter Summary

This chapter described actions you can take to protect your system and the cash in your checking account from forgery or embezzlement. Now that you know how to avoid risks such as these, you are ready to put Quicken to work for you.

Advanced Features

Includes

Accounting for Other Assets and Liabilities

Using Quicken's Reports

10

Accounting for Other
Assets and Liabilities

Quicken originally was designed as a checking account record-keeping tool. The newest release of Quicken, Version 3, however, can do much more than just keep track of your checking account. Using Quicken's familiar check-register format, you can maintain financial records for any asset or liability. With Version 3, you also can construct personal and business balance sheets.

This chapter describes how to use Quicken to perform record keeping for other assets and liabilities and then delivers information on why and how you can use Quicken to generate balance sheets.

Record Keeping for Other Assets and Liabilities

You need to set up an account for each asset or liability for which you want to keep records with Quicken. The accounts you want to appear together on a balance sheet must be set up in the same account group.

To set up accounts, use the **Select Account** option on Quicken's Main menu. **Select Account** displays the Select Account to Use screen shown in figure 10.1. This screen shows several accounts including a checking account, a savings account, a credit card, stock investments, a car loan, and a mortgage.

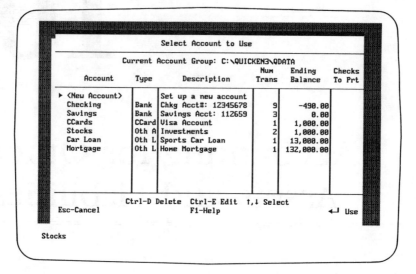

Fig. 10.1.

The Select Account to Use screen.

To add a new account, select the ‹New Account› item from the list. Quicken then displays the Set Up New Account screen shown in figure 10.2.

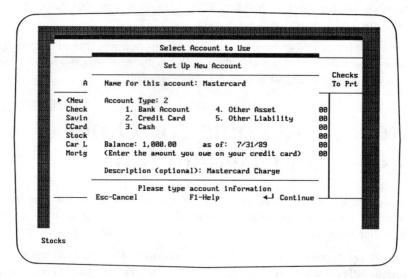

Fig. 10.2.

The Set Up New Account screen.

To complete this screen, you need to know the name, account type, description you want to use for the account, and the account balance.

Quicken provides three asset account types to choose from: bank account, cash, and other asset. If the asset is a bank account, set the account type as

1. If the asset is cash in your wallet or the petty cash box, set the account type as 3. For any other asset—accounts receivable, real estate, investments, and so on—enter the account type as 4.

Quicken also provides two liability account types: credit card and other liabilities. If the liability is the balance on your Visa or MasterCard account, set the account type as 2; otherwise, set the account type as 5. If you set up a credit card account, Quicken also prompts you for the credit card limit. Figure 10.3 shows the screen you complete to enter this piece of data.

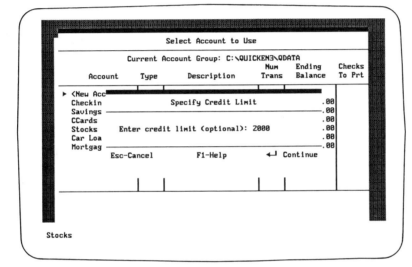

Fig. 10.3.

The Specify Credit Limit screen.

Using the Register

After you initially set up an account—whether an asset or a liability—you maintain the account in one of two ways.

First, you can select the account using **Select Account** from the Main menu or from the Acct/Print menu on the Write Checks and Register screens. You also can use the **Register** option to enter transactions that increase or decrease the account like you might for a checking account.

Figure 10.4 shows how a register of your investments might look. The other assets register looks almost identical to the regular bank account register and works the same way. Transaction amounts that decrease the investment account balance are recorded in the DECREASE column of the register. (On the bank account version of the Register screen, this column is labeled PAYMENT.) Transaction amounts that increase the investment

account are recorded in the INCREASE column of the register. (On the
bank account version of the check register, this column is labeled
DEPOSIT.) The total investment account balance shows at the bottom
right corner of the screen. If you have postdated transactions—those with
dates in the future, the current balance also shows. For other assets, the
only time you use the C column is if you want to indicate that you no
longer own an asset. (For example, if your certificate of deposit matures
and you withdraw the funds.)

Fig. 10.4.

*The register
used to track
your
investments.*

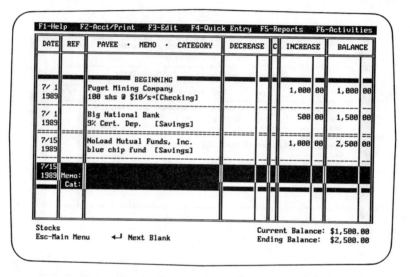

When working with the other asset register, you can access the same
menu options as when you are working with the bank account register,
except that **Update Account Balance** replaces **Reconcile**. (See "Updat-
ing Account Balances" later in this chapter.)

Figure 10.5 shows a register that you might use to track what you owe on
a home mortgage. The other liability register also mirrors the check register in appearance and operation. Transaction amounts that increase the
amount owed are recorded in the INCREASE column of the register. (On
the bank account version of the register screen, this column is labeled
PAYMENT.) Transaction amounts that decrease the amount owed are
recorded in the DECREASE column of the register. (On the bank account
version of the register, this column is labeled DEPOSIT.) The total liability
balance shows at the bottom right corner of the screen. If you have postdated transactions, the current balance also shows. You do not use the C
column when tracking a liability account.

```
 F1-Help   F2-Acct/Print   F3-Edit   F4-Quick Entry  F5-Reports   F6-Activities
┌────┬────┬──────────────────────────────┬──────────┬─┬──────────┬──────────┐
│DATE│REF │ PAYEE  ·  MEMO  ·  CATEGORY   │ INCREASE │C│ DECREASE │ BALANCE  │
├────┼────┼──────────────────────────────┼──────────┼─┼──────────┼──────────┤
│    │    │                              │          │ │          │          │
│    │    │ ═══════ BEGINNING ═══════     │          │ │          │          │
│8/ 1│    │Opening Balance               │132,000 00│ │          │132,000 00│
│1989│    │              [Mortgage]      │          │ │          │          │
│    │    │                              │          │ │          │          │
│9/ 1│    │September mortgage payment    │          │ │  112 00  │131,888 00│
│1989│    │              [Checking]      │          │ │          │          │
│    │    │                              │          │ │          │          │
│10/ 1│   │October mortgage payment      │          │ │  113 00  │131,775 00│
│1989│    │              [Checking]      │          │ │          │          │
│    │    │                              │          │ │          │          │
│11/ 1│   │November mortgage payment     │          │ │  115 00  │131,660 00│
│1989│    │              [Checking]      │          │ │          │          │
│    │    │                              │          │ │          │          │
│11/ 1│Memo:                             │          │ │          │          │
│1989│Cat: ████████████████████████████████████████████████████████████████│
└────┴────┴──────────────────────────────┴──────────┴─┴──────────┴──────────┘
 Mortgage                              Current Balance: $      0.00
 Esc-Main Menu    ↵ Next Blank         Ending Balance:  $131,660.00
```

Fig. 10.5.

The register used to track your mortgage balance.

When working with the other liability register, the menu options you can use are the same as when working with the bank account register, except that **Update Account Balance** replaces **Reconcile**.

CPA Tip: If you want to keep track of what you owe on a particular mortgage or loan, you may need an amortization schedule that the lender should provide. An amortization schedule shows the portion of your payments that goes to paying interest and the portion that goes to reducing the principal you owe. Only the principal reductions are recorded in the register for a loan or mortgage. The interest portion is reported as interest expense.

You can choose a second way to maintain correct account balances for other assets and liabilities. Quicken enables you to use an account name in the Category field on the Write Checks and Register screens. When you do so, Quicken uses the information from the checking account transaction to record the appropriate transaction in one of the other asset or liability accounts. If you are writing out a check to your stockbroker and enter the account name *[Stocks]* in the Category field, Quicken records an increase in the Stocks account equal to the payment you are making from your checking account. Figure 10.6 shows a $500 check being written to Washington, Adams, and Jefferson, your investment brokers. When you record the check, a $500 increase in your Stocks account also is recorded as shown in figure 10.7.

VERSION 3.0

Fig. 10.6.

A $500 check written to your stockbroker.

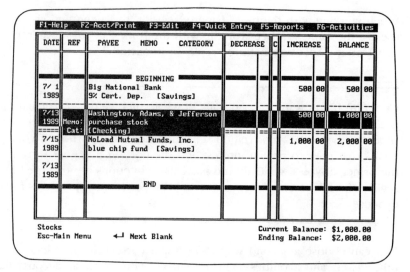

DATE	NUM	PAYEE · MEMO · CATEGORY	PAYMENT	C	DEPOSIT	BALANCE
		▬▬ BEGINNING ▬▬				
7/13 1989		Payroll Deposit Inc Sal			2,000 00	2,000 00
7/13 1989	Memo: Cat:	Washington, Adams, & Jefferson purchase stock [Stocks]	500 00			1,500 00
8/ 1 1989	1	Columbia Loan Company Car loan Auto Other	325 00	X		1,175 00
8/ 1 1989	2 SPLIT	Big National Bank [Savings]	75 00	X		1,100 00
8/ 1 1989	3	Bob's Car repair Change Oil Auto Other	25 00	X		1,075 00

Checking
Esc-Main Menu   ↵ Next Blank

Current Balance: $1,500.00
Ending Balance: $1,670.00

Fig. 10.7.

A $500 investment amount increase is recorded.

DATE	REF	PAYEE · MEMO · CATEGORY	DECREASE	C	INCREASE	BALANCE
		▬▬ BEGINNING ▬▬				
7/ 1 1989		Big National Bank 9% Cert. Dep. [Savings]			500 00	500 00
7/13 1989	Memo: Cat:	Washington, Adams, & Jefferson purchase stock [Checking]			500 00	1,000 00
7/15 1989		NoLoad Mutual Funds, Inc. blue chip fund [Savings]			1,000 00	2,000 00
7/13 1989		▬▬ END ▬▬				

Stocks
Esc-Main Menu   ↵ Next Blank

Current Balance: $1,000.00
Ending Balance: $2,000.00

VERSION 3.0

(*Note:* Remember that a convenient way to jump between different parts of the same transaction is to use the Edit menu option, **Go To Transfer**, or the shortcut key combination Ctrl-X.)

The register basically works the same—regardless of the account type. A few tips and techniques, however, can help you when using Quicken to account for other assets and liabilities. These tips and techniques include dealing with the nuances and subtleties of the cash account type, using the **Update Account Balance** option, dealing with the nuances and subtleties of the credit card account type, and using the **Pay Credit Card Bill** option accessed from the credit card register.

Dealing with Cash Accounts

The cash account option works well when you want to keep complete, detailed records of all your cash outlays. Often, you do not need this level of control or detail, but when you do, this account type provides just the tool to get the job done.

CPA Tip: For businesses, the cash account type is a convenient way to keep track of petty cash expenditures and reimbursements.

Figure 10.8 shows the cash account register screen. Notice that this screen is almost identical to the bank account register screen. Money flowing in and out of the account is recorded in the SPEND and RECEIVE columns. On the bank account register screen, money flowing out of the account is recorded in the PAYMENT column, and money flowing into the account is recorded in the DEPOSIT column. On the other asset and other liability account register screens, money flowing into and out of the account is recorded in the INCREASE and DECREASE columns.

DATE	REF	PAYEE · MEMO · CATEGORY	SPEND	RECEIVE	BALANCE
		F1-Help F2-Acct/Print F3-Edit F4-Quick Entry F5-Reports F6-Activities			
		══ BEGINNING ══			
7/31 1989		Opening Balance [Petty Cash]		200 00	200 00
8/ 1 1989		Parking Auto Other	5 00		195 00
8/ 1 1989		Lunch with Sam Hills discussed new p→Enter.	12 83		182 17
8/ 1 1989	Memo: Cat:				

Petty Cash
Esc-Main Menu ↵ Next Blank

Current Balance: $ 0.00
Ending Balance: $182.17

Fig. 10.8.

The cash account register screen.

As with the other asset and other liability account registers, the C column usually is not used. (You can use this column to match receipts against entries to indicate that you have back-up records.)

Updating Account Balances

On the Activities menu for cash accounts, other assets, and other liabilities accounts, **Update Account Balance** replaces **Reconcile**. (On the credit card account Activities menu, **Pay Credit Card Bill** replaces **Reconcile**. This option is described later in the chapter.) Figure 10.9 shows the cash account Activities menu.

Fig. 10.9.

The Activities menu for the cash account.

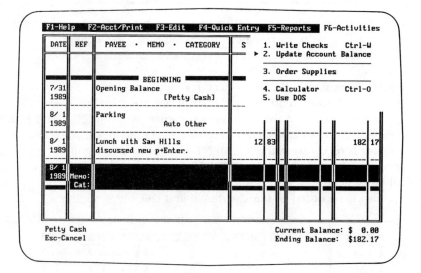

Update Account Balance provides a screen you use to reconcile, or adjust, an account. Suppose that the register you use to keep track of your cash shows $182.17 as the on-hand cash balance, but the actual balance is $161.88. You can use the Update Account Balance screen to record an adjustment as shown in figure 10.10.

Update Account Balance creates an adjustment transaction to reduce the cash balance. Figure 10.11 shows the adjustment transaction created by the Update Account Balance transaction so that the account balance shows as $161.88.

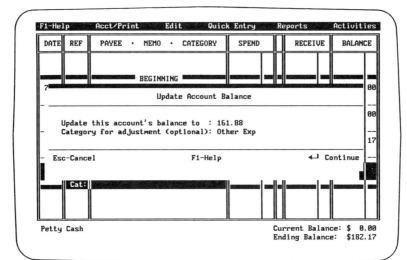

Fig. 10.10.

*The Update
Account
Balance screen.*

```
 F1-Help    Acct/Print    Edit    Quick Entry    Reports    Activities
 DATE  REF   PAYEE · MEMO · CATEGORY   SPEND       RECEIVE    BALANCE

                         BEGINNING
 7                                                                      00
                     Update Account Balance
                                                                        00
     Update this account's balance to  : 161.88
     Category for adjustment (optional): Other Exp
                                                                        17
   Esc-Cancel                    F1-Help              ↵ Continue

        Cat:

 Petty Cash                             Current Balance: $  0.00
                                        Ending Balance:  $182.17
```

```
 F1-Help  F2-Acct/Print  F3-Edit  F4-Quick Entry  F5-Reports  F6-Activities
 DATE  REF   PAYEE · MEMO · CATEGORY   SPEND       RECEIVE    BALANCE

                         BEGINNING
 7/31        Opening Balance                       200 00    200 00
 1989                  [Petty Cash]
 8/ 1        Parking                     5 00                195 00
 1989                  Auto Other
 8/ 1        Lunch with Sam Hills       12 83                182 17
 1989        discussed new p→Enter.
 8/ 3        Balance Adjustment         20 29                161 88
 1989 Memo:
      Cat: Other Exp
 8/ 1
 1989                      END

 Petty Cash                             Current Balance: $  0.00
 Esc-Main Menu    ↵ Next Blank          Ending Balance:  $161.88
```

Fig. 10.11.

*The Update
Account
Balance
adjustment
transaction.*

Dealing with Credit Card Accounts

The credit card account type is helpful if you want to keep track of the
details of your credit card spending and pay off your account balance over
time.

(*Note:* If you always pay your credit card in full every month, you do not
need to use the credit card account type, unless you want to track exactly

where and when charges are made. You usually can record the details of your credit card spending when you record the check payment to the credit card company. Version 3 of Quicken also can split your payments between various accounts such as transportation, clothing, and so on. Because the credit card balance always gets reduced to zero every month, you do not need to keep track of a zero balance.)

The steps involved in using the credit card account register to perform record keeping for your credit cards parallel the steps for using any other register. First, you set up the account and record the beginning balance. (Because you are working with a liability, the beginning balance is what you owe.) Second, you use the register to record credit card spending.

The check you write actually is recorded as a reduction in the amount owed on your credit card, for example [ccards]. You already have recorded the credit card spending by recording transactions in the credit card register.

As with the other asset and liability registers, some minor differences exist between the bank account register screen and menu options and the credit card register screen and menu options. The CHARGE column in the credit card register is where you record each use of your credit card. The PAYMENT column is where you record payments made to the credit card company. If you fill the credit limit field when you set up the credit card account, Quicken shows the credit remaining in the lower right corner of the screen above the Ending Balance field. Figure 10.12 shows the credit card register screen.

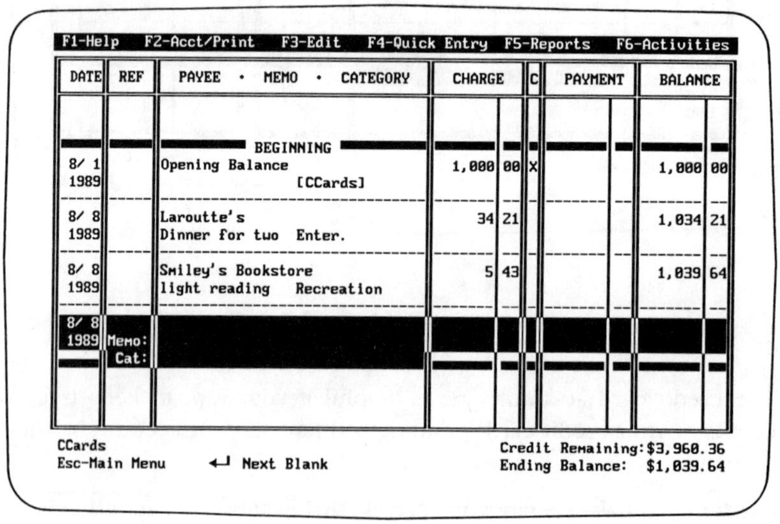

Fig. 10.12.

The credit card account register screen.

F1-Help	F2-Acct/Print	F3-Edit	F4-Quick Entry	F5-Reports	F6-Activities

DATE	REF	PAYEE · MEMO · CATEGORY	CHARGE	C	PAYMENT	BALANCE
		BEGINNING				
8/ 1 1989		Opening Balance [CCards]	1,000 00	X		1,000 00
8/ 8 1989		Laroutte's Dinner for two Enter.	34 21			1,034 21
8/ 8 1989		Smiley's Bookstore light reading Recreation	5 43			1,039 64
8/ 8 1989	Memo: Cat:					

```
CCards                                    Credit Remaining:$3,960.36
Esc-Main Menu      ↵ Next Blank           Ending Balance:   $1,039.64
```

Paying Credit Card Bill

The credit card Activities menu replaces the **Reconcile** option with **Pay Credit Card Bill** as shown in figure 10.13.

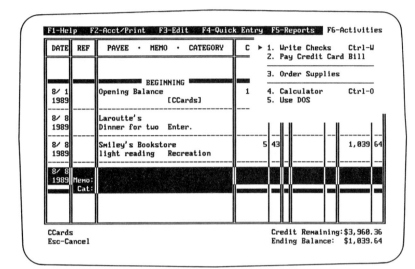

| F1-Help | F2-Acct/Print | F3-Edit | F4-Quick Entry | F5-Reports | F6-Activities |

Fig. 10.13.

The Activities menu for the credit card account.

If you select **Pay Credit Card Bill**, Quicken displays the Credit Card Statement Information screen shown in figure 10.14.

Pay Credit Card Bill enables you to reconcile your credit card register balance with the monthly credit card statement, record finance charges, and record a handwritten check or set up a check to be printed by Quicken.

You fill in several fields to begin this process. If you have used Quicken's **Reconcile** option or read about that feature in Chapter 8, you know that this screen closely resembles the one used to start the bank account reconciliation process. Enter the credit card charges and cash advances as a positive number in the Charges, Cash Advances field. Enter the total payments made in the Payments, Credits field also as a positive amount. If your statement shows credit slip transactions (because a store issued you a refund), also include these transactions in the Payments, Credits amount. Enter the ending credit card balance from your statement in the New Balance field. Assuming that you owe money to the credit card company, the number you enter is a positive one. Enter the monthly interest charges as a positive number in the Finance Charges field and the category to which you want finance charges assigned. Quicken uses this information to record a transaction for the monthly interest you are charged on the credit card. Figure 10.14 shows an example of a completed Credit Card Statement Information screen.

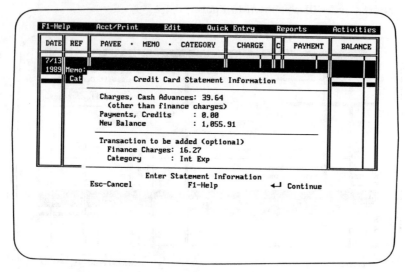

Fig. 10.14.

The Credit Card Statement Information screen.

When you press Enter, Quicken displays the credit card transactions list shown in figure 10.15. This screen and the abbreviated register screen, accessed by pressing F9, work like the reconciliation screens described in Chapter 8, "Reconciling Your Account."

Fig. 10.15.

The credit card transactions list.

```
 F1-Help        Acct/Print       Edit       Quick Entry       Reports       Activities
┌──────┬───┬──────────┬─────────┬──────────────────────┬────────────────────────┐
│ REF  │ C │  AMOUNT  │  DATE   │        PAYEE         │          MEMO          │
├──────┼───┼──────────┼─────────┼──────────────────────┼────────────────────────┤
│▶     │ ✕ │   16.27  │ 7/13/89 │ Finance Charges      │                        │
│      │   │   34.21  │ 8/ 8/89 │ Laroutte's           │ Dinner for two         │
│      │   │    5.43  │ 8/ 8/89 │ Smiley's Bookstore   │ light reading          │
│      │   │          │         │                      │                        │
│      │   │          │         │                      │                        │
│      │   │          │         │                      │                        │
│      │   │          │         │                      │                        │
└──────┴───┴──────────┴─────────┴──────────────────────┴────────────────────────┘
 ■ To Mark Cleared Items, press Space Bar  ■ To Add or Change Items, press F9

                        RECONCILIATION SUMMARY
      Items You Have Marked Cleared (✕)
      ─────────────────────────────────         Cleared (X,✕) Balance    1,016.27
         1    Charges, Debits      16.27         Statement Balance        1,055.91
         0    Payments, Credits     0.00         Difference                 -39.64

 F1-Help              F8-Mark Range        F9-View as Register      Ctrl-End Done
```

You mark credit card transactions as cleared by pressing the space bar when the transaction is highlighted. A cleared credit card transaction is one that appears on the credit card statement. After you have marked all the cleared credit card transactions, the cleared balance amount should equal the statement balance amount. If the two amounts do not equal each other, you missed recording a transaction or marking a transaction as cleared. (Chapter 8 gives tips on finding and correcting reconciliation errors for a checking account, but these tips also apply to reconciling a credit card statement.)

When you finish the reconciliation process—the difference amount shows as zero—press Ctrl-End. Quicken next displays the Make Credit Card Payment screen shown in figure 10.16.

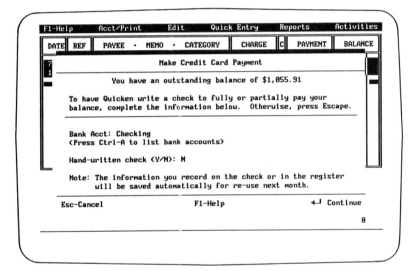

Fig. 10.16.

The Make Credit Card Payment screen.

If you press Ctrl-End prior to reconciling the balance to zero, Quicken makes the necessary adjustments to reconcile the balance.

Quicken uses the information from the Make Credit Card Payment screen to do one of two things: record a handwritten check, or set up a check to be printed. You fill two fields on the Make Credit Card Payment screen, the bank account name and the handwritten check flag. If the Hand-written check field is set to N, Quicken moves you to the Write Checks screen so that you can print a check to the credit card company on the specified bank account. If the Hand-written check field is set to Y, Quicken moves you to the register screen for the specified bank account so that you can record the check you wrote to the credit card company. In either case,

Quicken enters the payment amount as the entire credit card balance. If you want to pay less than that amount, change the amount in the payment amount field.

Building a Balance Sheet

A balance sheet is one of the traditional tools individuals and businesses can use to monitor their finances. A balance sheet lists the assets you own and the liabilities you owe. The difference between assets and liabilities is called owner's equity or net worth. Notice that a balance sheet is quite different from reports like income statements and cash flow reports that summarize what has happened over a period of time. A balance sheet provides a snapshot of your personal or business finances at a point in time. An income statement summarizes the activity between the last balance sheet date and the current balance sheet date.

Creating a balance sheet with Quicken is a two-step process. The first step is to set up an account for each of your assets along with a beginning balance amount that equals the asset's cost or value. Assets generally are items you have paid for and have lasting value. Personal assets include items like cash in your wallet, the surrender value of a life insurance policy, any investments, a home, and long-lived personal items like your car and furniture. Business assets usually include cash, accounts receivable, inventory, and other property and equipment.

First, determine the date at which you want to establish a balance sheet. You then can determine the cost of all your assets and liabilities as of the same date. All cost information needs to be accurate or your calculation of net worth will not be accurate. Use only one method for valuing your assets or liabilities, such as historical cost or fair market value. Mixing the different methods does not yield beneficial results. You also should note on your opening balances whether or not you used historical cost or fair market value, and if you used fair market value, where that value came from. For stocks and bonds, the daily New York Stock Exchange or American Exchange listings can help you determine fair market value. Have property appraised by a real estate appraiser to determine fair market value.

The second step in creating a balance sheet is to set up an account for each of your liabilities along with the balances owed. Liabilities are amounts you currently owe other people or businesses. Personal liabilities include items like credit card balances, income taxes owed, car loans, and a mortgage. Business liabilities usually include items like accounts payable, wages and salaries owed employees, income and payroll taxes, and bank credit lines and loans.

CPA Tip: The one crucial thing you need to do to produce a balance sheet is to make sure that all your assets and liability accounts are in the same account group.

You do not need to worry about the third step because Quicken does the work for you. The program calculates the difference between your assets and liabilities. Hopefully, the difference, called your financial net worth, is a positive one. For businesses and individuals, you want the net worth amount to grow larger over time because this amount acts as a financial cushion. Figure 10.17 shows an example of a personal balance sheet, or net worth statement, created by Quicken.

```
                        Example Personal Balance Sheet
                                As of 8/31/89
All Accounts                                                    Page 1
7/14/89
                                              8/31/89
                    Account                   Balance
    -------------------------------------     ------------------------
    ASSETS
      Cash and Bank Accounts
        Checking-Chkg Acct#: 12345678
          Ending Balance                         954.09
          plus: Checks Payable                 1,055.91
                                              ------------
          Total Checking-Chkg Acct#: 12345678              2,010.00
                                                           ------------
      Total Cash and Bank Accounts                         2,010.00

      Other Assets
        House-Home (appraised val.)                      150,000.00
        Stocks-Investments                                 2,000.00
                                                          ------------
      Total Other Assets                                 152,000.00
                                                          ------------
    TOTAL ASSETS                                         154,010.00

    LIABILITIES
      Checks Payable                                       1,055.91

      Credit Cards
        Mastercard-Mastercard Charge                       1,000.00
                                                          ------------
      Total Credit Cards                                   1,000.00

      Other Liabilities
        Mortgage-Home Mortgage                           132,000.00
                                                          ------------
      Total Other Liabilities                            132,000.00
                                                          ------------
    TOTAL LIABILITIES                                    134,055.91
                                                          ------------
    OVERALL TOTAL                                         19,954.09
                                                          ============
```

Fig. 10.17.

A sample personal balance sheet.

A business balance sheet looks the same, although the assets and liabilities listed are probably different. Chapter 11, "Using Quicken's Reports," describes how to print a balance sheet and each of Quicken's other reports.

Chapter Summary

With the new enhancements provided in Version 3, you easily can use Quicken for almost all of your personal or small-business accounting needs. This chapter described how to use Quicken to perform record keeping for assets like investments or accounts receivable and liabilities like credit card debts and loans. The chapter also described why and how you might use Quicken to generate a balance sheet.

11

Using Quicken's Reports

By using the **Write/Print Checks** and the **Register** options from the Main menu, you construct a database of the various transactions that determine your personal or business cash flows. The benefit of constructing any database is that you can sort, extract from, and summarize the information contained within the database. Quicken provides you with this same benefit through the **Reports** option. Using Quicken's reports turns your computer-based check book into a powerful tool for personal or business management.

This chapter describes the six options available on the Reports menu—accessed by selecting **Reports** from the Main menu or the Activities menu on the Write Checks and Register screens. Figure 11.1 shows the Reports menu.

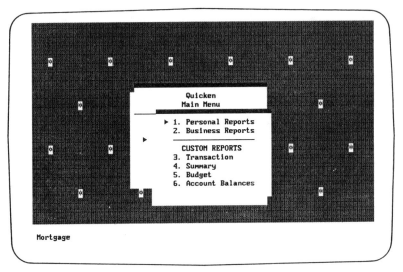

Fig. 11.1.

The Reports menu.

VERSION 3.0

The first two options on the Reports menu display menus of additional report choices. Figure 11.2 shows the Personal Reports menu. Figure 11.3 shows the Business Reports menu.

Fig. 11.2.

The Personal Reports menu.

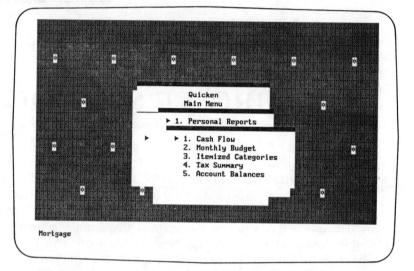

Fig. 11.3.

The Business Reports menu.

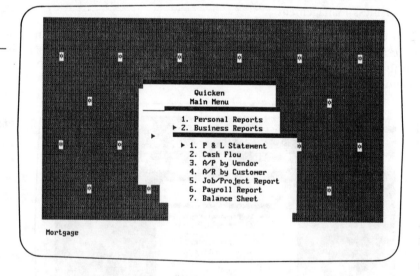

The other four options on the Reports menu enable you to create custom reports as discussed later in this chapter.

The Basics of Printing Reports

You need to take the following steps to print any of the six reports. First, you complete the create report screen. The Cash Flow Report screen is shown in figure 11.4, but this screen closely resembles the screens you use for several of the reports. (The rest of this chapter describes how you complete the individual create report screens.)

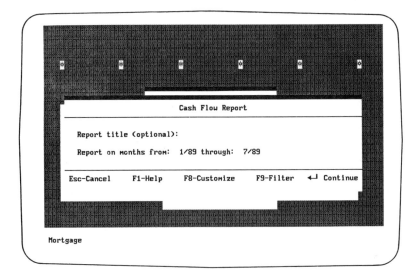

Fig. 11.4.

The Cash Flow Report screen.

When you complete the create report screen, press Enter, and Quicken generates and displays the report on-screen. You can use the arrow keys, PgUp, and PgDn to see different portions of the report. You also can use the Home and End keys to see the first and last pages of the report. On reports too wide to fit comfortably on-screen, you can use F9 to toggle between a full column-width and a half column-width version of the report.

The second step in printing a report is to press F8 or Ctrl-P. Either approach displays the Print Report screen shown in figure 11.5.

This screen enables you to specify where you want the report printed to. Answer the Print to field by typing a *1* for printer 1, *2* for printer 2, and so on. If you used printer names on the Printer Settings screen, you see those printer names on-screen. Figure 11.5 shows, for example, that the third printer is called HP LJetII-Checks.

Fig. 11.5.

*The Print
Report screen.*

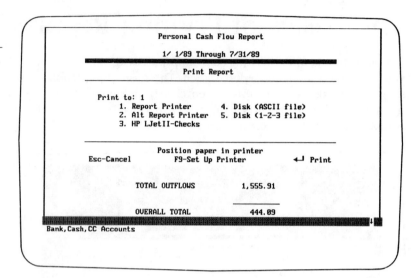

```
                    Personal Cash Flow Report

                    1/ 1/89 Through 7/31/89

                         Print Report


       Print to: 1
            1. Report Printer      4. Disk (ASCII file)
            2. Alt Report Printer  5. Disk (1-2-3 file)
            3. HP LJetII-Checks


                    Position paper in printer
       Esc-Cancel        F9-Set Up Printer          ↵ Print


            TOTAL OUTFLOWS          1,555.91


            OVERALL TOTAL            444.09

   Bank,Cash,CC Accounts
```

If you select 4 at the Print to field, Quicken prints an ASCII file. ASCII files are standardized text files that you can use to retrieve a Quicken report into a word processing program, such as Wordperfect or Microsoft Word. To create an ASCII file, Quicken requests three pieces of information: the file, lines per page, and the width. In the File field, enter a name for Quicken to use for the ASCII file. If you want to use a data directory different from the Quicken data directory, QUICKEN3, you also can specify a path name. (See your DOS user's manual for information on path names.) In the Lines per page field, set the number of report lines between page breaks. If you are using 11-inch paper, the page length usually is 66 lines. In the Width field, set the number of characters including blanks that Quicken prints on a line. If you are using 8 1/2-inch paper, the characters per line usually is 80. Figure 11.6 shows the completed Print To Disk screen with the file specified as PRNT_TXT.

If you select 5 at the Print to field on the Print Report screen, Quicken prints a 1-2-3 file. (1-2-3 is a popular spreadsheet program manufactured by Lotus Corporation.) To create a 1-2-3 file, Quicken requests the name of the file you want to create. As with the ASCII file creation option, if you want to use a data directory different than QUICKEN3, you also can specify a path name. Figure 11.7 shows the completed Print Report to Lotus File screen with the file specified as EXPENSES.

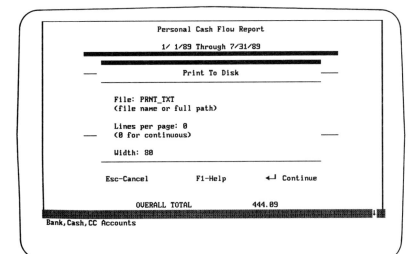

Fig. 11.6.

The Print To Disk screen.

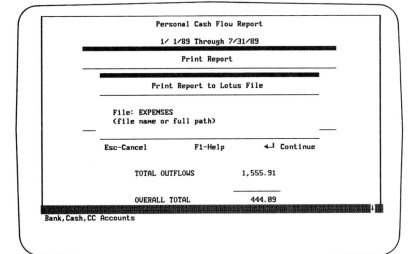

Fig. 11.7.

The Print Report to Lotus File screen.

The Personal Reports

On the Personal Reports menu, you have five choices. To request any of the five reports, you need to complete the create report screen that appears when you select a report from the Personal Reports menu.

Cash Flow

Figure 11.4 shows the Cash Flow Report screen completed so that the report title is *Personal Cash Flow Report* and so the report includes transactions between 1/89 and 7/89. The screen also identifies two special function keys, F8-Customize and F9-Filter, that you can use to modify the appearance of the report produced. Because these two function keys apply to all the personal and business reports, they are described under "Customizing and Filtering Reports," following the discussion of business reports.

Figure 11.8 shows an example of a personal cash flow report. The cash flow report shows the total money you have received and expended by category. The report also shows transfers. The last line of the outflows section of the cash flow report in figure 11.8 shows a transfer to the Stocks account. The report includes transactions from all the bank, cash, and credit card accounts in the current account group.

Fig. 11.8.

A sample cash flow report.

```
                              CASH FLOW REPORT
                           7/ 1/89 Through 7/31/89
         Bank,Cash,CC Accounts                                Page 1
         7/17/89
                                               7/ 1/89-
                         Category Description    7/31/89
                         -------------------- -----------
                         INFLOWS
                           Salary Income        4,000.00
                                               -----------
                         TOTAL INFLOWS          4,000.00

                         OUTFLOWS
                           Automobile Expense     175.00
                           Charitable Donations    25.00
                           Entertainment           25.00
                           Federal Tax Witholding 250.00
                           Groceries              432.91
                           Home Repair & Maint.   125.00
                           Housing                650.00
                           Interest Expense        25.00
                           Reg Retirement Sav Plan 40.00
                           Water, Gas, Electric    43.92
                           Outflows - Other     1,055.91
                           TO Stocks              500.00
                                               -----------
                         TOTAL OUTFLOWS         3,347.74

                                               -----------
                         OVERALL TOTAL            652.26
                                               ===========
```

Monthly Budget Report

The monthly budget report shows the total money you have received and expended by category and the amounts you budgeted to spend. The report also calculates the difference between what you budgeted and what you actually spent. This report includes transactions from all the bank, cash, and credit card accounts within the account group. Figure 11.9 shows the Monthly Budget Report screen.

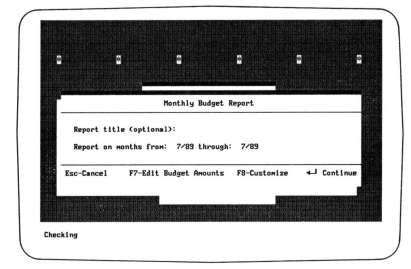

Fig. 11.9.

The Monthly Budget Report screen.

The Monthly Budget Report screen provides two special function keys: F7-Edit Budget Amounts and F8-Customize. "Customizing and Filtering Reports" describes how to use the F8-Customize function key. F7 enables you to change the budgeted amounts for categories using the Specify Budget Amounts screen (see fig. 11.10).

This screen is the one you used to initially set your budget. (See Appendix A for more on budgeting and Chapter 7 for more on using categories and classes.)

Figure 11.11 shows a sample monthly budget report. Although figure 11.11 shows only one month, if you specify the period to be covered by the report as beginning at the start of the year, Quicken provides a month-by-month comparison of actual expenses to the budgeted amount.

Fig. 11.10.

Pressing F7 accesses the Specify Budget Amounts screen.

```
                        Specify Budget Amounts

                                                    Budget      Monthly
         Category     Type       Description        Amount      Detail

      ▶ Bonus         Inc    Bonus Income
        Canada Pen    Inc    Canadian Pension
        Div Income    Inc    Dividend Income
        Family Allow  Inc    Family Allowance
        Inc Sal       Inc    Salary Income          2,000.00
        Int Inc       Inc    Interest Income
        Invest Inc    Inc    Investment Income
        Oldage Pen    Inc    Old Age Pension
        Other Inc     Inc    Other Income
        Auto Fuel     Expns  Automobile Fuel
        Auto Other    Expns  Automobile Expense       175.00
        Bank Chrg     Expns  Bank Charge

                            ↑,↓ Select
      Esc-Cancel     F1-Help   Ctrl-E Edit Monthly Detail      Ctrl↵ Done


   Checking
```

Fig. 11.11.

A sample monthly budget report.

```
                            MONTHLY BUDGET REPORT
                          7/ 1/89 Through 7/31/89
        Bank,Cash,CC Accounts                                      Page 1
        7/17/89
                                    7/ 1/89    -      7/31/89
                 Category Description  Actual    Budget    Diff
        -------------------------- ---------- ---------- ----------
        INFLOWS
          Salary Income             4,000.00   2,000.00   2,000.00
                                   ---------- ---------- ----------
        TOTAL INFLOWS               4,000.00   2,000.00   2,000.00

        OUTFLOWS
          Automobile Expense          175.00     175.00       0.00
          Charitable Donations         25.00      25.00       0.00
          Entertainment                25.00      25.00       0.00
          Federal Tax Witholding      250.00     250.00       0.00
          Groceries                   432.91     453.90     -20.99
          Home Repair & Maint.        125.00     125.00       0.00
          Housing                     650.00     650.00       0.00
          Interest Expense             25.00      25.00       0.00
          Reg Retirement Sav Plan      40.00      40.00       0.00
          Water, Gas, Electric         43.92      50.00      -6.08
                                   ---------- ---------- ----------
        TOTAL OUTFLOWS             1,791.83   1,818.90     -27.07

                                   ---------- ---------- ----------
        OVERALL TOTAL              2,208.17     181.10   2,027.07
                                   ========== ========== ==========
```

The monthly budget report only shows categories for which amounts have been spent or budgeted. Transfers are not included on the report.

Itemized Category Report

The itemized category report shows each transaction in an account group sorted and subtotaled by category. This type of report provides a convenient way to see the detailed transactions that add up to a category total. The Itemized Category Report screen, shown in figure 11.12, works like the other report request screens.

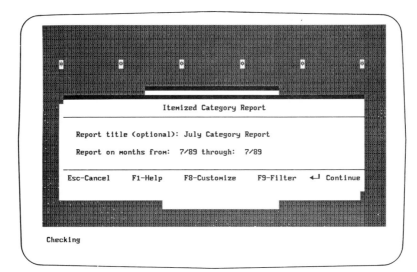

Fig. 11.12.

The Itemized Category Report screen.

Again, you can replace the default report title, "Itemized Category Report," with a more specific title such as "July Category Report" by using the optional report title field. You also can specify a range of months to be included on the report and use the F8-Customize and F9-Filter function keys to change the appearance of the data on a report. Figure 11.13 shows a sample of the itemized category report.

Tax Summary

The tax summary report shows all the transactions assigned to categories you marked as tax-related. Transactions are sorted and subtotaled by category. The Tax Summary Report screen, shown in figure 11.14, works like the other request screens, enabling you to give the tax summary report a more unique title or to include only transactions from specified months.

Fig. 11.13.

*A sample
itemized
category report.*

```
                           July Category Report
                          7/ 1/89 Through 7/31/89
       All Accounts                                             Page 1
       7/17/89

        Date   Acct   Num      Payee        Memo      Category   Clr  Amount
       -----  ------- ------ --------------- ---------- ----------------- - -----------
                             INCOME/EXPENSE
                               INCOME
                                 Salary Income
                                 -------------
        7/13 Checkin       Payroll Deposit          Inc Sal       2,000 00
        7/17 Checkin     S Monthly payroll Gross wage Inc Sal     2,000.00
                                                                 -----------
                               Total Salary Income               4,000.00

                                 Income - Other
                                 --------------
        7/ 1 Stocks        Big National Ba 9% Cert. D               500.00
        7/15 Stocks        NoLoad Mutual F blue chip              1,000.00
                                                                 -----------
                               Total Income - Other              1,500.00
                                                                 -----------
                             TOTAL INCOME                         5,500.00


                             EXPENSES
                               Automobile Expense
                               ------------------
        7/17 Checkin       Motors Acceptan monthly ca Auto Other   -175.00
                                                                 -----------
                               Total Automobile Expense            -175.00

                               Charitable Donations
                               --------------------
        7/17 Checkin       United Way      monthly Un Charity       -25.00
                                                                 -----------
                               Total Charitable Donations          -25.00

                               Entertainment
                               -------------
        7/17 Checkin     S Big National Ba July enter Enter.        -25.00
                                                                 -----------
                               Total Entertainment                 -25.00

                               Federal Tax Witholding
                               ----------------------
        7/17 Checkin     S Monthly payroll income tax Tax Fed      -250.00
                                                                 -----------
                               Total Federal Tax Witholding       -250.00

                               Groceries
                               ---------
        7/22 Checkin       Save-On-Foods   food and b Groceries   -432.91
                                                                 -----------
                               Total Groceries                    -432.91
```

The F8-Customize and F9-Filter function keys are available in case you want to produce a custom-tailored version of the report. (See "Customizing and Filtering Reports" later in the chapter.) Figure 11.15 shows a sample tax summary report.

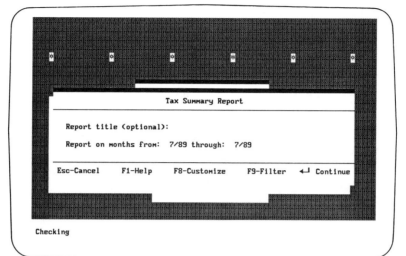

Fig. 11.14.

The Tax Summary Report screen.

```
                        Tax Summary Report

      Report title (optional):

      Report on months from:  7/89 through:  7/89


   Esc-Cancel    F1-Help    F8-Customize    F9-Filter   ↵ Continue



Checking
```

Fig. 11.15.

A sample tax summary report.

```
                        TAX SUMMARY REPORT
                       7/ 1/89 Through 7/31/89
All Accounts                                              Page 1
7/17/89

  Date   Acct     Num      Payee        Memo      Category   Clr Amount
 ------ -------- ------ --------------- ----------- --------------- - ---------
                 INCOME/EXPENSE
                   INCOME
                     Salary Income
                     -------------
  7/13 Checking       Payroll Deposit              Inc Sal      2,000.00
  7/17 Checking     S Monthly payroll  Gross wages Inc Sal      2,000.00
                                                              ---------
                     Total Salary Income                       4,000.00
                                                              ---------
                   TOTAL INCOME                                4,000.00
                                                              ---------

                   EXPENSES
                     Charitable Donations
                     --------------------
  7/17 Checking       United Way        monthly Uni Charity      -25.00
                                                              ---------
                     Total Charitable Donations                  -25.00

                     Federal Tax Witholding
                     ----------------------
  7/17 Checking     S Monthly payroll  income tax  Tax Fed      -250.00
                                                              ---------
                     Total Federal Tax Witholding               -250.00

                     Interest Expense
                     ----------------
  7/22 Checking       Student Loan Ser July studen Int Exp       -25.00
                                                              ---------
                     Total Interest Expense                      -25.00
                                                              ---------
                   TOTAL EXPENSES                               -300.00

                                                              ---------
                   TOTAL INCOME/EXPENSE                        3,700.00
                                                              =========
```

Account Balances

An account balances report shows the balance in each of the accounts in an account group on a particular date. If the account group includes all your assets and liabilities, the resulting report is a balance sheet. (Balance sheets are described in Chapter 10, "Accounting for Other Assets and Liabilities.") Figure 11.16 shows the Account Balances Report screen.

Fig. 11.16.

The Account Balances Report screen.

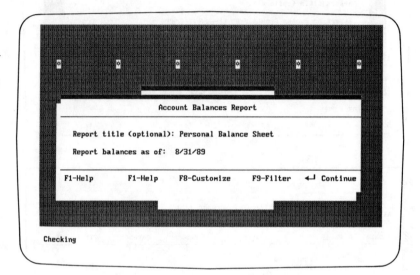

```
                        Account Balances Report

        Report title (optional): Personal Balance Sheet

        Report balances as of:  8/31/89

    F1-Help         F1-Help       F8-Customize     F9-Filter   ↵ Continue
```

```
Checking
```

The Account Balances Report screen differs from other personal reports because you cannot enter a range of dates; you can enter only one date. The account balances report does not report on activity for a period of time, but provides a snapshot of certain aspects of your financial condition—the account balances in your account group—at a point in time. Figure 11.17 shows a sample account balances report.

The Business Reports

The Business Reports menu provides seven reports as shown in figure 11.3. To request any of the reports, complete the report request screen with an optional title and the period of time you want the report to cover.

```
                    Personal Balance Sheet
                       As of 8/31/89
  All Accounts                                              Page 1
  7/17/89
                                              8/31/89
              Account                         Balance
  ----------------------------------------  ------------
  ASSETS
     Cash and Bank Accounts
        Checking-Chkg Acct#: 12345678
           Ending Balance                     1,162.26
           plus: Checks Payable               1,055.91
                                            ------------
        Total Checking-Chkg Acct#: 12345678               2,218.17
                                                        ------------
     Total Cash and Bank Accounts                         2,218.17

     Other Assets
        House-Home (appraised val.)                      150,000.00
        Stocks-Investments                                 2,000.00
                                                        ------------
     Total Other Assets                                  152,000.00

                                                        ------------
  TOTAL ASSETS                                           154,218.17

  LIABILITIES
     Checks Payable                                        1,055.91

     Credit Cards
        Mastercard-Mastercard Charge                       1,000.00
                                                        ------------
     Total Credit Cards                                    1,000.00

     Other Liabilities
        Mortgage-Home Mortgage                           132,000.00
                                                        ------------
     Total Other Liabilities                             132,000.00

                                                        ------------
  TOTAL LIABILITIES                                       134,055.91

                                                        ------------
  OVERALL TOTAL                                            20,162.26
                                                        ============
```

Fig. 11.17.

A sample account balances report.

Profit and Loss Statement

A profit and loss statement shows the total income and expense transactions by category for all the accounts on a monthly basis. Transactions from any of the accounts in the account groups are included, but transfers between accounts are not. Figure 11.18 shows the Profit & Loss Statement screen. Like most of the report request screens, you have two options: to use your own report title and to specify the months to be included on the report.

Figure 11.19 shows a sample profit and loss statement.

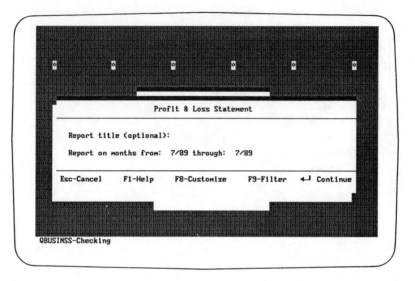

Fig. 11.18.

The Profit & Loss Statement screen.

```
                    Profit & Loss Statement

     Report title (optional):

     Report on months from:  7/89 through:  7/89


  Esc-Cancel     F1-Help     F8-Customize     F9-Filter    ←┘ Continue
```

QBUSINSS-Checking

Fig. 11.19.

A sample profit and loss statement.

```
                              PROFIT & LOSS STATEMENT
                               7/ 1/89 Through 7/31/89
QBUSINSS-All Accounts                                                    Page 1
7/17/89
                                              7/ 1/89-
                        Category Description     7/31/89
                    ---------------------------- -----------
                    INCOME/EXPENSE
                      INCOME
                        Gross Sales             12,300.00
                                                -----------
                    TOTAL INCOME                12,300.00

                      EXPENSES
                        Car & Truck                350.00
                        Entertainment              581.05
                        Insurance                  432.97
                        Interest Paid               95.30
                        Legal & Prof. Fees         125.00
                        Office Expenses            329.00
                        Painting subcontracters  5,000.00
                        Rent Paid                  750.00
                                                -----------
                    TOTAL EXPENSES              7,663.32

                                                -----------
                    TOTAL INCOME/EXPENSE         4,636.68
                                                ===========
```

The Cash Flow Report

A cash flow report resembles a profit and loss statement. This report includes all bank, cash, and credit card accounts and shows the money received and spent by category for each month. The cash flow report also shows transfers between accounts. Figure 11.20 shows the Cash Flow Report screen.

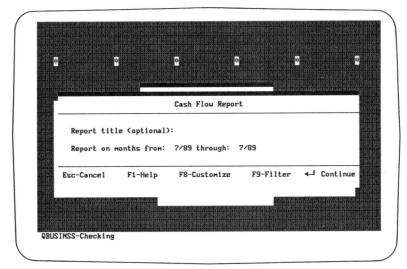

Fig. 11.20.

*The Cash Flow
Report screen.*

Like the Profit & Loss Statement screen, you enter the range of months for which you want the cash flow report prepared. You have the option of entering your own report title that Quicken prints on the cash flow report in place of the default title, "Cash Flow Report." You also have the option of using the F8-Customize and F9-Filter keys to fine-tune the ultimate report produced.

Figure 11.21 shows a sample cash flow report. The major difference between this report and the profit and loss statement is that the transfer to the Loan account is shown on the cash flow report. The transfer to Loan is the last outflow listed.

A/P By Vendor Report

The A/P by vendor report lists all the unprinted checks sorted and subtotaled by payee. (A/P is an abbreviation for accounts payable, the unpaid bills of a business.) Figure 11.22 shows the A/P (Unprinted Checks) by Vendor screen. You do not enter a date or a range of dates on this screen. You can enter a substitute report title for Quicken to use in place of the default report title, "A/P by Vendor Report." You also can use the F8-Customize and F9-Filter function keys as described later in the chapter to change the appearance of the report and the data it uses.

Fig. 11.21.

A sample cash flow report.

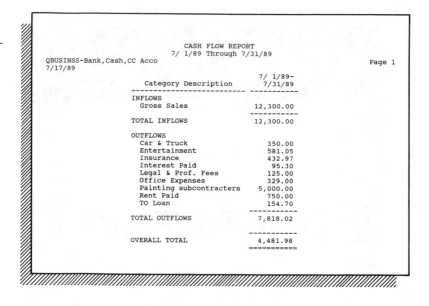

Figure 11.23 shows a sample A/P by vendor report. Two vendor totals appear to be for the same vendor: one for Hughes Office Supplies and another for Hughes Office Supply Store. Quicken subtotals unprinted checks with the exact payee names. If you type the payee name differently for different checks, the payee is not recognized by Quicken as the same payee and, therefore, the amounts are not subtotaled. If you are going to use this report (or the A/R by customer report described next), you should use the memorized transactions feature. When you use this feature, the payee name is identical for each transaction.

Fig. 11.22.

The A/P (Unprinted Checks) by Vendor screen.

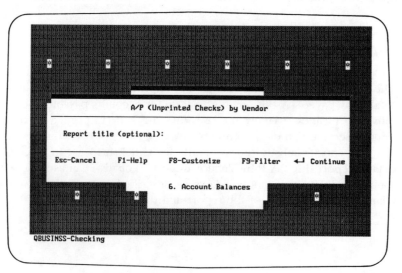

```
                       A/P (UNPRINTED CHECKS) BY VENDOR
                              7/ 1/89 Through 7/31/89
QBUSINSS-All Accounts                                         Page 1
7/17/89

                               Payee            7/89
                    --------------------------- ----------
                    Hughes Office Supplies         -47.57
                    Hughes Office Supply Store     -53.91
                    Parker Bennett              -1,075.00
                                                ----------
                    OVERALL TOTAL               -1,176.48
                                                ==========
```

Fig. 11.23.

A sample accounts payable by vendor report.

A/R by Customer Report

The A/R by customer report shows the transactions in all of the other asset accounts sorted and subtotaled by payee. The report, however, does not include transactions marked as cleared—those transactions marked with an * or X in the C column of the register. (A/R is an abbreviation for accounts receivable, the amounts a business's customers owe.) Figure 11.24 shows the A/R by Customer screen. You can enter a title to replace the default report title Quicken uses, "A/R by Customer Report." You also can use the F8-Customize and F9-Filter function keys as described later in the chapter.

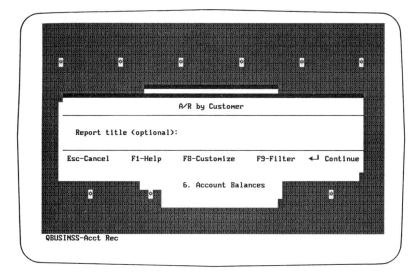

Fig. 11.24.

The A/R by Customer screen.

After you complete the request screen, press Enter. Quicken displays the Select Accounts to Include screen (see fig. 11.25).

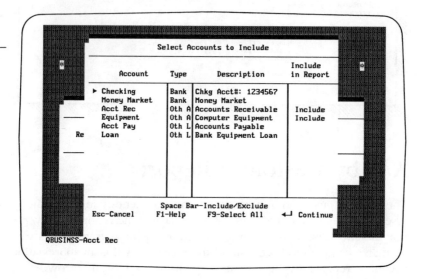

Fig. 11.25.

The Select Accounts to Include screen.

Quicken initially selects all asset account types for inclusion on the A/R by customer report. If you have other asset accounts besides accounts receivable, you want to exclude these. For example, figure 11.25 shows two accounts marked for inclusion: Acct Rec and Equipment. To exclude an account, use the up- and down-arrow keys to move the selection triangle to the left of the account you want to exclude and press the space bar. The space bar acts as a toggle switch, alternately marking the account for inclusion or exclusion. If you want to select all the accounts, press F9.

Figure 11.26 shows a sample A/R by customer report.

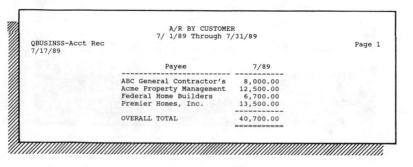

Fig. 11.26.

A sample accounts receivable by customer report.

Job/Project Report

The job/project report shows category totals by month for each month in the specified date range. The report also shows account balances at the end of the last month. (If you are using classes, the report shows category totals by classes in separate columns across the report page.) Figure 11.27 shows the Job/Project Report screen. Figure 11.28 shows a sample job/project report.

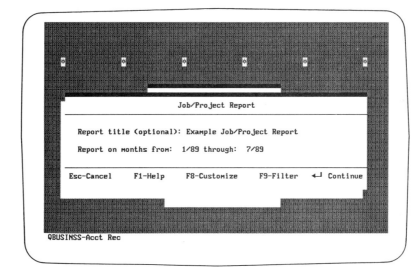

Fig. 11.27.

The Job/Project Report screen.

Payroll Report

The payroll report shows the total amounts paid to individual payees when the transaction category starts with "payroll." (The precise search argument used is, *payroll...* See the discussions of exact and key-word matches in Chapters 4 and 6 for more information.) This report type includes transactions from all accounts. Figure 11.29 shows the Payroll Report screen. Figure 11.30 shows a sample payroll report.

Fig. 11.28.

A sample job/ project report.

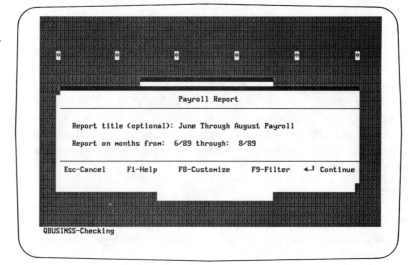

```
                              Example Job/Project Report
                              1/ 1/89 Through 7/31/89
QBUSINSS-All Accounts                                              Page 1
7/17/89

                    Category Description          Other
                 ------------------------------ --------------
                 INCOME/EXPENSE
                   INCOME
                     Gross Sales                    46,300.00
                                                 --------------
                   TOTAL INCOME                      46,300.00

                   EXPENSES
                     Car & Truck                        350.00
                     Entertainment                      581.05
                     Insurance                          432.97
                     Interest Paid                       95.30
                     Legal & Prof. Fees                 125.00
                     Office Expenses                    430.48
                     Painting subcontracters          6,075.00
                     Rent Paid                          750.00
                                                 --------------
                   TOTAL EXPENSES                     8,839.80

                                                 --------------
                   TOTAL INCOME/EXPENSE             37,460.20

                 TRANSFERS
                   TO Loan                            -154.70
                   FROM Checking                       154.70
                                                 --------------
                 TOTAL TRANSFERS                        0.00

                 BALANCE FORWARD
                   Acct Pay                         -3,211.95
                   Acct Rec                          6,700.00
                   Loan                             -8,743.01
                   Checking                          1,000.00
                   Equipment                        12,300.00
                   Money Market                      6,543.87
                                                 --------------
                 TOTAL BALANCE FORWARD              14,588.91

                                                 --------------
                 OVERALL TOTAL                      52,049.11
                                                 ==============
```

Fig. 11.29.

The Payroll Report screen.

```
                        Payroll Report

   Report title (optional): June Through August Payroll

   Report on months from:  6/89 through:  8/89

 Esc-Cancel    F1-Help    F8-Customize    F9-Filter   ← Continue

QBUSINSS-Checking
```

```
                         July Payroll
                   7/ 1/89 Through 7/31/89
QBUSINSS-All Accounts                                          Page 1
7/17/89
                            INC/EXP         INC/EXP         INC/EXP
                           EXPENSES        EXPENSES        EXPENSES
            Payee        Gross Wages       Soc. Sec.          TOTAL
         ----------------  --------------  --------------  --------------
         Angel Barnes        1,500.00         112.65        1,612.65
         Bonnie Chapman      1,000.00          75.10        1,075.10
         Cat Dosewallips       500.00          37.55          537.55
         William Lake        1,000.00          75.10        1,075.10
                           --------------  --------------  --------------
         OVERALL TOTAL       4,000.00         300.40        4,300.40
                           ==============  ==============  ==============
```

Fig. 11.30.

A sample payroll report.

Balance Sheet

The balance sheet report shows the account balances for all the accounts in the account group at a specific point in time. If the account group includes accounts for all of your assets and liabilities, the resulting report is a balance sheet and shows the net worth of your business. (Chapter 10, "Accounting for Other Assets and Liabilities," describes balance sheets in more detail.) Figure 11.31 shows the Balance Sheet screen. Figure 11.32 shows an example of a business balance sheet.

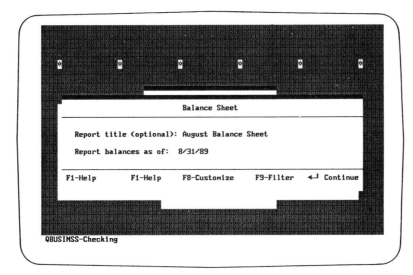

Fig. 11.31.

The Balance Sheet screen.

Fig. 11.32.

A sample balance sheet.

```
                        August Balance Sheet
                          As of 8/31/89
QBUSINSS-All Accounts                                           Page 1
8/31/89
                                               8/31/89
                      Account                  Balance
------------------------------------------  ----------------------
ASSETS
  Cash and Bank Accounts
    Checking-Chkg Acct#: 1234567
      Ending Balance                              5.10
      plus: Checks Payable                    1,176.48
                                              -----------
      Total Checking-Chkg Acct#: 1234567                   1,181.58
    Money Market-Money Market                              6,543.87
                                                           -----------
    Total Cash and Bank Accounts                           7,725.45

  Other Assets
    Acct Rec-Accounts Receivable                          40,700.00
    Equipment-Computer Equipment                          12,300.00
                                                          -----------
    Total Other Assets                                    53,000.00

                                                          -----------
  TOTAL ASSETS                                            60,725.45

LIABILITIES
  Checks Payable                                           1,176.48

  Other Liabilities
    Acct Pay-Accounts Payable                              3,211.95
    Loan-Bank Equipment Loan                               8,588.31
                                                          -----------
  Total Other Liabilities                                 11,800.26

                                                          -----------
  TOTAL LIABILITIES                                       12,976.74

                                                          -----------
  OVERALL TOTAL                                           47,748.71
                                                          ===========
```

Customizing and Filtering Reports

Each personal report, except the monthly budget report, and each business report provide two special function keys on the report screen: F8-Customize and F9-Filter. (The monthly budget report provides just the first function key, F8-Customize.) F8-Customize enables you to modify the way data is organized and presented on a report. F9-Filter enables you to include or exclude certain transactions from a report. These two function keys give you complete flexibility over the way Quicken generates personal and business reports. The F9-Filter function key also enables you to change the way Quicken prepares custom reports.

Customizing

If you press F8-Customize from one of the report screens, Quicken displays the Create Summary Report screen shown in figure 11.33.

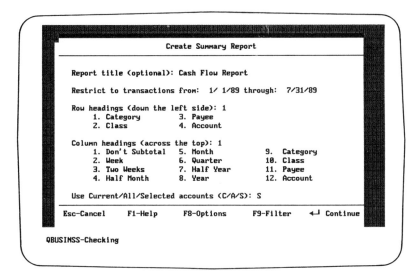

Fig. 11.33.

The Create Summary Report screen enables you to customize your report.

Quicken fills out the Create Summary Report screen to generate the report default type. Not all of the fields on the Create Summary Report screen are displayed every time—only those fields that make sense for the report you are generating. However, you can fill in a combination or perhaps all of the fields shown in figure 11.33. These fields are described in the following paragraphs.

Using the Report Title Field

You can use this field to substitute a more precise or specific report title in place of the default report title. The Report title field provides space for up to 39 characters.

Note: The default report title that Quicken uses to identify a report corresponds to the report screen title. For example, if you press F8-Customize from the Cash Flow Report screen, the default report title is "Cash Flow Report."

Using the Restrict to Transactions From and Through Date Fields

You may want to see account transactions for a specific period of time. For example, when assessing your cash flows for the month of June, you only want account transactions from the month of June. Use the date restriction fields for this purpose. By entering a from date and a through date in these fields, you limit the transactions included on a report to those with transaction dates falling between the from and through date.

Both date fields need to be filled using the standard date format. As with the date fields found elsewhere in the Quicken, you can move the date ahead one day at a time by pressing the + key and move the date back one day at a time by pressing the − key.

Using the Row Headings Field

The Row headings field enables you to select the order by which transactions are sorted and the subtotals that are calculated. You usually have four choices: Category, Class, Payee, or Account. The names of the row headings you select appear down the left side of the printed report.

Using the Column Headings Field

The Column headings field enables you to select the order by which transactions are segregated and subtotaled in columns across the report page. You can have as many as twelve options:

1. Don't Subtotal
2. Week
3. Two Weeks
4. Half Month
5. Month
6. Quarter
7. Half Year
8. Year
9. Category
10. Class
11. Payee
12. Account

You select the scheme you want to use by typing the number that appears to the left of the column heading you want to use.

Using the Use Current/All/ Selected Accounts Field

The Use Current/All/Selected accounts field enables you to specify which accounts from the selected account group should be included on the report. A *C* designates that only the current account should be included. An *A* designates that every account should included. An *S* designates that only selected accounts should be included. If you choose *S*, Quicken displays the Select Accounts to Include screen shown in figure 11-25. To include an account, use the up- and down-arrow keys to move the selection triangle to the left of the account you want to include and press the space bar. The space bar acts as a toggle switch, alternately marking the account for inclusion or exclusion. If you want to select all the accounts, press F9.

(***Note:*** For the account balances and balance sheet reports, you have three choices that the space bar toggles you between. You can include an account, exclude an account, or show any class detail. Pressing the space bar alternately displays Include, Detail, or nothing next to the option.)

Filtering

If you press F9-Filter from one of the report request screens, Quicken displays the Filter Report Transactions screen shown in figure 11.34.

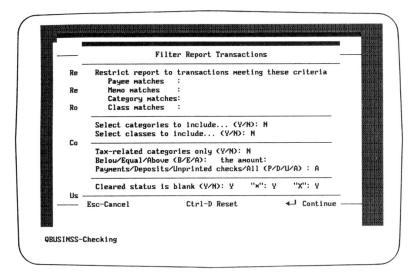

Fig. 11.34.

The Filter Report Transactions screen.

You can use a variety of fields to include or exclude transactions from a report. If you start modifying these field and then want to reset them to the original values, press Ctrl-D.

Using the Payee Matches Field

The Payee matches field enables you to instruct Quicken to include or exclude a certain payee or transaction description from a transaction report based on exact or key-word matches. (Chapters 4 and 6 describe in detail the mechanics of exact and key-word matches. See figure 6.4 in Chapter 6.) If you leave this field blank, you do not affect transactions being included or excluded from the report.

Using the Memo Matches Field

The Memo matches field works similarly to the Payee matches, except that Quicken compares the Memo matches field to the transactions' memo fields. This field affects the transactions included or excluded on the report like the Payee matches field. You do not have to use this field.

Using the Category Matches Field

The Category matches field enables you to instruct Quicken to include or exclude transactions assigned to certain categories based on exact or key-word matches. If you leave this field blank, the transactions being included or excluded from the report are not affected.

Using the Class Matches Field

The Class matches field works similarly to the Category matches field, except that Quicken compares the class field to class entries in the trans-actions' Category field. Like the Category matches field, this optional field affects the transactions included or excluded on the report.

Using the Select Categories to Include Field

The Select categories to include field enables you to specify an entire set of categories to be included on a report. If you set this field to Y for yes, Quicken displays the Select Categories To Include screen that you can use to mark the categories you want included on a report (see fig. 11.35).

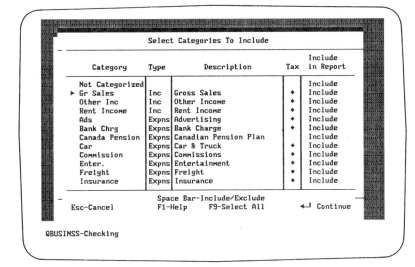

Fig. 11.35.

*The Select
Categories To
Include screen.*

To include a category, use the up- and down arrow keys to move the selection triangle to the left of the category you want to include and press the space bar. The space bar acts as a toggle switch, alternately marking the category for inclusion or exclusion. If you want to select all the categories, press F9.

Using the Select Classes To Include Field

The Select classes to include field enables you to specify an entire set of classes to be included on a report. If you set this field to Y for yes, Quicken displays the Select Classes To Include screen that you can use to mark individual categories you want included on a report (see fig. 11.36).

To include a class, use the up- and down-arrow keys to move the selection triangle to the left of the class you want to include and press the space bar. The space bar acts as a toggle switch, alternately marking the class for inclusion or exclusion. If you want to select all the classes, press F9.

Using the Tax-related Categories Only Field

The Tax-related categories only field enables you to include each of the categories you marked as tax-related when initially defining the category.

Fig. 11.36.

*The Select
Classes To
Include screen.*

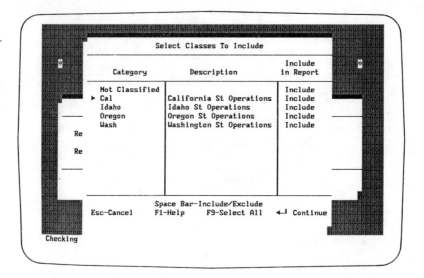

Using the Below/Equal/Above and Amount Fields

The Below/Equal/Above and amount fields enable you to include transactions on a report based on the transaction amount. By using these two fields, you are telling Quicken that you want transactions included on your report only when the transaction amount is less than, equal to, or greater than some amount. You type a B to indicate below, E to indicate equal, or A to indicate above. Enter the amount you want transaction amounts compared to in the amount field.

Using the Payments/Deposits/Unprinted Checks/All Field

The Payments/Deposits/Unprinted checks/All field enables you to include only certain types of transactions. To include only payments, enter a *P* in this field. To include only deposits, enter a *D* in this field. To include only unprinted checks, enter a *U* in this field. To include all transactions, enter an *A* in this field.

You can use this report to determine your cash flow requirements. If you have entered all of your bills and then want to know the total, you can select U for unprinted checks. Your report then tells you the total cash required for all unpaid bills.

Using the Cleared Status Field

The Cleared status is blank field enables you to include transactions on a report based on the contents of the C column in the register. The C column shows whether or not a transaction has been marked as cleared. Three valid entries exist for the C field: *, X, and nothing. As the Create Summary Report screen shows, you can include transactions on a report by entering a *Y* for yes next to the is blank, is "*", or is "X" fields. You also can exclude transactions by entering a *N* for no next to the same three fields.

F8-Report Options

You access the Create Summary Report screen, shown in figure 11.33, in one of two ways: pressing F8-Customize from one of the personal or business report screens or by selecting one of the custom report options. No matter how you arrive at the Create Summary Report screen, you have another function key available to you when you get there: F8-Option. Like the F8-Customize and F9-Filter function keys, the F8-Report Options vary slightly depending on which report you are preparing. Figure 11.37 shows the Report Options screen for creating a transaction report. (Transaction reports are described next.)

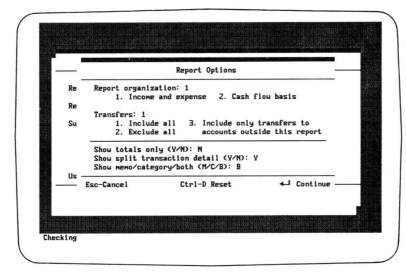

Fig. 11.37.

The Report Options screen.

You can have as many as five additional fields that are similar to the F8-Customize function key's effect on the appearance and organization of a report. Using Report organization determines whether the report includes only transactions assigned to categories (income and expense transactions), or transactions assigned to categories and transactions representing transfers. Using the Transfers field determines whether all transfers are included; all are excluded, or only transfers involving an account outside of the set of selected accounts are included. Using the Show totals only field determines whether a report shows the detail transactions that make up a total along with the actual total. Show split transaction detail applies only when the Show totals only field is set to N for no and determines whether split transaction detail is printed on the report. Using the Show memo/category/both field determines whether just the memo, just the category, or the memo and category entries appear on the report.

Creating a Transaction Report

You may want to view your register transactions arranged in some order other than chronologically by date. For example, you may find value in sorting and summarizing transactions by the payee or for time periods such as a week or month. The transaction report gives you the ability to see your account transactions in any of these ways.

To print a transaction report, select the first choice on the Reports menu to display the Create Transaction Report screen shown in figure 11.38. You can use the four available fields to control the way the transaction report looks and the information the report includes.

Using the Report Title Field

The default report title that Quicken uses to identify a transaction report is "Transaction Report." You should title reports more descriptively. You can substitute another report title by typing the title in the Report title field. For example, you may title a report listing all of the June income and expense transactions as *June Income and Expense Statement*. The Report title field has room for up to 39 characters.

Using the Restrict Transactions From and Through Date Fields

You usually want to see account transactions for a specific period of time. For example, when filling out your tax returns, you want to see how much you spent on mortgage interest last year. Maybe you want to keep track of monthly car expenses. In either case, you need to limit the transactions included on a report to a certain range of dates. You can use the restrict transaction fields. Both date fields need to be filled using the standard mm/dd/yy date format. As with the date field elsewhere in Quicken, you can move the date ahead one day at a time by pressing the + key and move the date back one day at a time by pressing the − key.

Using the Subtotal by Field

You can subtotal transactions with one of the choices identified on the Create Transaction Report screen (see figure 11.38).

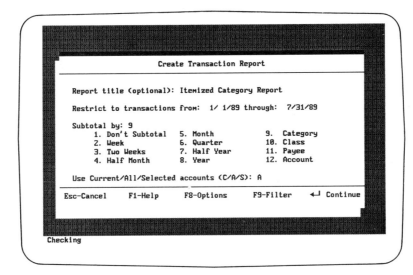

Fig. 11.38.

The Create Transaction Report screen.

You pick one of the twelve subtotal choices by typing the number that appears the left of the choice. For example, if you do not want to subtotal, type *1*. To subtotal for each week, type *2*. To subtotal for each two weeks, type *3*, and so on.

Using the Use Current/All/Selected Accounts Field

You can use the Use Current/All/Selected accounts field to determine whether just the current account's transactions are included; just selected account's transactions are included, or all the account's transactions are included on the report. If you choose the Selected accounts option, Quicken displays the Select Accounts to Include screen, shown in figure 11.25. (The Use Current/All/Selected accounts field is described in more detail in the earlier chapter section on customizing reports.)

The Create Transaction Report screen also provides you with the F8-Options and F9-Filter function keys that you can use to further tailor your transaction reports. (The preceding section describes the F8-Options and F9-Filter functions keys.)

Creating a Summary Report

Like a transaction report, a summary report enables you to see information from your registers. A summary report, however, automatically gives you totals by category, class, payee, or account in addition to any of the other subtotals you request. With this type of report, you also can select the accounts you want to include.

To print a summary report, select the **Summary** custom report from the Reports menu to display the Create Summary Report screen shown in figure 11.39.

You can use the five available fields to control the way a category report looks and the information contained in the report.

Using the Report Title Field

You can use the Report title field to more precisely identify summary reports. The title field allows up to 39 characters.

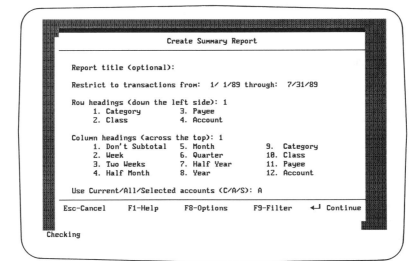

```
                    Create Summary Report

    Report title (optional):

    Restrict to transactions from:  1/ 1/89 through:  7/31/89

    Row headings (down the left side): 1
         1. Category       3. Payee
         2. Class          4. Account

    Column headings (across the top): 1
         1. Don't Subtotal  5. Month          9.  Category
         2. Week            6. Quarter        10. Class
         3. Two Weeks       7. Half Year      11. Payee
         4. Half Month      8. Year           12. Account

    Use Current/All/Selected accounts (C/A/S): A

    Esc-Cancel    F1-Help     F8-Options     F9-Filter    ↵ Continue

Checking
```

Fig. 11.39.

The Create Summary Report screen.

Using the Restrict Transactions From and Through Date Fields

You usually want to see account transactions for a specific period of time. For example, at the end of the month you may want to see how much you spent on various items. You can limit the transactions included on a summary report to a range of dates beginning with the first day of the month and ending with the last day of the month. As with date fields elsewhere in Quicken, you can move the date ahead one day at a time by pressing the + key and move the date back one day at a time by pressing the − key.

Using the Row Headings Field

You use the Row headings field to tell Quicken how you want transactions sorted and summarized. You type *1* to designate by category, *2* to designate by class, *3* to designate by payee, and *4* to designate by account.

Using the Column Headings Field

You pick one of the twelve subtotal choices by typing the number that appears the left of the choice. For example, if you do not want to subtotal, type *1*. To subtotal for each week, type *2*. To subtotal for each two weeks, type *3*, and so on.

Subtotal amounts are shown in separate columns across the report page. The payroll report, shown in figure 11.30, shows category subtotals in columns across the report page.

Using the Use Current/All/Selected Accounts Field

The Use Current/All/Selected accounts field gives you the option of including only certain accounts in a report.

You can use this field to determine whether just the current account's transactions are included, just the selected account's transactions are included, or all the account's transactions are included on the report. If you choose the Selected accounts option, Quicken displays the Select Accounts to Include screen (see fig. 11.25).

The Create Transaction Report screen also provides you with the F8-Options and F9-Filter function keys that you can use to further tailor your transaction reports.

Creating a Budget Report

Appendix A describes budgeting as a fundamental tool that individuals and businesses can use to better manage their finances. One of the on-going steps in using a budget as a tool is to compare what you spent with what you planned to spend, or budgeted. Quicken's **Budget** option on the Reports menu enables you to create customized budget reports tailored specifically to your personal or business needs.

To print a custom budget report, select the fifth choice on the Reports menu. This option displays the Create Budget Report screen shown in figure 11.40. This screen closely resembles the other create report screens.

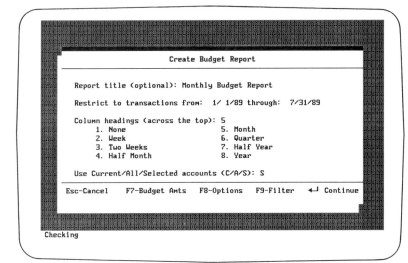

Fig. 11.40.

The Create Budget Report screen.

As with the other report screens, you have four fields on this screen plus the F8-Options and F9-Filter function keys with which to control the way the report looks and the information the report contains. (The F8-Options and F9-Filter function keys are described earlier in the chapter.)

Using the Report Title Field

The standard report title that Quicken uses to identify a budget report is "Monthly Budget Report." As with the other create report screens, however, you can substitute another report title by typing the title in this field. The title field is large enough for 39 characters.

Using the Restrict Transactions From and Through Date Fields

If you want to see transactions and budgeted amounts for a specific period of time, you can use the Restrict to transactions from and through fields. The restrict from date sets the start of the period and the restrict to date sets the end of the period. Fill both date fields using the standard mm/dd/yy date format. You can move the date ahead one day at a time by pressing the + key and move the date back one day at a time by pressing the − key.

Using the Column Headings Field

The Column headings field enables you to calculate subtotals—and show them across a report page in columns—in one of eight ways as listed on the Create Budget Report screen. You can pick one of the eight subtotal choices by typing the number appearing to the left of the choice (see fig. 11.40).

Using the Use Current/All/Selected Accounts Field

You can use the Use Current/All/Selected accounts field to determine which accounts in the current account group are included on a report. Your choices are C for just the current account, S for selected accounts, and A for all accounts in the account group. If you choose the Selected accounts option, Quicken displays the Select Accounts to Include screen shown in figure 11.25.

The Create Budget Report screen also provides you with the F7-Budget Amts, F8-Options, and F9-Filter function keys that you can use to further tailor your budget reports. F7 accesses the Specify Budget Amounts screen shown in figure 11.10. You can use the Specify Budget Amounts screen to change or add budgeted amounts from categories. (Chapter 7, "Using Categories and Classes," discusses this topic in more detail.)

Creating an Account Balances Report

You use the sixth and final option on the Reports menu to create customized account balances reports. If you had extensive investments with several brokers and wanted a report that specified only those accounts, you would create this report or any specialized report with this option. Figure 11.41 shows the Create Account Balances Report screen that you use to construct customized account balances reports.

You can use four fields to tailor an account balances report. These fields are described in the following paragraphs. (You also can use the F8-Options and F9-Filter function keys.)

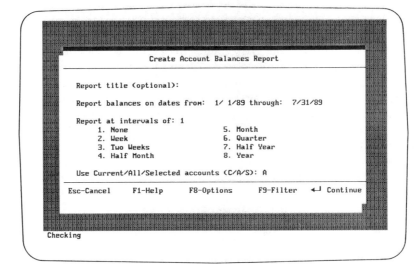

Fig. 11.41.

The Create Account Balances Report screen.

Using the Report Title Field

You can use the optional, 34-character Report title field to label reports exactly as you want. If you leave this field blank, Quicken supplies the title, "Account Balances Report."

Using the Report Balances on Dates From and Through Fields

The Report balances on dates from and through fields are slightly different than the Restrict Transactions from and through date fields on other screens. Remember that the account balances report shows the account balances at a specific point in time. This field sets a boundary around the points in time for which an account balances report is generated. The points in time for which an account balances report is generated are determined by the next field, the Report at intervals of field.

Using the Report at Intervals of Field

The Report at intervals of field determines the points in time for which an account balances report is generated. The start of the first interval is the first day of the year. Assuming that the Report balances on dates from field is 1/1/89, the first account balances column is for 1/1/89. The next date depends on the interval. If the interval is weekly, the second column is 1/7/89. If the interval is biweekly, the second column is for 1/14/89. If the interval is by half month, the second column is for 1/18/89, and so on. The report shows account balances for each interval between the from date and through date. The last column of the report shows the account balances on the through date.

If the Report at intervals of field is set to 1 for none, the only point in time for which the account balances report is generated is the Report balances on dates through field.

Using the Use Current/All/Selected Accounts Field

The Use Current/All/Selected accounts field enables you to determine which accounts get their balances reported on the account balances report. A C designates just the current account; an S designates only the selected accounts; an A designates all accounts. If you choose the Selected accounts option, Quicken displays the Select Accounts to Include screen shown in figure 11.25.

Chapter Summary

This chapter reviewed the basics of printing any Quicken report and detailed the steps and tricks for printing each of Quicken's personal, business, and custom reports. These reports use the information stored in your account registers to provide you with a wealth of financial information that you can use to better manage your personal or business finances.

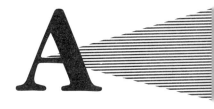

A Review of Budgeting

Budgeting has an undeserved bad reputation. Budgeting is a simple tool with astonishingly positive benefits for businesses and households.

Because one of Quicken's most significant benefits—and maybe even the program's biggest benefit—is that you can monitor your success in achieving a budget, this appendix reviews the three steps of budgeting, describes how Quicken helps, and provides some tips on how to budget successfully.

Overview of Budgeting

Basically, budgeting consists of the following three steps:

1. Setting your business or personal financial goals

2. Using your list of goals as a guide to developing a financial game plan, or budget, that covers what you want to spend your money on

3. Using the budget to monitor your spending to determine how closely you are progressing toward your business or personal goals

Setting Your Goals

Budgeting begins with identifying your goals in business or life. You are on your own here. When building a list of your goals, however, keep the following two things in mind:

1. Keep your goals general.

2. Involve other people—particularly those who have to live within the budget—in setting the goals.

By stating your goals in more general terms, you don't start with built-in constraints and conflicts among your goals. Suppose that your goal is to live in an opulent fashion where the weather is warm and sunny. With this goal, you have a world of choices and an incredible range of prices. If your goal is to live in a mansion in Beverly Hills, you have limited yourself. Living in a Beverly Hills mansion is one way to live in an opulent fashion where the weather is warm and sunny, but it is not the only way. Keep your options open as you build a list of life goals, and you are more likely to get more of the things you want out of life.

A second point about setting goals is to involve other people. The often stated and obvious reason for this rule is that people who work together to build a list of goals later will work together to achieve the goals. Working together also produces better goal lists.

The United States Air Force and many businesses used to play a game called Desert Survival that demonstrates the results of better goals. You pretend that a plane on which you are a passenger crashes in the desert. You are 30 miles off course and at least that far from civilization; it's over a hundred degrees in the shade, and you can salvage about fifteen or twenty items before the plane bursts into flames. First, you decide by yourself whether you will stay with the wreckage or start towards civilization and which of the items you will keep. Next, you repeat the analysis in groups of four or five people, and this time the entire group must agree on the plan and which items to keep.

The interesting thing about the game and the reason that this whole issue applies to budgeting is that in almost every case, when people make the survival decisions together, they dramatically increase their chances of survival.

Hopefully, making the wrong budgeting decision will not cost you your life, but the moral of the desert survival game still applies. Whether you are budgeting your personal finances or a small business, you build better goal lists when you get more people involved. Your spouse may end up discovering some option you would never have considered. A daughter may admit that she is not interested in piano lessons or charm school. Your partner may point out a subtle flaw you overlooked.

When you finish setting your goals, write them down. Do not limit yourself to just financial goals. You may have financial goals, such as accumulating the down payment for a new car or taking a special vacation.

You also may have non-financial goals, such as spending more time with your family or beginning some recreational or charitable activity.

Designing a Game Plan

After you build a list of goals, you are ready to achieve them. As you work through the details, you undoubtedly modify your goals and make compromises.

If you described your goals in general terms and if you included everybody's good ideas, you should be able to come up with a detailed list of the costs of pursuing and achieving your business or personal goals. At this stage, you decide what you are going to spend on entertainment or vacations, how much you can spend on housing, and other such issues. As a rough yardstick to use to build your own detailed game plan, table A.1 summarizes what most people spend on the average as a percent of their income. (This list comes from a survey made in 1986 by *CONSUMER REPORTS* magazine.)

Table A.1
Average Spending Based on Income©

Spending Category	Percent Spent, by Income Level		
	$15,000–$30,000	$30,000–$50,000	$50,000–$150,000
Taxes			
Federal income	7%	11%	15%
Social security	7%	8%	7%
State and local	6%	6%	7%
Housing			
Mortgage or rent	11%	11%	9%
Other housing costs	13%	12%	11%
Food	20%	15%	10%
Transportation	12%	10%	7%
Vacation, recreation	5%	4%	5%
Health care, insurance	5%	4%	3%
Clothing	3%	3%	3%
Savings and investments	5%	8%	12%
Other, specified*	5%	4%	5%
Other, unspecified	1%	4%	8%

Table A.1—*continued*

* includes tuition, educational supplies, books, magazines, contributions and gifts, finance charges other than mortgage and auto loans, day-care, child support, alimony

Copyright © 1986 by Consumers Union of United States, Inc., Mount Vernon, NY 10553. Reprinted by permission from CONSUMER REPORTS, September 1986.

If you are budgeting for a business, you can visit your local public library to obtain similar information. Dun and Bradstreet and Robert Morris Associates annually publish financial information on businesses grouped by industry and business size.

For business or personal budgeting, however, do not interpret the averages as anything other than general guidelines. Seeing other people's spending provides a useful perspective on your own spending, but your goals should determine the details of your financial game plan.

CPA Tip: When budgeting for taxes, you should be able to estimate amounts fairly precisely. You can pick up one of the personal income tax guides to give you all the details, but the following general rules apply: social security amounts to 7.51 percent of your earnings up to a maximum amount of $48,000 of taxable income for 1989. Federal income taxes depend on your filing status and your taxable income. Generally, you can calculate your taxable income as:

(Total Income) − (your deductions) − (your personal exemptions)

Your income includes wages, salaries, interest, dividends, and so on. Deductions include individual retirement accounts, alimony, and your itemized deductions or your standard deduction. Personal exemptions are $1,950 of allowances you get to subtract from your total income for each person in your family. Your filing status relates to whether you are single or married or have dependents. The standard deductions for the various filing statuses for 1989 are shown in table A.2. The tax-rate schedules for the various filing statuses that show the taxes you pay on your taxable income are shown in table A.3. For 1990, the dollar amounts for personal exemptions, the standard deduction amounts, and the tax-rate schedules are adjusted for inflation.

Table A.2
Standard Deductions for 1989

Filing Status	Amount*
Married, filing joint return and Qualifying widow(er)	$5,200
Head of household	$4,550
Single	$3,100
Married, filing separately	$2,600

* To the amounts, an additional standard deduction of $600 is allowed for a married individual (whether filing jointly or separately) or a qualifying widow(er) who is 65 or over or blind ($1,200 if the individual is 65 or over and blind, $2,400 if both spouses are 65 or over and blind). An additional standard deduction of $750 is allowed for an unmarried individual (single or head of household) who is 65 or over or blind ($1,500 if 65 or over and blind).

Table A.3
1989 Tax-Rate Schedules

Schedule X—Single

If taxable income is:	tax is:	plus:	of the amount over:
$0–$18,550	$0	15%	$0
$18,550–$44,900	$2,782.50	28%	$18,550
$44,900–$93,130	$10,160.50	33%	$44,900
$93,130+	$26,076.40	28%*	$93,130

Schedule Y-1—Married, Filing Jointly or Qualifying Widow(er)

If taxable income is:	tax is:	plus:	of the amount over:
$0–$30,950	$0	15%	$0
$30,950–$74,850	$4,642.50	28%	$30,950
$74,850–$155,320	$16,934.50	33%	$74,850
$155,320+	$43,489.60	28%	$155,320

Schedule Z—Head of Household

If taxable income is:	tax is:	plus:	of the amount over:
$0–$24,850	$0	15%	$0
$24,850–$64,200	$3,727.50	28%	$24,850

Table A.3—*continued*

If taxable income is:	tax is:	plus:	of the amount over:
$64,200–$128,810	$14,745.50	33%	$64,200
$128,810+	$36,066.80	28%	$128,810

Schedule Y-2—Married Filing Separately

If taxable income is:	tax is:	plus:	of the amount over:
$0–$15,475	$0	15%	$0
$15,475–$37,425	$2,321.25	28%	$15,475
$37,425–$117,895	$8,467.25	33%	$37,425
$117,895+	$22,672.10	28%*	$117,895

* A special 5 percent surtax applies when you re-enter the 28 percent tax bracket. The 5 percent surtax, which has the effect of removing the benefits of the personal exemptions you claim, needs to be calculated using the worksheet provided with your filing instructions and then added to the amounts in these rate schedules.

When you finish setting your goals, write down your spending game plan. Now that you know how much time and money you can allocate to each of your goals, you often can expand your list of goals to include estimates of costs and time. Table A.4 lists a set of sample personal goals, and table A.5 lists a set of sample business goals. Table A.6 shows an example of an annual personal budget with monthly breakdowns supporting the goals from table A.4. Table A.7 shows an example of an annual business budget that supports the goals from table A.5.

Table A.4
Sample Personal Budget Goals

Goals	Cost	Timing
Visit Egypt and see pyramids	$5,000	1995
Start fishing again	$50	ASAP
Begin preparing for retirement	$100,000	2025
Spend more time with family	$0	ASAP

Table A.5
Sample Business Budget Goals

Goals	Cost	Timing
Generate 20% more annual sales	$20,000	over year
Pay down credit line	$5,000	year-end
Make profits of $25,000	$25,000	over year
Provide better quality service	$0	ASAP

Table A.6
Example Budget To Support Personal Goals

Personal Budget	Annual	Monthly
Income	$25,000	$2,083
Outgo		
Income taxes	$1,750	$146
Social security	1,878	156
Rent	6,000	500
Other housing	3,000	250
Food	4,800	400
Transportation	2,500	208
Vacation, recreation	1,200	100
Fishing gear	50	4
Clothing	1,250	104
Savings—IRA	500	42
Other	1,200	100
Total Expenses	24,628	2,052
Leftover/Contingency	373	31

Table A.7
Example Budget To Support Business Goals

Business Budget	Annual	Monthly
Sales	$125,000	$10,417
Expenses		
Materials	$30,000	2,500
Labor	30,000	2,500
Rent	12,000	1,000

Table A.7—*continued*

Business Budget	Annual	Monthly
Expenses		
Transportation	12,500	1,042
Supplies	12,000	1,000
Legal/Accounting	1,200	100
Other	2,100	175
Total Expenses	99,800	8,317
Profits	25,200	2,100

You should notice a few things about the relationships between the goals and budget. First, some of your goals represent things you can achieve almost immediately while others may take much longer. Second, some goals on your list do not directly affect your budget. Third, some expenditures do not tie to formal, or stated, goals, but still represent implied goals. For example, you do not list feeding the children or staying in business as goals, but these goals may be your most important ones.

Monitoring Your Progress

The third and final step in budgeting relates to monitoring your progress in achieving your personal or business goals. On a periodic basis—every month or every quarter—you should compare what you budgeted to spend with what you actually spent. Sometimes, people view these comparisons as negative, but the idea is that if you are following your budget, you are moving toward your goals. For example, if you get through the first month of the year and are operating under the budget shown in table A.6, you can compare what you spent with your budget. If you see that you are having difficulty salting away extra money for the trip to Egypt and into your individual retirement account, you know that your spending or your goals need to change.

How Quicken Helps

Quicken provides two related features that enable you to budget more effectively for your personal finances and for small businesses: categories and reporting.

Using Categories

With categories, you can identify each of the checks you record as falling into a spending category such as housing, contributions, entertainment, taxes, and so on. The steps and benefits of using categories are discussed in more detail in Chapter 7. By noting the category into which every check you record belongs, you can produce reports that summarize and total the amounts spent for each category. Figure A.1 shows an example of a Quicken spending report.

```
                        Example Category Report
                         7/ 1/89 Through 7/31/89
  Checking                                                     Page 1
  7/13/89
                                          7/ 1/89-
                  Category Description     7/31/89
                  -------------------------  -----------
                  INFLOWS
                    Salary Income           2,000.00
                                           -----------
                  TOTAL INFLOWS             2,000.00

                  OUTFLOWS
                    Automobile Expense        178.12
                    Entertainment              34.56
                    Federal Tax Witholding    245.21
                    Groceries                 453.90
                    Home Repair & Maint.      125.00
                    Housing                   650.00
                    Interest Expense           32.46
                    Reg Retirement Sav Plan    50.00
                    Water, Gas, Electric       54.32
                                           -----------
                  TOTAL OUTFLOWS            1,823.57

                                           -----------
                  OVERALL TOTAL              176.43
                                           ===========
```

Fig. A.1.

An example of a Quicken spending report.

Budget Reporting

Quicken also enables you to enter any amounts budgeted for a category and calculates the difference, called a *variance*, between the total spent on a category and the budgeted amount for a category. In this way, Quicken does the arithmetic related to monitoring how closely you follow your budget and how successfully you are marching toward your life goals. Figure A.2 shows an example of a Quicken budget report.

Fig. A.2.

An example of a Quicken budget report.

```
                           Example Budget Report
                          7/ 1/89 Through 7/31/89
          Checking                                                    Page 1
          7/13/89
                                      7/ 1/89     -      7/31/89
                  Category Description  Actual    Budget    Diff
                  ------------------- --------- --------- ---------
                  INFLOWS
                    Salary Income       2,000.00  2,000.00      0.00
                                        --------- --------- ---------
                  TOTAL INFLOWS         2,000.00  2,000.00      0.00

                  OUTFLOWS
                    Automobile Expense    178.12    175.00      3.12
                    Charitable Donations    0.00     25.00    -25.00
                    Entertainment          34.56     25.00      9.56
                    Federal Tax Witholding 245.21    250.00     -4.79
                    Groceries             453.90    453.90      0.00
                    Home Repair & Maint.  125.00    125.00      0.00
                    Housing               650.00    650.00      0.00
                    Interest Expense       32.46     25.00      7.46
                    Reg Retirement Sav Plan 50.00     40.00     10.00
                    Water, Gas, Electric   54.32     50.00      4.32
                                        --------- --------- ---------
                  TOTAL OUTFLOWS        1,823.57  1,818.90      4.67

                                        --------- --------- ---------
                  OVERALL TOTAL          176.43    181.10     -4.67
                                        ========= ========= =========
```

Tips for Successful Budgeting

Even if you started out listing your personal or business goals, involved the entire family or company in the process, and created a budget compatible with your stated and implied goals, you can take other precautions to succeed in budgeting. These precautions include paying yourself first, recognizing after-tax shares, providing for unplanned or emergency events, and using zero-based budgeting.

Paying Yourself First

Families need savings to provide cushions for financial emergencies, money for major expenditures such as a home or a child's education, and the means for financial support during retirement. Small businesses need savings to provide funds for growing the business and for replacing assets.

You always have bills to pay, however, and you have to resist a lot of financial temptations. Getting to the end of the month with extra money is difficult—which is why you need to pay yourself first. For many people, paying oneself first is the only way you successfully can save money.

Figure A.3 shows the amount you ultimately accumulate if you put away $25 a month and earn 10 percent interest assuming various income tax rates. (The logic behind including income taxes is that if you earn $100 in interest and are taxed on the money at the 33 percent tax rate, you need to withdraw $33 of the $100 to pay income taxes.)

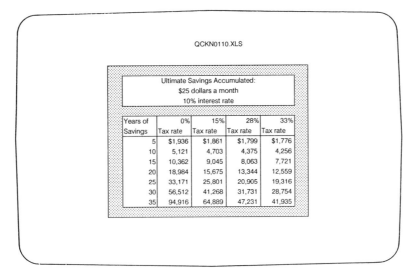

If you save $50 a month, double the amounts shown in the figure. If you save $100, quadruple the amounts shown in the table, and so on.

CPA Tip: If you save money for retirement, try to use options like individual retirement accounts and 401(k) plans. Figure A.3 shows that when you save $25 a month for 35 years in one of these investment vehicles where you pay 0 percent income tax, you end up with roughly twice as much as if you were paying a 28 or 33 percent income tax on your interest income.

Recognizing After-Tax Shares of Bonuses and Raises

A second important budgeting consideration in personal and business situations is that you need to recognize that if you receive an extra $1,000 as a bonus, raise, or windfall, you cannot spend the entire $1,000. For 1989, a 7.51 percent social security tax and a 15.01 percent self-employment tax is levied on up to $48,000 of earned income. You also have to pay any federal income taxes of 15, 28, or 33 percent plus any state income taxes. You may even have other expenses that, like income taxes, decrease your take-home share of any bonus or windfall such as an automatic contribution to a deferred compensation plan or charitable giving to which you have made a commitment. Totaled up, you typically need to deduct at least 20 percent and as much as 60 percent from any bonus or windfall to figure out what you have available for spending.

Allowing for Unplanned and Emergency Expenses

Unfortunately, people lose their jobs, cars break down, and children get sick. Over the time period your budget covers, all sorts of unforeseen and unplanned events will occur and cost you money. If you can afford to, the best approach is to budget and set aside a little each month to cover these little unexpected expenses of life.

CPA Tip: In the past, budget planners have used several rules of thumb regarding how much emergency savings is enough. If your primary reason for emergency savings is in case you lose your job—because you are well-insured for medical, disability, and life claims—the following is an approach you should use:

1. Consider the length of time you need to find a new job.

2. Take the salary you would have earned over the period of unemployment and subtract any employment benefits or severance pay you receive.

3. Reduce that remainder by the income taxes you do not pay and any amounts you do not save because you have no income.

For example, suppose that it will take as long as six months to find a job; you currently earn $2,500 a month; you get half a month's severance pay if you lose your job; unemployment amounts to $100 a week, and you pay 7.51 percent social security tax and a 15 percent income tax. You then can calculate your emergency savings as:

$$((6*\$2500)-(26*\$100)-\$1250)*(1-7.51\%-15\%) = \$8,640$$

Using Zero-Based Budgeting

Large businesses use zero-based budgeting with success. So can individuals and small businesses. Basically, zero-based budgeting says that while you spent money on some category last year, you should not necessarily spend money on the same category this year.

Certainly, looking at what you spent last year can provide a valuable perspective, but this year's spending should be determined by this year's goals. Saying, "Well, last year I spent $500 on furniture, and therefore I will spend $500 this year," is dangerous. The danger with this approach is that your house or apartment may not have room for any more furniture. Now, you can say that you will not buy any more furniture if your house is packed. What about the dues for the athletic club you haven't used for months or years? Or the extra term life insurance you bought when your kids were living at home? Or the advertising money you spent to attract your first customers? Budgeting and spending amounts as you have in the past is easy to do even though your goals, your lifestyle, or your business have since made the expense unnecessary.

Appendix Summary

This appendix outlined the budgeting process and why budgeting is important in managing your personal finances, described how Quicken helps with the process, and provided some tips on how to budget and manage your finances more successfully. With this information as a background, you should not have any problem deciding whether or not you want to use the budgeting tools that Quicken provides.

B

Using This Book with
Version 2

If you are working with Version 2 of Quicken, you should find *Using Quicken* helpful, even though the book is written for Version 3 of Quicken. To use this book for Version 2, you need to be aware of the differences between the Version 2 and Version 3 features. As an aid to Quicken Version 2 users, margin icons indicate material that applies only to Version 3. Version 2 users should skip this material unless you are exploring the functionality of the new version. Besides some minor changes, Quicken Version 3 provides a different menu structure and two major new features.

Reconciling the Menu Differences

One major change from Version 2 to Version 3 is the menu structure including where menu options appear and how they are named.

The **Reconcile** option no longer appears on Quicken's Main menu. Instead, this option is on the Activities submenu available from the Register screen. On the Main menu **Select Account** replaces **Reconcile**. **Select Account** enables you to choose the account you want to work with. If you have trouble finding a specific option or the screen required for a certain report, the menu maps in the back of this book provide a quick reference source.

Some of the menu names have changed. The Edit/Find menu that Version 2 provides is called Edit in Version 3, and the Bank Account menu that Version 2 provides is called Acct/Print in Version 3 because the menu now accesses not just account data, but also the print menus.

Version 3 also provides a few new menu options. Version 2 does not have the Edit menu options **Void Transaction** (Ctrl-V) nor **Go To Transfer** (Ctrl-X). Version 2 also does not have the Change Settings menu option **Passwords** or the Activities menu options **Calculator** and **DOS**. If you are working with Version 2, skip over the material on the options new to Version 3.

Recognizing Version 3's Two New Features

The major new feature of Version 3 is the new account types and account group concept that enables you to easily transfer money from one account to another. This feature may seem like a small enhancement, but in fact, the feature is very powerful. To transfer money, Version 3 creates account groups that amount to collections, or sets, of accounts between which money can be transferred. For example, if you tell Quicken that you are writing a check to deposit to your savings account, Quicken records the increase in savings for you on the basis of the check you are recording in your checking account.

Because you can transfer money between accounts and, therefore, are more likely to use Quicken for all your personal or business accounting, Version 3 also provides some special tools to manage other assets besides bank accounts and to manage other liabilities. Basically, these features, which are described in Chapter 10, enable you to reconcile credit card balances and update account balances for items like investments and loans. If you are working with Version 2, you should not need to read Chapter 10.

The third major new feature in Version 3 is that Quicken now provides some predefined reports. Quicken fills out the report request screen for you. However, you still have the option of using the report request screens, and the only changes to the screens are cosmetic. Chapter 11, "Using Quicken's Reports," should prove a valuable reference for users of both versions. The predefined reports Quicken provides also give Version 2 users examples of the sorts of reports that you can create.

Other Miscellaneous Changes

If you are using this book for Version 2, you need to be aware of some other minor differences. First, the Category and Memo fields are split into two separate fields in Version 3, but are combined as one field in Version 2. You need to tell Quicken Version 2 when you are entering a category in the Memo field by preceding the category name with the "@" character. If you want to use a subcategory, you separate the categories with a space instead of the colon used for Version 3. Classes also do not exist in Version 2.

When you define a category in Version 2, you do not need to tell Quicken whether the category is for income or expense transactions as you do in Version 3. Quicken uses the sign (positive or negative) of the category total to determine whether the category is an income or expense.

The predefined category lists provided by Version 2 also slightly differ from Version 3. This should not be a problem, however, because both lists are just starting points you can use to build your own categorization scheme.

Quicken Version 2 stores the Quicken program and data files in a directory named QUICKEN2. Version 3 stores the Quicken program and data files in a directory name QUICKEN3.

Knowing about these differences not only helps you use this book for Version 2, but also can help you decide whether to upgrade from Version 2 to Version 3.

Converting Files from Version 2 to Version 3

Users of Version 2 should know that Version 3 has a utility disk to convert 2.0 files to 3.0 files.

After placing the Help disk in drive A, type *A:CONVERT* at the prompt and press Enter. Quicken displays the introductory CONVERT screen, shown in figure B.1, that tells you that the program is making Version 3 files using your Version 2 files.

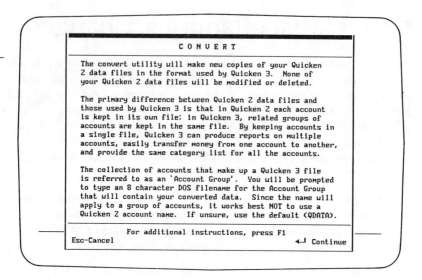

Fig. B.1.

The CONVERT program introduction screen.

C O N V E R T

The convert utility will make new copies of your Quicken 2 data files in the format used by Quicken 3. None of your Quicken 2 data files will be modified or deleted.

The primary difference between Quicken 2 data files and those used by Quicken 3 is that in Quicken 2 each account is kept in its own file; in Quicken 3, related groups of accounts are kept in the same file. By keeping accounts in a single file, Quicken 3 can produce reports on multiple accounts, easily transfer money from one account to another, and provide the same category list for all the accounts.

The collection of accounts that make up a Quicken 3 file is referred to as an 'Account Group'. You will be prompted to type an 8 character DOS filename for the Account Group that will contain your converted data. Since the name will apply to a group of accounts, it works best NOT to use a Quicken 2 account name. If unsure, use the default (QDATA).

For additional instructions, press F1
Esc-Cancel   ◄┘ Continue

As the menus come up, you need to fill in the name you have selected for the Version 3 account grouping. The program provides a default name, QDATA, if you are unsure about what name you want to use (see fig. B.2). (This default name also is used for the Version 3 Install program.)

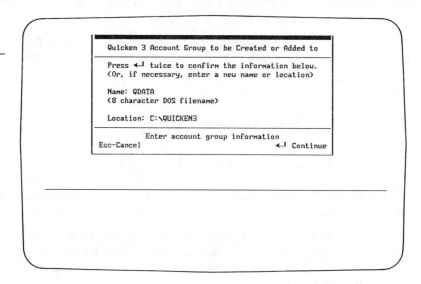

Fig. B.2.

The program provides the default file name, QDATA.

Quicken 3 Account Group to be Created or Added to

Press ◄┘ twice to confirm the information below. (Or, if necessary, enter a new name or location)

Name: QDATA
(8 character DOS filename)

Location: C:\QUICKEN3

Enter account group information
Esc-Cancel   ◄┘ Continue

You also need to provide the drive and directory for Quicken to locate the Version 2 files. Figure B.3 shows the screen you use to specify the location of the Version 2 files.

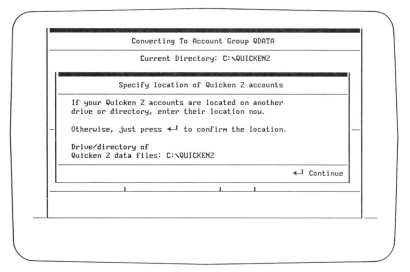

Fig. B.3.

The Specify location of Quicken 2 accounts screen.

When you press Enter, Quicken provides you with a listing of files to be converted (see fig. B.4).

```
                   Converting To Account Group QDATA

                   Current Directory: C:\QUICKEN2

    Press the Space Bar to mark the Quicken 2 accounts which are to be
    converted into this Quicken 3 account group. (Press the Space Bar
    repeatedly to cycle through the account type options.)

        Quicken 2                                Quicken 3
        Account Name      Description     Size    Account Type

      ▶ 2NDNATNL     First National Bank    5K   None (Don't Convert)
        3RDNATNL     Third National Bank    1K   None (Don't Convert)
        1STNATNL     1st National #123456   6K   None (Don't Convert)
        QSMPLE_H                            4K   None (Don't Convert)


          Space Bar-Specify Account Type     F9-Change Directory
    Esc-Exit                    F1-Help               ↵ Continue
```

Fig. B.4.

The Converting To Account Group screen.

After using the space bar to toggle the selection of accounts you want to convert, press Return. Quicken may notify you that some data becomes lost during the conversion because address and split description fields are one character shorter in Version 3 (see fig. B.5).

Fig. B.5.

The program warns you when characters are lost in the conversion process.

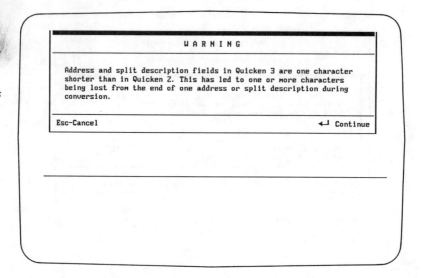

```
                        W A R N I N G

   Address and split description fields in Quicken 3 are one character
   shorter than in Quicken 2. This has led to one or more characters
   being lost from the end of one address or split description during
   conversion.

   Esc-Cancel                                        ↵ Continue
```

When CONVERT finishes, Quicken informs you that the accounts are successfully converted (see fig. B.6).

Fig. B.6.

Quicken tells you when the files have been converted successfully.

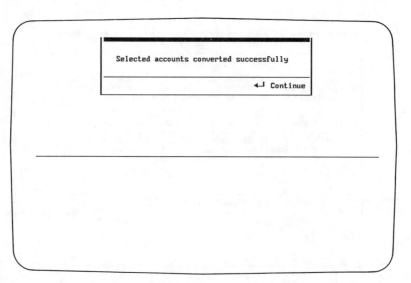

```
   Selected accounts converted successfully

                                   ↵ Continue
```

Quicken also asks what you want to do next: finish, convert more Version 2 files to Version 3, or create another Version 3 account group (see fig. B.7).

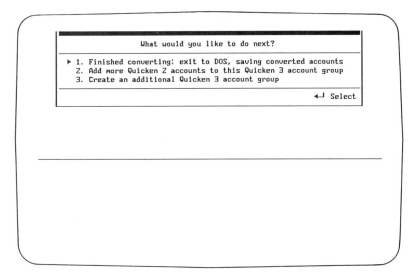

Fig. B.7.

Quicken asks you what you want to do next.

For more information on Quicken Version 3, contact Intuit, 540 University Ave., Palo Alto, CA 94301; (415) 322-0573 or 800-624-8742.

Using Quicken
in Your Business

You may be surprised to learn that more people use Quicken as a business accounting package than as a home accounting package. The reasons for this usage are logical; you do not have to know double-entry bookkeeping (as you do for many other small-business accounting packages), and you use a simple and familiar tool, the register. This appendix covers some of the special techniques and procedures to use Quicken for business accounting.

Because the mechanical procedures of using Quicken are well-documented within the pages of this book, this appendix is based on the assumption that you know how to enter transactions into a register, set up accounts, define categories, and print reports. If you are not familiar with these features of Quicken, review the material covered in Chapter 2, "Selecting Accounts and Changing Settings"; Chapter 5, "Using the Register"; Chapter 6, "Using the Register Menu Options"; Chapter 7, "Using Categories and Classes"; Chapter 10, "Accounting for Other Assets and Liabilities"; and Chapter 11, "Using Quicken's Reports."

This appendix begins by discussing the overall approach for using Quicken in a business. That discussion is followed by short sections that detail the seven basic accounting tasks: invoicing customers, tracking receivables, tracking inventory, accounting for fixed assets, preparing payroll, job costing, and tracking loans and notes.

When you combine basic bill paying and check writing described throughout the chapters of *Using Quicken* with the details of the seven basic accounting tasks described in this appendix, you should have the information you need to perform your business accounting with Quicken Version 3.0.

Understanding the Basics

Using Quicken for business accounting is easier if you understand the following three basic concepts: what you do to use Quicken accounts, what should be recorded in a register, and what categories count.

What You Do To Use Quicken Accounts

You use Quicken accounts to track the values of business assets or liabilities, and you need to set up one account for each business asset or liability you want to track.

A *business asset* is anything you own. Common examples of business assets include the cash in a checking account, the receivable that some customer or client owes you, an investment in stock, inventory you resell, a piece of furniture, a piece of equipment, and real estate.

A *business liability* is anything you owe. Common examples of business liabilities include the loan on a car or delivery truck, payroll taxes you owe the government, the mortgage on your building, and the balance on a bank credit line.

Assets and liabilities have something in common; at any time, you can calculate the value of the asset or liability. Usually, you are not so much interested in the day-to-day or week-to-week change in a particular asset but rather the value at a specific time.

All the accounts you set up for a business must be included in the same account group. If you perform accounting for several businesses, each business needs its own account group. If you use Quicken at your business and at home, you need one account group for each (see Chapter 2).

Note: By default, Quicken enables you to define up to 64 accounts within an account group. You can increase this figure to 99 accounts.

What a Transaction Is

Transactions are what you record in a register to show the change in the value of an asset or liability. If you use Quicken for business accounting, however, you need to record the change of the asset or liability you use to complete the transaction and the effect of the change on other accounts, income, or expenses. No change ever affects only one asset or liability.

Whenever you record the change in the value of some asset or liability, you also need to record how the change affects other accounts, income, or expenses. You actually perform double-entry bookkeeping without having to think or worry about debits and credits.

This discussion of transactions may seem redundant to you. But you need to verify that your assets and liabilities really are assets and liabilities. You also need to verify that the things you want to record as transactions in a register really are transactions and not assets or liabilities.

Suppose that you want to track your receivables and record customer payments on those receivables. You need to set up an account each time you create an individual receivable. Changes in the value of that asset—such as when you receive the customer's payment—need to be recorded as transactions in the register. If you invoice Johnson Manufacturing $1,000 for a service, you need to set up an account for this asset. The temptation with a group of similar assets, such as receivables, is to group them as one asset using one account group. Using the grouping approach, however, obscures information on specific accounts. You cannot tell whether Johnson Manufacturing still owes the $1,000 or how the $1,000 original asset value has changed.

The key to using Quicken as a small-business accounting system is knowing what your assets, liabilities, and transactions are. The paragraphs that follow offer many tips and suggestions to assist you in this analysis.

Which Categories Count

The term *bottom line* refers to the figure at the bottom of a profit and loss statement that shows whether you made or lost money in your business. The reason you use categories within Quicken is to calculate whether you are making or losing money. You use two kinds of categories: Income and Expense. Income categories count your business revenues, or inflows. Common income categories include sales of products or services, interest and dividends from investments, and even the proceeds from the sale of some asset. Expense categories count your business costs, or outflows. Examples of expense categories include the cost of advertising, insurance, utilities, and employee wages.

Income and expense categories have something in common: they enable you to count business inflows and outflows over a period of time—such as for the week, month, or year. For the week, month, or year, you can use the income and expense category information to tell whether you made or lost money.

When you use Quicken to track only cash inflows and outflows—your bank and cash accounts—you are using *cash-basis* accounting. Cash-basis accounting means that you record income only when you deposit money, and you record expenses only when you pay the money. This system makes sense. When you make the bank deposit or the check payment, you are categorizing the transaction as income or expense.

When you use Quicken to keep track of other assets and liabilities, however, you move toward *accrual-* or *modified accrual*-basis accounting. Accrual-basis accounting means that you record income when you earn it, and you record expenses when you use the goods or services from which the expenses stem. If you start using Quicken to track other assets and liabilities, you are using accrual-basis accounting. For example, if you use Quicken to account for customer receivables, you recognize the transaction as income when you record the receivable. If you use Quicken to account for fixed assets and depreciation, you categorize the expense of using the asset when you record depreciation.

Accrual-basis accounting gives you much better estimates of your income and expenses so that it better measures your profits. Accrual-basis accounting also results in better record-keeping because you keep registers for all your assets and liabilities—not just cash.

Invoicing Customers

Quicken does not provide an invoicing feature, but you can create a report that works as an invoice. Set up an account to record the asset you have because some customer or client now owes you money. You probably want to name the account by combining "invoice" with the actual invoice number. The account type should be 4, indicating another asset. Set the balance to zero and leave the description blank. Figure C.1 shows an example of the Set Up New Account screen filled to define such an account.

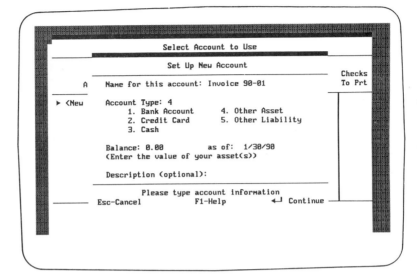

Fig. C.1.

The Set Up New Account screen filled to define the receivable that results from creating an invoice.

Select the account so that you can access the register for the account. To record the invoice, edit the opening balance entry that Quicken makes when you set up an account. You enter the customer name in the PAYEE field, the total invoice amount in the INCREASE field, and any customer reference number in the MEMO field. Select **Split Transaction** from the F3 Edit menu or its speed key equivalent, Ctrl-S, to provide details on the total invoice amount. Anything that has an amount associated with it must be categorized and described—even if every item has the same category. Suppose that you are an attorney and want to create a $1,000 invoice to a client, Johnson Manufacturing, for $300 of work on a real estate lease, $600 of work on a bank loan agreement, and $100 for out-of-pocket expenses. Figure C.2 shows an example of the completed Register screen and the Split Transaction window to record just such an invoice. (Remember that you can split a transaction into as many as 30 lines, so you can create an invoice that lists up to 30 charges.)

Now you are ready to record and print the invoice. Record the invoice by pressing Ctrl-Enter. To print the invoice, press F5 to access the Reports menu and select **Transactions**. Quicken then displays the Create Transaction Report screen. Enter your company name as the Report title, enter the billing period or the billing date in the Restrict transactions to and from fields, and set the Subtotal by field to 12 for subtotaling by account (see fig. C.3). Press F8 (Options) to access the Report Options screen, set the Split transaction detail to Y for yes and the Show memo/category/ both field to M for memo only (see fig. C.4). After you complete the

Fig. C.2.

The Register and Split Transaction screens completed for creating an invoice.

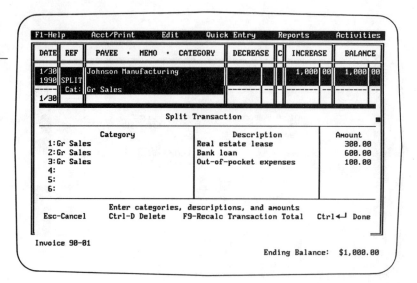

Report Options screen, press Ctrl-Enter to return to the Create Transaction Report screen. To generate an on-screen version of the invoice, press Ctrl-Enter again. If you want to print the invoice, press F8 (Print), complete the Print Report screen, and press Ctrl-Enter.

Fig. C.3.

The Create Transaction Report screen for an invoice.

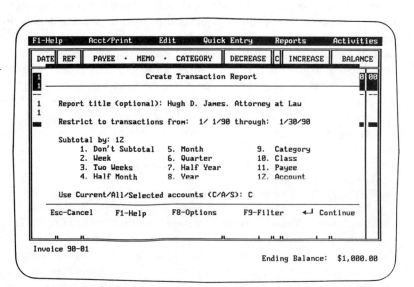

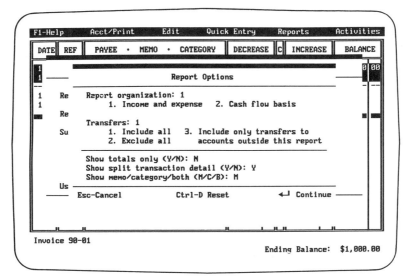

Fig. C.4.

The Report Options screen for an invoice.

Figure C.5 shows the resulting invoice. Your business name shows at the top of the invoice as well as the billing period or billing date. JAMES is the name of the account group for the business. The Payee field shows the customer or client name. The Memo field shows the descriptions and amounts of the various charges that make up the invoice. Finally, the total shows the invoice amount.

```
                        Hugh D. James. Attorney at Law
                          1/ 1/90 Through 1/30/90
     JAMES-Invoice 90-01                                    Page 1
     1/30/90

     Date    Num            Payee                Memo        Clr Amount
     -----  ------  ---------------------------  ----------------------  - --------

                    Invoice 90-01
                    -------------
     1/30    S Johnson Manufacturing    Real estate lease       300.00
                                        Bank loan               600.00
                                        Out-of-pocket expenses  100.00
                                                             ---------
                    Total Invoice 90-01                       1,000.00
                                                             =========
```

Fig. C.5.

An invoice generated with Quicken.

To be candid, the invoice is not as sophisticated or custom-tailored as those produced by accounting packages designed to generate invoices. Depending on the requirements on your business, however, this invoice can be satisfactory. Remember that you can export the report to an ASCII file that can be edited with almost any word processing program.

CPA Tip: Customers need the due date, your address, and your federal tax identification number so that they can report payments to you to the Internal Revenue Service. If you generate your invoices solely with Quicken, make sure that your customers already have this information some other way. If you export the invoice as an ASCII text file so that you can edit the invoice, add the due date, your federal tax identification number, and your address.

Tracking Customer Payments and Receivables

If you use Quicken to generate customer invoices, you create an account that records the asset a customer receivable represents. If you do not create invoices with Quicken, you still need to follow the steps described in the preceding section to record the receivable as an asset. After you record the receivable as an asset, you must record customer payments on the receivable and monitor your receivables—topics covered in the following sections.

Recording Customer Payments

To record customer payments, select the bank account you use to deposit the check and record the deposit in the usual way. To categorize the transaction, record the deposit as a transfer from the actual receivable account. For example, if you received a $500 check from Johnson Manufacturing as a partial payment on the $1,000 receivable created by Invoice 90-01, you complete the Register for the bank account you are depositing the money into as shown in figure C.6. (Remember that Quicken lists the categories and the accounts when you select **Categorize/Transfer** from the F4 Quick Entry menu.)

Quicken records a $500 reduction in the account you use to track the $1,000 receivable. Figure C.7 shows the Register for the Invoice 90-01 account after you record the $500 partial payment from Johnson Manufacturing as a deposit to the bank account. Quicken records the decrease in the Invoice 90-01 receivable. After a receivable is reduced to zero, you should print a copy of the register as a record of the receivable and the customer's payments. Then delete the account to make room for more accounts.

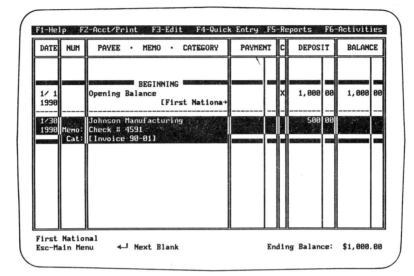

Fig. C.6.

Recording a $500 partial payment on the $1,000 receivable created by the invoice.

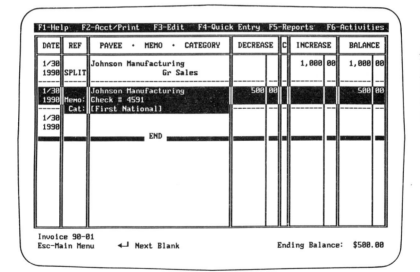

Fig. C.7.

Quicken records the second half of a transfer transaction.

CPA Tip: Some businesses offer a discount to customers who pay invoices early, but you should know that giving your customers such discounts is an expensive way to borrow money from your customers. Suppose that you normally require payment within 30 days of the invoice date but allow a two percent discount for payments received within 10 days. If your customer pays within 10 days, you essentially pay the customer a 2 percent interest charge by receiving the money 20 days early. Because one year contains roughly 18 twenty-day periods, the 2 percent for 20 days equals approximately 36 percent interest annually.

Similarly, a 1 percent discount equals approximately 18 percent annually, and a 3 percent discount equals 54 percent. Even if you need to borrow the money for cash flow reasons, you probably can find money to borrow at much lower interest rates.

Tracking Customer Receivables

Another basic receivables accounting task is tracking how much customers owe and how long they have owed you. Create a summary report that shows receivables account balances grouped by their age by following these steps:

1. To begin, select the **Summary** option from the Reports menu by pressing F5. Quicken displays the Create Summary Report screen (see fig. C.8).

2. To complete the screen to show only receivables balances, enter a report title and a range of dates, in the Restrict to transactions from and through fields, that begins with the date of your oldest receivable and ends with the current date.

Fig. C.8.

The Create Summary Report screen completed for a receivables aging.

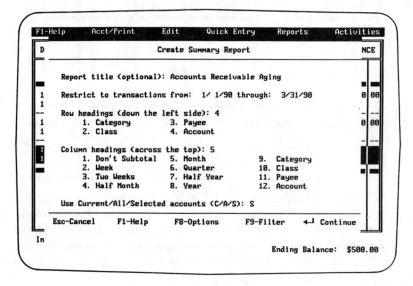

```
 F1-Help     Acct/Print      Edit       Quick Entry      Reports      Activities
 D                              Create Summary Report                      NCE

     Report title (optional): Accounts Receivable Aging

  1  Restrict to transactions from:  1/ 1/90 through:  3/31/90         0 00
  1
     Row headings (down the left side): 4
  1     1. Category        3. Payee                                     0 00
  1     2. Class           4. Account

     Column headings (across the top): 5
  1     1. Don't Subtotal  5. Month         9.  Category
  1     2. Week            6. Quarter      10.  Class
        3. Two Weeks       7. Half Year    11.  Payee
        4. Half Month      8. Year         12.  Account

     Use Current/All/Selected accounts (C/A/S): S

     Esc-Cancel     F1-Help     F8-Options     F9-Filter    ↵ Continue
  In

                                         Ending Balance:  $500.00
```

3. Set the Row headings field to 4. Next, set the Column headings field to whatever time intervals you want to use to age receivables. (Usually, businesses age their receivables on a monthly basis.)

4. Finally, set the Current/All/Selected accounts field to S for selected, and press Enter.

Quicken next displays the Select Accounts to Include screen. You want to exclude accounts that are not receivables. To exclude these accounts, move the cursor to the account you want to exclude and press the space bar. After you complete the Select Accounts to Include screen, press Ctrl-Enter, and Quicken displays the Accounts Receivable Aging report Summary (see fig. C.9).

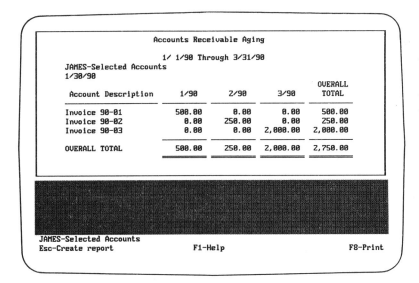

Fig. C.9.

The Accounts Receivable Aging report.

The summary report shows you each of the receivables customers owe you and the ages of the receivables. Invoice 90-01, for example, shows up in January because the date of that account's first transaction is in January.

Note: One problem with this approach is that the account names do not indicate the customers. If you do not use Quicken to generate invoices, you can mitigate this problem by naming accounts with the invoice number and the customer name. For example, you can name the account that tracks invoice 90-01 from Johnson Manufacturing as I-9001 Johnson.

CPA Tip: The Quicken user's manual offers another approach for recording receivables and two other approaches for recording payments on the receivables. The manual suggests that you record all your receivables, or at least all of a specific customer's receivables, in one account. With regard to recording payments, the manual suggests that you enter the payment as a decrease transaction in a large Receivables register or as a negative transfer amount for a specific receivable transaction by using the split transaction window. (If you have more questions about these approaches, refer to the user's manual.) The benefit of the manual's two approaches is that you do not use up as many accounts—the limit is 99. These suggestions have several problems, however:

❏ If you record invoices and payment transactions in a large register, you have difficulty seeing how much a customer owes you or has previously paid you on a specific invoice.

❏ If you use the split transaction window to record payments on an invoice, a second problem crops up. Applying a payment to five invoices, you have to go into the Receivables register and edit five transactions to show the payment. Your bank reconciliation also is more difficult because you recorded the payment as five deposits rather than one.

❏ You cannot generate invoices if you do not set up receivables in separate accounts.

Accounting for Fixed Assets

Accounting for fixed assets represents another activity that most businesses need to address. You may own furniture, equipment, and even real estate that needs to be depreciated. Although the assets you depreciate can be different, the mechanics of recording depreciation are consistent.

Note: If you need to record depletion for natural resources like timber or you need to record amortization expense for intangible assets like copyrights, the procedures are the same.

Understanding Depreciation

Suppose that you purchase a delivery truck for $12,000. You plan to use the truck for five years and then sell the truck for $2,000. The rationale for depreciating the truck is that over the five years, you need to include the expense of the truck when measuring your profits. Depreciation is a way of allocating the cost of an asset over two or more years. Several methods to make this allocation exist, but a common one is straight-line depreciation that works as follows: If you buy the truck for $12,000, intending to sell it five years later for $2,000, the overall cost of using the truck over the five years is $10,000. To calculate the yearly cost, divide the $10,000 by five years, and $2,000 is your annual depreciation expense to be included in your calculations of profits.

On balance sheets, assets get listed at an amount equal to the original cost minus the depreciation already taken. Continuing with the delivery truck example, at the end of the first year the balance sheet lists the truck at $10,000—calculated as $12,000 original cost minus $2,000 of depreciation. Similarly, at the end of the second, third, fourth, and fifth years, the balance sheet lists the truck at the original cost minus the depreciation taken to date. After the end of the fifth year, when the truck is listed at $2,000—calculated as $12,000 minus $10,000 of depreciation—you stop depreciating the asset because you do not depreciate the asset below its salvage value.

CPA Tip: Other depreciation methods exist, and those that the federal tax laws prescribe can be confusing. In essence, however, how you use Quicken to record depreciation works the same no matter what depreciation method you use. Within the scope of this appendix, I cannot give you complete information about how to calculate the depreciation on your assets, but if you want more information on the tax laws, call the Internal Revenue Service and ask for Internal Revenue Service Publication 534. If you want more information on how to calculate depreciation according to accepted accounting principles, which is different from depreciation calculated for the tax laws, consult your certified public accountant.

Recording Fixed Assets and Depreciation

To record fixed assets and the depreciation expense related to fixed assets, set up an account for each asset that needs to be depreciated. Enter something descriptive as the account name, set the account type to 4 for other assets, and enter the purchase price as the initial balance. Figure C.10 shows the Set Up New Account screen filled to define a new account for a $12,000 delivery truck.

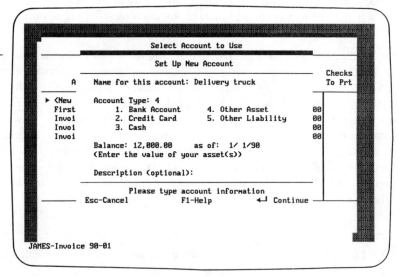

Fig. C.10.

The Set Up New Account screen filled to define a new account for a $12,000 delivery truck.

If you have groups of similar assets with similar life spans, you usually can depreciate them as a group. For example, you probably would not depreciate individually each piece of furniture you buy during the year. Rather, you would aggregate and depreciate them together as one asset.

To record depreciation, you can enter a decrease transaction that categorizes $2,000 a year to the Depreciation expense category. Remember that Quicken does not use a transaction in its calculations of profit unless the date is within the range you specify on the Create Report screens. Accordingly, you can enter all five years of depreciation at once by using transaction dates in each of the five years. Figure C.11 shows the Register screen for the delivery truck completed with the depreciation expense record for 1990, 1991, and 1992.

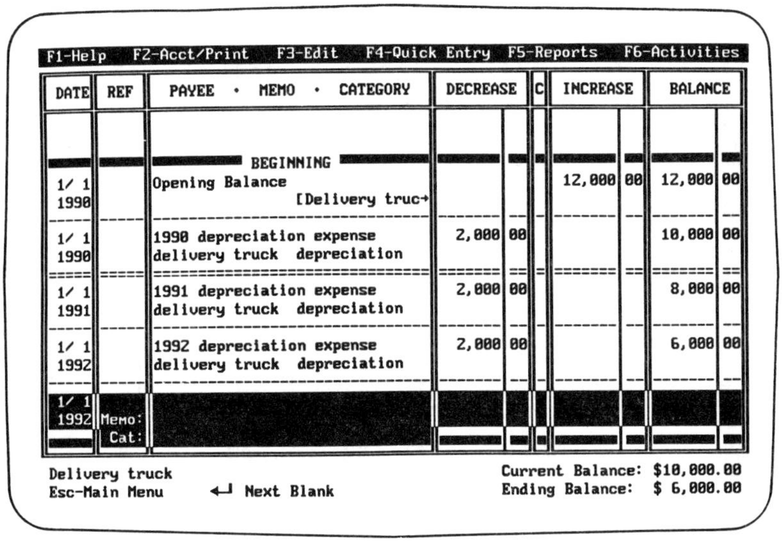

```
F1-Help   F2-Acct/Print   F3-Edit   F4-Quick Entry   F5-Reports   F6-Activities
┌────┬────┬─────────────────────────────┬──────────┬─┬─────────┬─────────┐
│DATE│REF │ PAYEE  ·  MEMO  ·  CATEGORY │ DECREASE │C│ INCREASE│ BALANCE │
├────┴────┴─────────────────────────────┴──────────┴─┴─────────┴─────────┤
│                    ▬▬▬▬▬ BEGINNING ▬▬▬▬▬                                 │
│ 1/ 1│    │Opening Balance              │          │ │12,000│00│12,000│00│
│ 1990│    │             [Delivery truc→ │          │ │      │  │      │  │
│ 1/ 1│    │1990 depreciation expense    │ 2,000│00 │ │      │  │10,000│00│
│ 1990│    │delivery truck  depreciation │          │ │      │  │      │  │
│ 1/ 1│    │1991 depreciation expense    │ 2,000│00 │ │      │  │ 8,000│00│
│ 1991│    │delivery truck  depreciation │          │ │      │  │      │  │
│ 1/ 1│    │1992 depreciation expense    │ 2,000│00 │ │      │  │ 6,000│00│
│ 1992│    │delivery truck  depreciation │          │ │      │  │      │  │
│ 1/ 1│Memo:│                            │          │ │      │  │      │  │
│ 1992│Cat: │                            │          │ │      │  │      │  │
└─────────────────────────────────────────────────────────────────────────┘
 Delivery truck                          Current Balance: $10,000.00
 Esc-Main Menu      ↵ Next Blank         Ending Balance:  $ 6,000.00
```

Fig. C.11.

The delivery truck register showing the asset depreciation transactions.

Preparing Payroll

One of the more common business applications of Quicken is to prepare employee payroll checks and reports. For a simple example, assume the following: You want to prepare a payroll check for an employee who earns $1,000 a month; the employee's social security tax is $76.50; and the employee's federal income tax withholding amount is $100. Also assume that the employer's matching share of social security is $76.50, and you must pay $10 for federal unemployment tax.

Getting Ready for Payroll

To record this payroll transaction, set up a liability account for each of the payroll taxes payable accounts. Enter the account type as 5, for Other Liability, and enter the initial amount (the amount you already owe). In this example, this amount includes the federal income tax withholding, the employee's social security amount, your matching social security taxes, and the federal unemployment tax. To define each of the payroll taxes accounts, use the Set Up New Account screen. Figure C.12 shows how to set up the account for the federal income tax withholding amount. Use the screen, filled out in similar fashion, to define each of the payroll taxes amounts.

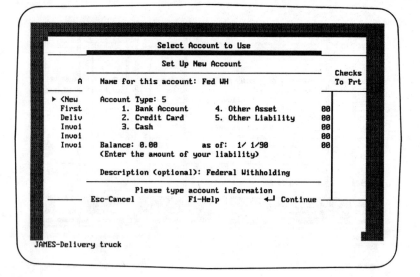

Fig. C.12.

The Set Up New Account screen filled to define the federal income tax withholding liability.

You also need to define a category for each of the employer's payroll expenses: the employee's wages, the employer's matching share of the social security tax, and the federal unemployment tax. You do not, however, define categories for the employee's social security tax or the employee's federal income tax withholding amounts because these amounts are expenses of the employee, not the employer.

Paying Employees

To record the payroll check, enter a transaction as shown in figure C.13. If you write payroll checks using the same bank account you use to write other checks, enter the Memo description as *payroll*, or *payroll* and the pay date, so that you can use the Memo field as the basis for including transactions on reports. If you use checks with vouchers—as you should for payroll—the employee's gross wages and the employee's deductions should appear on the first 16 lines of the split transaction screen, so that the split transaction shows on the voucher. On the Other Settings screen, make sure that the Print categories on voucher checks switch is set to yes so that the gross wages and deductions information prints on the voucher.

The other wages expenses—such as the employer's matching share of FICA and the federal unemployment tax—should be entered starting on line 17 of the split transaction screen, so that the expense does not appear on the payroll check's voucher (see fig. C.14).

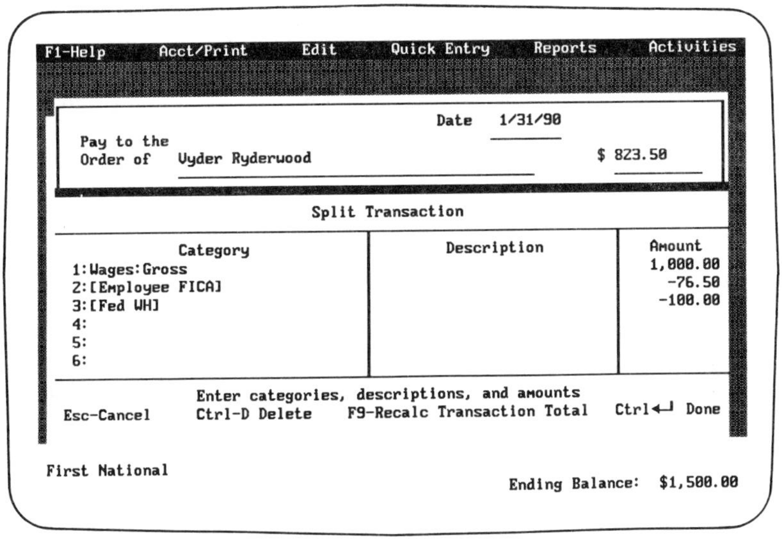

Fig. C.13.

The gross wages and employee deductions should be entered on the first 16 lines of the split transaction screen.

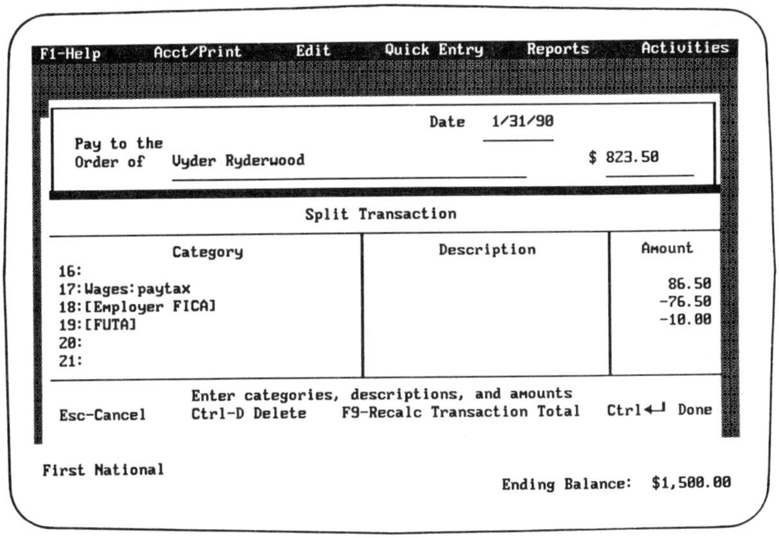

Fig. C.14.

The other wages expenses start on line 17.

When you complete the split transaction screen, press Ctrl-Enter. Figure C.15 shows the completed check. The net wages amount is $823.50, which is $1,000 in gross wages minus $100 in federal withholding and minus $76.50 in social security.

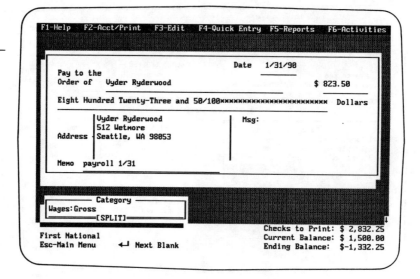

Fig. C.15.

The completed payroll check.

Paying Payroll Taxes

When you pay the government, you already have recorded the expense of the taxes and are carrying the payroll taxes you still owe as a liability. When you write the check to the government, the Category field needs to show the payroll tax liability account. For example, if you write a check to pay the $10 in federal unemployment taxes, you enter the category as [FUTA], because FUTA is the name of the liability account you use to track what you owe in federal unemployment tax.

You also use the same approach to record paying any of the other payroll tax liabilities you owe. You write a check to the government and categorize the transaction as a transfer from the payroll taxes liability account.

In real life, of course, you probably have several more payroll tax expenses and liabilities for items like state and local income taxes, state unemployment insurance, and disability insurance. The accounting procedures you follow to record and then pay each of these liabilities, however, are the same.

CPA Tip: You need to segregate the payroll tax liability money. The best approach is to set up a separate bank account that you use to collect and disburse payroll taxes. Do not, for any reason, "borrow" money from your payroll taxes bank account. Although the act may seem innocuous, the money is not yours to spend. The money belongs to an employee or the federal government; you only hold the money in trust.

Completing Quarterly and Annual Tax Reports

The final aspect of preparing payroll relates to the filing of the quarterly and annual payroll forms and reports to the state and local government. You actually have a series of federal reporting requirements for W-2s, W-3s, 940s, and 941s. Depending on where you live, you also may have several state and local payroll forms and reports to complete. You should be able to retrieve the numbers for these forms by printing a summary report based on the bank account you use to write payroll checks (see fig. C.16).

To print the summary report, select the **Summary** option from the Reports menu. You should subtotal the report by category. If you write the payroll checks on the same account you use to write other checks and include *payroll* in the Memo field, you can use the F9 (Filter) option to specify that only transactions with "payroll" appear on the summary report.

Completing the W-2 and W-3

You use the gross wages figures ($2,500 for Batum Schrag and $1,000 for Vyder Ryderwood) as the total wages amounts on the employees' W-2s. You use the transfers from withholding figures ($300 for Schrag and $100 for Ryderwood) as the federal income tax withholding amounts. You use the transfers from employee's FICA ($191.25 for Schrag and $76.50 for Ryderwood) as the social security taxes withheld amounts.

The W-3 summarizes the W-2 forms you complete. You enter the employer totals for each of the individual amounts on the employee W-2s you complete. You can use the totals from the summary report for these employer totals.

```
                               Payroll Summary Report
                                1/ 1/90 Through 3/31/90
        JAMES-First National                                              Page 1
        1/30/90
                             INC/EXP          INC/EXP          INC/EXP        INC/EXP
                             EXPENSES         EXPENSES         EXPENSES       EXPENSES
                          Wages & Job Cr   Wages & Job Cr   Wages & Job Cr     TOTAL
            Payee         Employee's gro   payroll taxes        TOTAL
        ---------------   --------------   --------------   --------------  --------------
        Batum Schrag           2,500.00          216.25         2,716.25       2,716.25
        Vyder Ryderwood        1,000.00           86.50         1,086.50       1,086.50
                          --------------   --------------   --------------  --------------
        OVERALL TOTAL          3,500.00          302.75         3,802.75       3,802.75
                          ==============   ==============   ==============  ==============
```

```
                               Payroll Summary Report
                                1/ 1/90 Through 3/31/90
        JAMES-First National                                              Page 2
        1/30/90
                             INC/EXP         TRANSFERS        TRANSFERS      TRANSFERS
                              TOTAL            FROM             FROM            FROM
                                           Employee FICA    Employer FICA      FUTA
            Payee
        ---------------   --------------   --------------   --------------  --------------
        Batum Schrag          -2,716.25          191.25           191.25          25.00
        Vyder Ryderwood       -1,086.50           76.50            76.50          10.00
                          --------------   --------------   --------------  --------------
        OVERALL TOTAL         -3,802.75          267.75           267.75          35.00
                          ==============   ==============   ==============  ==============
```

```
                               Payroll Summary Report
                                1/ 1/90 Through 3/31/90
        JAMES-First National                                              Page 3
        1/30/90
                            TRANSFERS        TRANSFERS        OVERALL
                              FROM             TOTAL           TOTAL
                             Fed WH
            Payee
        ---------------   --------------   --------------   --------------
        Batum Schrag             300.00          707.50        -2,008.75
        Vyder Ryderwood          100.00          263.00          -823.50
                          --------------   --------------   --------------
        OVERALL TOTAL            400.00          970.50        -2,832.25
                          ==============   ==============   ==============
```

Note: One difference between the transaction report shown in figure C.16
and the one you use to prepare the W-2 and W-3 forms is that your range
of transaction dates encompasses the entire year.

Completing Other Forms and Reports

The federal and the state governments have other tax forms and reports
you must complete. You use the 940 form, for example, to calculate and
report annual federal unemployment tax liability. You also use the 941
form each quarter to calculate and report federal income and social security taxes withheld and the employer's share of the social security taxes.
Again, you should be able to use the summary report like the one shown
in figure C.16 to complete the quarterly return.

Note: For the Employer's Annual Unemployment Tax (form 940), the range of transaction dates must encompass the entire year. For the Employer's Quarterly Federal Tax (form 941), the range of transaction dates must cover the quarter.

CPA Tip: Typically, the Internal Revenue Service provides you with a great deal of help and information about federal payroll taxes. You should take advantage of their help. Specifically, you need the Employer's Tax Guide (often called Circular E). If you do not already have one, call the nearest Internal Revenue Service Office and request a guide. If you are a sole proprietor, you also may want to request the information packet, "Your Business Tax Kit for Sole Proprietor," which provides information about the taxes you pay as a sole proprietor. Some IRS locations provide free small-business tax education seminars. You also should call your state revenue office and request any information they have on the state income and payroll taxes.

Inventory Accounting

An inventory accounting system is supposed to answer two questions: How much inventory do I currently hold? How much inventory did I sell over the year? A perpetual inventory system can answer both questions. Unfortunately, Quicken does not provide you with the tools to maintain a perpetual system. A *perpetual inventory system* tracks every change in inventory as the changes occur, in dollars and in units. As a result, you always know exactly how much inventory in dollars and in units you hold. Because Quicken tracks only dollars, not units, you can answer only the second question: How much inventory did I sell over the year? You can answer this question with a simple periodic inventory system.

Understanding Periodic Inventory Systems

A periodic system works as follows. At the end of every year, you count the inventory you are holding and add up its cost. Calculate the cost of the goods, or inventory, you sold by taking the inventory purchases you made over the year and subtracting the change in inventory.

Suppose that you sell cars and that each car costs $10,000. You held three cars in inventory at the beginning of the year, purchased ten cars over the year, and have four cars in inventory at the end of the year. Using the equation described previously, you can calculate the value of the inventory you sold over the year as follows:

Car purchases: ($10K * 10)		$100,000
Change over year:		
Ending ($10K * 4 cars)	$40,000	
Beginning ($10K * 3 cars)	$30,000	
Minus change over year		− $10,000
Cost of inventory sold over year		$90,000

You know that over the year you bought $100,000 of cars and that you are holding $10,000 more inventory than you were last year, which means that you did not sell all the cars you bought.

Implementing a Periodic Inventory System

The following steps describe how you implement a periodic inventory system using Quicken:

1. Set up an Other Asset account for the inventory you buy and sell. The name can be inventory. The account type should be 4. The starting balance should be the starting inventory balance. (If you are just starting your business, the starting inventory balance can be zero if you have not yet begun to purchase inventory.)

2. When you purchase inventory, do not categorize the purchase as an expense—transfer the total purchase amount to the inventory account.

3. When you want to calculate your net income, select the inventory account and use the **Update Account Balance** option to reset the inventory account balance to whatever your physical count shows. The adjustment transaction should be categorized as cost of goods sold.

Figure C.17 shows an inventory account register after a month of purchases and the adjustment transaction that calculates the actual cost of goods sold amount.

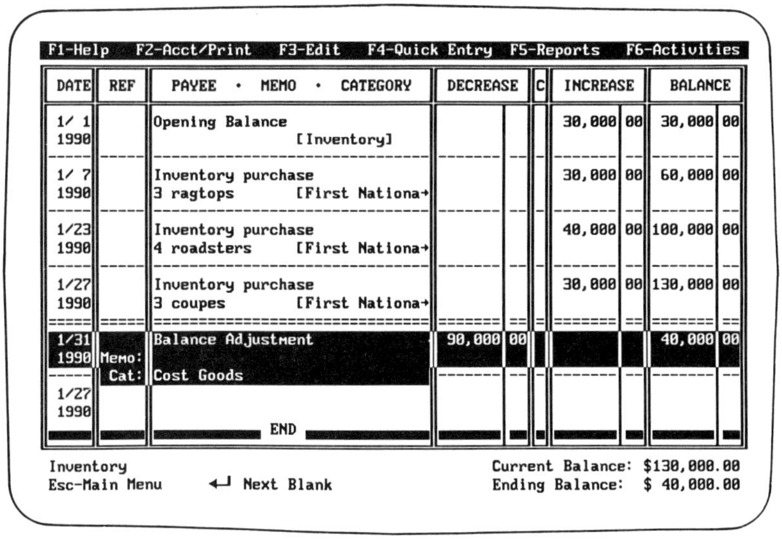

Fig. C.17.

An inventory account register with sample transactions.

Reviewing the Problems of a Periodic System

You should make sure that you can live with the problems of a periodic inventory system before you spend a large amount of time and energy on implementing such a system.

- Although you have accurate measures of your cash flow, you have an accurate measure of profits only through the last adjustment transaction. If you need to measure profits frequently, you must take frequent physical counts of your inventory and make the physical adjustment transaction.

- You don't know the details or components of the cost of goods sold because you get the cost of goods sold from an adjustment transaction. As a result, you do not know the portion of cost of goods sold that stems from sales to specific customers or the portion that stems from breakage, shoplifting, or spoilage.

- You also never really know how much inventory you are actually holding, except when you make physical counts of your inventory. You never can use your inventory system, therefore, to see which items need to be reordered or how many units you are stocking of a specific item.

Job Costing

Job costing refers to tracking the costs of a specific project, or job, and comparing these costs to what you planned to spend. Home builders, advertising agencies, and specialty manufacturers are examples of businesses with projects that must be monitored for actual and planned costs.

The Quicken user's manual suggests one approach for job costing: categorize expenses as belonging to a category and a class. When you print a transaction or summary report, you can choose to subtotal by the classes. Because you used classes to represent jobs, the total for a class is the total for a job. The following paragraphs describe alternative approaches that help you avoid two problems you encounter when categorizing expenses as belonging to a category and class.

The first problem with using classes as the basis for your job costing system is that within Quicken you do not budget by classes, but by categories. If you use the classes approach, you omit one of the basic job costing function tasks: comparing what you planned to spend with what you actually spent. Fortunately, you can solve this problem by setting up a group of categories that you use only for a specific job. You may even include some code or abbreviation in the category name to indicate the job.

For example, suppose that you are a home builder constructing a house on lot 23 in Deerfield and that you use three rough categories of expenses on all your homes: land, material, and labor. In this case, you can create three special categories: 23D Land, 23D material, and 23D labor, which you can use exclusively to budget and track the costs of the house you are constructing. Remember, you cannot budget for subcategories; you can budget only for categories.

A second problem with using classes as the basis for your job costing system is that the costs you expend on a job should not always be categorized as an expense but should often be treated as an asset. The costs of building the home on lot 23 in the Deerfield subdivision should be carried as inventory until the home is sold. When the home is sold, the total costs of the home should be categorized as the cost of goods sold. During the job, if you categorize the costs of building the home as expenses when you pay the costs, you overstate your expenses (which understates your profits), and you understate your assets (which understates your net worth). These understatements of profits and net worth can be a real problem if you have investors or lenders looking carefully at your financial performance and condition.

To solve this problem, create a transaction in which you move cost dollars out of the job cost categories into an asset account. The basic steps for moving these dollars from the expense categories to an asset account are as follows:

1. Set up an asset account for the job.

2. Print the budget report to see your actual costs and to show, if you choose, your planned costs.

3. Create an entry in the new asset account register that increases the balance of the asset and categorizes the increase as the budget report shows the actual spending.

Figure C.18 shows the on-screen version of the budgeting report that, if you follow the approaches described in the preceding paragraphs, you can generate to monitor job costs. Figure C.19 shows a copy of the new asset account register with the transaction that shows the reasons for the increase in the asset. Figure C.20 shows the business balance sheet with the asset being created by the job correctly displayed on the balance sheet.

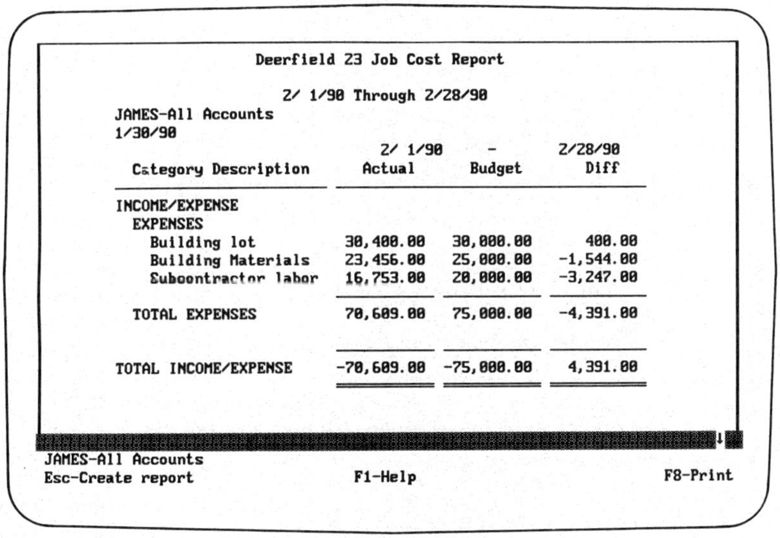

```
                    Deerfield 23 Job Cost Report

                    2/ 1/90 Through 2/28/90
        JAMES-All Accounts
        1/30/90
                                2/ 1/90      -        2/28/90
            Category Description   Actual    Budget      Diff

        INCOME/EXPENSE
          EXPENSES
            Building lot         30,400.00  30,000.00     400.00
            Building Materials   23,456.00  25,000.00  -1,544.00
            Subcontractor labor  16,753.00  20,000.00  -3,247.00

          TOTAL EXPENSES         70,609.00  75,000.00  -4,391.00


        TOTAL INCOME/EXPENSE    -70,609.00 -75,000.00   4,391.00



        JAMES-All Accounts
        Esc-Create report            F1-Help                    F8-Print
```

Fig. C.18.

A budget report for a job.

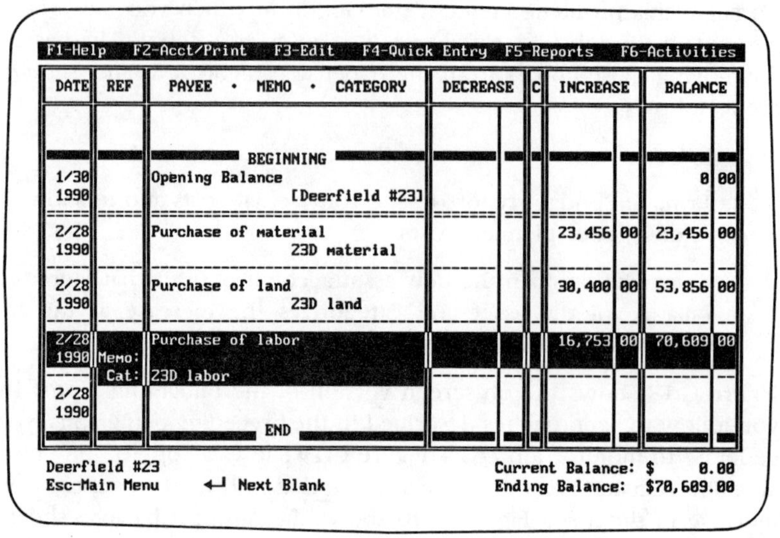

Fig. C.19.

A transaction register showing how to record an asset.

```
 F1-Help   F2-Acct/Print   F3-Edit   F4-Quick Entry  F5-Reports   F6-Activities

  DATE  REF    PAYEE  ·  MEMO  ·  CATEGORY    DECREASE  C  INCREASE    BALANCE

                        ====== BEGINNING ======
  1/30        Opening Balance                                                 0 00
  1990                     [Deerfield #23]
  =====  ===========================================  ===  =======  == =======  ==
  2/28        Purchase of material                              23,456 00  23,456 00
  1990                     23D material
  -----       -------------------------------------       -------  -- -------  --
  2/28        Purchase of land                                  30,400 00  53,856 00
  1990                     23D land
  -----       -------------------------------------       -------  -- -------  --
  2/28  Memo: Purchase of labor                                 16,753 00  70,609 00
  1990
  -----  Cat: 23D labor
  2/28
  1990
                        ====== END ======

  Deerfield #23                                Current Balance: $      0.00
  Esc-Main Menu    ←┘ Next Blank               Ending Balance:  $70,609.00
```

Fig. C.20.

A balance sheet showing the asset.

```
                          ACCOUNT BALANCES REPORT
                              As of 2/28/90
  JAMES-All Accounts                                               Page 1
  1/30/90
                                              2/28/90
                    Account                   Balance
  -----------------------------------    --------------------------
  ASSETS
    Cash and Bank Accounts
      First National
        Ending Balance            28,058.75
        plus: Checks Payable       2,832.25
                                 ------------
        Total First National                     30,891.00
                                              ------------
    Total Cash and Bank Accounts               30,891.00

    Other Assets
      Deerfield #23                             70,609.00
      Delivery truck                            10,000.00
      Inventory                                 40,000.00
      Invoice 90-01                                500.00
      Invoice 90-02                                250.00
                                              ------------
    Total Other Assets                         121,359.00

                                              ------------
  TOTAL ASSETS                                 152,250.00

  LIABILITIES
    Checks Payable                               2,832.25

    Other Liabilities
      Employee FICA                                267.75
      Employer FICA                                267.75
      Fed WH-Federal Withholding                   400.00
      FUTA-Federal Unemployment                     35.00
                                              ------------
    Total Other Liabilities                        970.50

                                              ------------
  TOTAL LIABILITIES                              3,802.75

                                              ------------
  OVERALL TOTAL                                148,447.25
                                              ============
```

Tracking Loans and Notes

Keeping accurate records of what you pay and owe on a loan is not always easy—but is important. Interest expense often is a valid business and personal income tax deduction. You need to report how much you owe on various loans for financial statements and credit applications.

Consider using Quicken for loan record-keeping. To begin, set up another liability account for the loan. The starting account balance equals what you currently owe. Define categories for the loan interest expense and any of the other expenses you pay when you make a loan payment. For a mortgage, other expense categories may include the property taxes and private mortgage insurance. For an equipment loan or lease, other expense categories may include sales tax and property insurance. Begin recording transactions. For example, you want to record a $796 loan payment—$740 of interest and $56 of principal. Suppose that you pay an additional $30 of property taxes, so that the check amount equals $826. You split portions of the payment, $740 to interest expense and $30 to property taxes. You also record the $56 of principal reduction by transferring the $56 to the liability account you set up to track the loan balances. Figure C.21 shows the Split Transaction screen filled to record a loan payment.

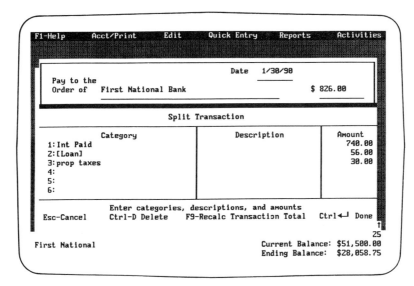

Fig. C.21.

Recording a loan payment.

At the end of the year, you want to adjust for interest-principal breakdown errors. Such errors can occur for several reasons. For example, the amortization schedule shows the interest and principal components of pay-

CPA Tip: For amortization loans, you should get an amortization schedule from the bank. The schedule shows the principal and interest portions of the payments you make and the loan balances after each payment. The easiest place to get one is from the lender. If you are an expert with a spreadsheet like Lotus 1-2-3 or Microsoft Excel, you can construct your own amortization schedule. Figure C.22 shows an amortization schedule created with a spreadsheet.

Fig. C.22.

An amortization schedule created with a spreadsheet program.

FIXRATE.XLS

Loan Amortization Schedule

Payment Date	Period	Total Payment	Interest Component	Principal Component	Principal Balance
15-Jan-90	1	$796	$740	$56	$99,944
15-Feb-90	2	796	740	56	99,888
15-Mar-90	3	796	739	57	99,831
15-Apr-90	4	796	739	57	99,773
15-May-90	5	796	738	58	99,716
15-Jun-90	6	796	738	58	99,658
15-Jul-90	7	796	737	59	99,599
15-Aug-90	8	796	737	59	99,540
15-Sep-90	9	796	737	59	99,481
15-Oct-90	10	796	736	60	99,421
15-Nov-90	11	796	736	60	99,361
15-Dec-90	12	796	735	61	99,300
15-Jan-91	13	796	735	61	99,239
15-Feb-91	14	796	734	62	99,177
15-Mar-91	15	796	734	62	99,115
15-Apr-91	16	796	733	63	99,052
15-May-91	17	796	733	63	98,989
15-Jun-91	18	796	733	63	98,926
15-Jul-91	19	796	732	64	98,862
15-Aug-91	20	796	732	64	98,798

ments assuming that you pay the same day every month, but some months you may pay earlier and incur less interest, and other months you may pay later and incur more interest.

To identify a breakdown error, compare the ending balance the lender shows on the year-end statement with what your loan register shows. After you identify the dollar size of the error, making the correction is easy. If your loan register balance is $3 too high, for example, you edit the last loan payment split transaction amounts in the checking account register so that the interest is $3 less and the loan account transfer is $3 more. To double-check, compare the ending balance in the loan account register with what the lender's annual statement shows. The two amounts should equal.

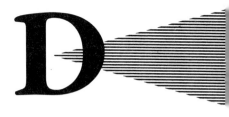

D

Tips for Specific Business Situations

The purpose of this appendix is to give you tips for using Quicken in specific business situations. This appendix assumes that you have read the previous sections of the book and does not focus on the mechanics
of menu options or the way in which you complete screens. The focus of this appendix is how you use Quicken within the framework of specific businesses.

Because the tips are broken down into 15 groups, you need to read only those tips that apply to your situation. After reading this appendix, you should have a firmer grasp of how to apply Quicken to your financial management needs.

Income Tax Accounting Tips

You must complete some type of federal income tax form at the end of the year to report your income and expenses. Real estate investors complete the Schedule E tax form (see fig. D.1); farmers complete the Schedule F tax form (see fig. D.2); sole proprietors complete the Schedule C tax form (see fig. D.3); partnerships complete the Schedule 1065 tax form (see fig. D.4); and corporations complete one of the three corporate income tax forms: 1120-A for small corporations (see fig. D.5), 1120S for S corporations (see fig. D.6), and 1120 for all other corporations (see fig. D.7).

Fig. D.1.

The Schedule E form indicates which income and expense categories real estate investors use to report profits and losses.

SCHEDULE E
(Form 1040)
Department of the Treasury
Internal Revenue Service

Supplemental Income and Loss
(From rents, royalties, partnerships, estates, trusts, REMICs, etc.)
▶ Attach to Form 1040 or Form 1041.
▶ See Instructions for Schedule E (Form 1040).

OMB No. 1545-0074
1989
Attachment Sequence No. **13**

Name(s) shown on return | **Your social security number**

Part I Income or Loss From Rentals and Royalties **Caution:** *Your rental loss may be limited. See Instructions.*

1 Show the kind and location of **rental property:**
A ....
B ....
C ....

	Yes	No
2 For each rental property listed on line 1, did you or your family use it for personal purposes for more than the greater of 14 days or 10% of the total days rented at fair rental value during the tax year? A		
B		
C		
3 For each **rental real estate property** listed on line 1, did you actively participate in its operation during the tax year? (See Instructions.) A		
B		
C		

		Properties A	Properties B	Properties C		D Totals (Add columns A, B, and C)
Rental and Royalty Income:						
4 Rents received	4				4	
5 Royalties received	5				5	
Rental and Royalty Expenses:						
6 Advertising	6					
7 Auto and travel	7					
8 Cleaning and maintenance	8					
9 Commissions	9					
10 Insurance	10					
11 Legal and other professional fees	11					
12 Mortgage interest paid to banks, etc. (see Instructions)	12				12	
13 Other interest	13					
14 Repairs	14					
15 Supplies	15					
16 Taxes	16					
17 Utilities (see Instructions)	17					
18 Wages and salaries	18					
19 Other (list) ▶	19					
20 Add lines 6 through 19	20				20	
21 Depreciation expense or depletion (see Instructions)	21				21	
22 Total expenses. Add lines 20 and 21	22					
23 Income or (loss) from rental or royalty properties. Subtract line 22 from line 4 (rents) or line 5 (royalties). If the result is a (loss), see Instructions to find out if you must file **Form 6198**	23					
24 Deductible rental loss. **Caution:** *Your rental loss on line 23 may be limited. See Instructions to find out if you must file Form 8582*	24	( )	( )	( )		

25 **Income.** Add rental and royalty income from line 23. Enter the total income here	25	
26 **Losses.** Add royalty losses from line 23 and rental losses from line 24. Enter the total losses here	26	( )
27 Combine amounts on lines 25 and 26. Enter the net income or (loss) here	27	
28 Net farm rental income or (loss) from Form 4835. (Also complete line 43 on page 2.)	28	
29 Total rental and royalty income or (loss). Combine amounts on lines 27 and 28. Enter the result here. If Parts II, III, and IV on page 2 do not apply to you, enter the amount from line 29 on Form 1040, line 18. Otherwise, include the amount from line 29 in the total on line 42 on page 2	29	

For Paperwork Reduction Act Notice, see Form 1040 Instructions. **Schedule E (Form 1040) 1989**

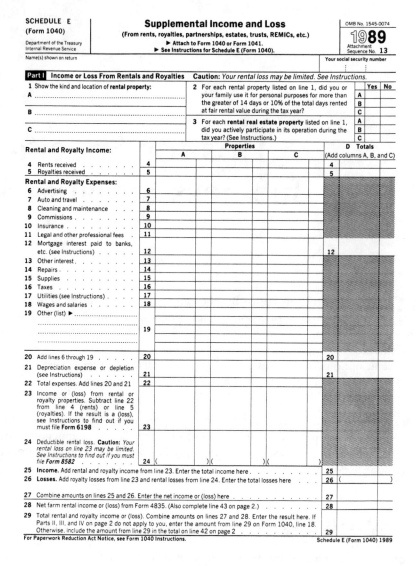

If you live in a state with income taxes, you also may have an equivalent state income tax form. Make sure that you or your accountant can easily prepare your tax return with the information Quicken produces. (The more time your accountant takes, the more money you pay to have your return prepared.)

Verify that you use categories that are easily reconcilable with the income and expense categories shown on the actual tax forms. The most straight-

Schedule E (Form 1040) 1989 — Attachment Sequence No. 13 — Page 2

Name(s) shown on return. (Do not enter name and social security number if shown on other side.) | Your social security number

Note: *If you report amounts from farming or fishing on Schedule E, you must include your gross income from those activities on line 43 below.*

Part II Income or Loss From Partnerships and S Corporations

If you report a loss from an at-risk activity, you MUST check either column **(e)** or **(f)** to describe your investment in the activity. See Instructions. If you check column **(f)**, you must attach **Form 6198.**

30	(a) Name	(b) Enter P for partnership; S for S corporation	(c) Check if foreign partnership	(d) Employer identification number	Investment At Risk? (e) All is at risk	(f) Some is not at risk
A						
B						
C						
D						
E						

	Passive Income and Loss		Nonpassive Income and Loss		
	(g) Passive loss allowed from Form 8582	(h) Passive income from Schedule K-1	(i) Nonpassive loss from Schedule K-1	(j) Section 179 deduction (see Instructions for limits)	(k) Nonpassive income from Schedule K-1
A					
B					
C					
D					
E					
31a Totals					
b Totals					

32 Add amounts in columns (h) and (k) of line 31a. Enter the total income here . . . 32

33 Add amounts in columns (g), (i), and (j) of line 31b. Enter the total here . . . 33 ( )

34 Total partnership and S corporation income or (loss). Combine amounts on lines 32 and 33. Enter the result here and include in the total on line 42 below . . . 34

Part III Income or Loss From Estates and Trusts

35	(a) Name	(b) Employer identification number
A		
B		
C		

	Passive Income and Loss		Nonpassive Income and Loss	
	(c) Passive deduction or loss allowed from Form 8582	(d) Passive income from Schedule K-1	(e) Deduction or loss from Schedule K-1	(f) Other income from Schedule K-1
A				
B				
C				
36a Totals				
b Totals				

37 Add amounts in columns (d) and (f) of line 36a. Enter the total income here . . . 37

38 Add amounts in columns (c) and (e) of line 36b. Enter the total here . . . 38 ( )

39 Total estate and trust income or (loss). Combine amounts on lines 37 and 38. Enter the result here and include in the total on line 42 below . . . 39

Part IV Income or Loss From Real Estate Mortgage Investment Conduits (REMICs)—Residual Holder

40	(a) Name	(b) Employer identification number	(c) Excess inclusion from Schedules Q, line 2c (see Instructions)	(d) Taxable income (net loss) from Schedules Q, line 1b	(e) Income from Schedules Q, line 3b

41 Combine amounts in columns (d) and (e) only. Enter the result here and include in the total on line 42 below. . . . 41

Part V Summary of Parts I Through IV

42 TOTAL income or (loss). Combine amounts on lines 29, 34, 39, and 41. Enter the result here and on Form 1040, line 18 . . . ▶ 42

Part VI Reconciliation of Farming and Fishing Income

43 Farmers and fishermen: Enter your **gross** farming and fishing income reported in Parts I, II, and III (see Instructions) . . . 43

Fig. D.1. cont.

Schedule E, Form 1040.

forward approach is to create categories for each of the income and expense lines on the income tax form you file and to use these categories to account for income and expense transactions. If you want more detail than the tax form income and expense lines provide, you can use subcategories that fall under the income and expense categories. Chapter 7, "Using Categories and Classes," describes how to create and use categories and subcategories.

Fig. D.2.

The Schedule F form indicates which income and expense categories farmers use to report profits and losses.

SCHEDULE F (Form 1040)	**Farm Income and Expenses**	OMB No. 1545-0074
Department of the Treasury Internal Revenue Service	► Attach to Form 1040, Form 1041, or Form 1065. ► See Instructions for Schedule F (Form 1040).	**1989** Attachment Sequence No. **14**

Name of proprietor | Social security number (SSN)

A Principal product. (Describe in one or two words your principal crop or activity for the current tax year.) | **B** Agricultural activity code (from Part IV) ►

C Accounting method: ☐ Cash ☐ Accrual | **D** Employer ID number (Not SSN)

E Did you make an election in a prior year to include Commodity Credit Corporation loan proceeds as income in that year? ☐ Yes ☐ No
F Did you "materially participate" in the operation of this business during 1989? (If "No," see Instructions for limitations on losses.) ☐ Yes ☐ No
G Do you elect, or did you previously elect, to currently deduct certain preproductive period expenses? (See Instructions.) ☐ Does not apply ☐ Yes ☐ No
If you choose to revoke a prior election for animals, see the Instructions.

Part I **Farm Income—Cash Method—Complete Parts I and II** (Accrual method taxpayers complete Parts II and III, and line 11 of Part I.)
Do not include sales of livestock held for draft, breeding, sport, or dairy purposes; report these sales on Form 4797.

1	Sales of livestock and other items you bought for resale	**1**			
2	Cost or other basis of livestock and other items you bought for resale	**2**			
3	Subtract line 2 from line 1			**3**	
4	Sales of livestock, produce, grains, and other products you raised			**4**	
5a	Total cooperative distributions (Form(s) 1099-PATR) **5a**		5b Taxable amount	**5b**	
6a	Agricultural program payments (see Instructions) **6a**		6b Taxable amount	**6b**	
7	Commodity Credit Corporation (CCC) loans:				
a	CCC loans reported under election (see Instructions)			**7a**	
b	CCC loans forfeited or repaid with certificates **7b**		7c Taxable amount	**7c**	
8	Crop insurance proceeds and certain disaster payments (see Instructions):				
a	Amount received in 1989 **8a**		8b Taxable amount	**8b**	
c	If election to defer to 1990 is attached, check here ► ☐	8d Amount deferred from 1988		**8d**	
9	Custom hire (machine work) income			**9**	
10	Other income, including Federal and state gasoline or fuel tax credit or refund (see Instructions)			**10**	
11	Add amounts in the right column for lines 3 through 10. If accrual method taxpayer, enter the amount from page 2, line 51. This is your **gross income** ►			**11**	

Part II **Farm Expenses—Cash and Accrual Method** (Do not include personal or living expenses such as taxes, insurance, repairs, etc., on your home.)

12	Breeding fees	**12**		24	Labor hired (less jobs credit)	**24**		
13	Chemicals	**13**		25	Pension and profit-sharing plans	**25**		
14	Conservation expenses (you must attach **Form 8645**)	**14**		26	Rent or lease:			
15	Custom hire (machine work)	**15**		a	Machinery and equipment	**26a**		
16	Depreciation and section 179 deduction not claimed elsewhere (from **Form 4562**)	**16**		b	Other (land, animals, etc.)	**26b**		
				27	Repairs and maintenance	**27**		
17	Employee benefit programs other than on line 25	**17**		28	Seeds and plants purchased	**28**		
18	Feed purchased	**18**		29	Storage and warehousing	**29**		
19	Fertilizers and lime	**19**		30	Supplies purchased	**30**		
20	Freight and trucking	**20**		31	Taxes	**31**		
21	Gasoline, fuel, and oil	**21**		32	Utilities (see Instructions)	**32**		
22	Insurance (other than health)	**22**		33	Veterinary fees and medicine	**33**		
23	Interest:			34	Other expenses (specify):			
a	Mortgage (paid to banks, etc.)	**23a**		a		**34a**		
b	Other	**23b**		b		**34b**		
				c		**34c**		
				d		**34d**		
				e		**34e**		

35	Add amounts on lines 12 through 34e. These are your **total expenses** ►	**35**	
36	**Net farm profit or (loss)**. Subtract line 35 from line 11. If a profit, enter on Form 1040, line 19, and on Schedule SE, line 1. If a loss, you MUST go on to line 37. (Fiduciaries and partnerships, see Instructions.)	**36**	
37	If you have a loss, you MUST check the box that describes your investment in this activity (see Instructions). If you checked 37a, enter the loss on Form 1040, line 19, and Schedule SE, line 1. If you checked 37b, you MUST attach **Form 6198**.	**37a** ☐ All investment is at risk. **37b** ☐ Some investment is not at risk.	

For Paperwork Reduction Act Notice, see Form 1040 Instructions. | Schedule F (Form 1040) 1989

You also can work with categories that you need to add together with other categories to calculate a tax form entry. Suppose that you are a sole proprietor and own a restaurant. Although total wages goes on one line of the Schedule C tax form, you may want to track several categories of wages including waitresses, dishwashers, cooks, bartenders, and so on. In this case, you actually have several wages categories that must be added to calculate the wages amount that goes on the tax form.

Schedule F (Form 1040) 1989   Page **2**

Part III   **Farm Income—Accrual Method**

Do not include sales of livestock held for draft, breeding, sport, or dairy purposes; report these sales on Form 4797 and do not include this livestock on line 46 below.

38	Sales of livestock, produce, grains, and other products during year	38
39a	Total cooperative distributions (Form(s) 1099-PATR) [39a] 39b Taxable amount	39b
40a	Agricultural program payments (see Instructions) [40a] 40b Taxable amount	40b
41	Commodity Credit Corporation (CCC) loans:	
a	CCC loans reported under election (see Instructions)	41a
b	CCC loans forfeited or repaid with certificates [41b] 41c Taxable amount	41c
42	Crop insurance proceeds	42
43	Custom hire (machine work) income	43
44	Other income, including Federal and state gasoline or fuel tax credit or refund (see Instructions)	44
45	Add amounts in the right column for lines 38 through 44	45
46	Inventory of livestock, produce, grains, and other products at beginning of year 46	
47	Cost of livestock, produce, grains, and other products purchased during year 47	
48	Add lines 46 and 47 48	
49	Inventory of livestock, produce, grains, and other products at end of year 49	
50	Cost of livestock, produce, grains, and other products sold. Subtract line 49 from line 48*	50
51	Subtract line 50 from line 45. Enter the result here and on page 1, line 11. This is your **gross income** ▶	51

*If you use the unit-livestock-price method or the farm-price method of valuing inventory and the amount on line 49 is larger than the amount on line 48, subtract line 48 from line 49. Enter the result on line 50. Add lines 45 and 50. Enter the total on line 51.

Part IV   **Principal Agricultural Activity Codes**

Select one of the following codes and write the 3-digit number on page 1, line B. (Note: If your principal source of income is from providing agricultural services such as soil preparation, veterinary, farm labor, horticultural, or management for a fee or on a contract basis, you should file **Schedule C** (Form 1040), Profit or Loss From Business.)

120	**Field crop,** including grains and nongrains such as cotton, peanuts, feed corn, wheat, tobacco, Irish potatoes, etc.
160	**Vegetables and melons,** garden-type vegetables and melons, such as sweet corn, tomatoes, squash, etc.
170	**Fruit and tree nuts,** including grapes, berries, olives, etc.
180	**Ornamental floriculture and nursery products**
185	**Food crops grown under cover,** including hydroponic crops

211	**Beefcattle feedlots**
212	**Beefcattle,** except feedlots
215	**Hogs, sheep, and goats**
240	**Dairy**
250	**Poultry and eggs,** including chickens, ducks, pigeons, quail, etc.
260	**General livestock,** not specializing in any one livestock category
270	**Animal specialty,** including fur-bearing animals, pets, horses, etc.
280	**Animal aquaculture,** including fish, shellfish, mollusks, frogs, etc., produced within confined space
290	**Forest products,** including forest nurseries and seed gathering, extraction of pine gum, and gathering of forest products
300	**Agricultural production,** not specified

Fig. D.2. cont.

Schedule F, Form 1040.

If you are using Quicken for a sole proprietorship and you hold and resell inventory, you need Part III of the Schedule C form to calculate your cost of goods sold and your inventory balances (see fig. D.3). You can use the periodic inventory approach described in Appendix C to produce the information for Part III of the Schedule C form.

Fig. D.3.

*The Schedule C
form indicates
which income
and expense
categories sole
proprietors use
to report profits
and losses.*

SCHEDULE C
(Form 1040)

Department of the Treasury
Internal Revenue Service

Profit or Loss From Business
(Sole Proprietorship)
Partnerships, Joint Ventures, Etc., Must File Form 1065.
▶ Attach to Form 1040 or Form 1041. ▶ See Instructions for Schedule C (Form 1040).

OMB No. 1545-0074

1989

Attachment
Sequence No. **09**

Name of proprietor

Social security number (SSN)

A Principal business or profession, including product or service (see Instructions)

B Principal business code
(from page 2) ▶

C Business name and address ▶

D Employer ID number (Not SSN)

E Method(s) used to value closing inventory: **(1)** ☐ Cost **(2)** ☐ Lower of cost or market **(3)** ☐ Other (attach explanation) **(4)** ☐ Does not apply (if checked, skip line G)

F Accounting method: **(1)** ☐ Cash **(2)** ☐ Accrual **(3)** ☐ Other (specify) ▶ ....

Yes | No

G Was there any change in determining quantities, costs, or valuations between opening and closing inventory? (If "Yes," attach explanation.)

H Are you deducting expenses for business use of your home? (If "Yes," see Instructions for limitations.)

I Did you "materially participate" in the operation of this business during 1989? (If "No," see Instructions for limitations on losses.)

J If this schedule includes a loss, credit, deduction, income, or other tax benefit relating to a tax shelter required to be registered, check here . ▶☐
If you checked this box, you MUST attach **Form 8271.**

Part I Income

1 Gross receipts or sales . . . . | 1 |
2 Returns and allowances . . . . | 2 |
3 Subtract line 2 from line 1. Enter the result here . . . . | 3 |
4 Cost of goods sold and/or operations (from line 39 on page 2) . . . . . | 4 |
5 Subtract line 4 from line 3 and enter the **gross profit** here . . . . . . | 5 |
6 Other income, including Federal and state gasoline or fuel tax credit or refund (see Instructions) . . . | 6 |
7 Add lines 5 and 6. This is your **gross income** . . . . ▶ | 7 |

Part II Expenses

8 Advertising . . . . . . | 8 |
9 Bad debts from sales or services (see Instructions) . . | 9 |
10 Car and truck expenses . . . | 10 |
11 Commissions . . . . . | 11 |
12 Depletion . . . . . | 12 |
13 Depreciation and section 179 deduction from **Form 4562** (not included in Part III) . . | 13 |
14 Employee benefit programs (other than on line 20) . . | 14 |
15 Freight (not included in Part III) | 15 |
16 Insurance (other than health) . | 16 |
17 Interest:
a Mortgage (paid to banks, etc.) . | 17a |
b Other . . . . | 17b |
18 Legal and professional services . | 18 |
19 Office expense . . . . . | 19 |
20 Pension and profit-sharing plans . | 20 |
21 Rent or lease:
a Machinery and equipment . . . | 21a |
b Other business property . . . | 21b |

22 Repairs . . . . . . | 22 |
23 Supplies (not included in Part III) | 23 |
24 Taxes . . . . . . | 24 |
25 Travel, meals, and entertainment:
a Travel . . . . . . | 25a |
b Meals and entertainment .
c Enter 20% of line 25b subject to limitations (see Instructions) .
d Subtract line 25c from line 25b | 25d |
26 Utilities (see Instructions) . . | 26 |
27 Wages (less jobs credit) . . . | 27 |
28 Other expenses (list type and amount):
....
....
....
....
....
....
| 28 |

29 Add amounts in columns for lines 8 through 28. These are your **total expenses** . . . . ▶ | 29 |
30 Net profit or **(loss)**. Subtract line 29 from line 7. If a profit, enter here and on Form 1040, line 12, and on Schedule SE, line 2. If a loss, you MUST go on to line 31. (Fiduciaries, see Instructions.) . . . . . . | 30 |
31 If you have a loss, you MUST check the box that describes your investment in this activity (see Instructions) . . | 31a ☐ All investment is at risk.
If you checked 31a, enter the loss on Form 1040, line 12, and Schedule SE, line 2. | 31b ☐ Some investment is not at risk.
If you checked 31b, you MUST attach **Form 6198.**

For Paperwork Reduction Act Notice, see Form 1040 Instructions.

Schedule C (Form 1040) 1989

If you are using Quicken for a partnership or a corporation, you must report asset and liability amounts on the tax return (see figs. D.4 through D.7). You also want to verify that Quicken provides the raw data necessary to complete these lines of the tax return. The easiest approach is

Schedule C (Form 1040) 1989   Page **2**

Part III Cost of Goods Sold and/or Operations (See Instructions.)

32 Inventory at beginning of year. (If different from last year's closing inventory, attach explanation.)	32	
33 Purchases less cost of items withdrawn for personal use	33	
34 Cost of labor. (Do not include salary paid to yourself.)	34	
35 Materials and supplies	35	
36 Other costs	36	
37 Add lines 32 through 36	37	
38 Inventory at end of year	38	
39 Cost of goods sold and/or operations. Subtract line 38 from line 37. Enter the result here and on page 1, line 4	39	

Part IV Principal Business or Professional Activity Codes (*Caution: Codes have been revised. Check your code carefully.*)

Locate the major business category that best describes your activity (for example, Retail Trade, Services, etc.). Within the major category, select the activity code that most closely identifies the business or profession that is the principal source of your sales or receipts. **Enter this 4-digit code on page 1, line B.**
(*Note: If your principal source of income is from farming activities, you should file Schedule F (Form 1040), Farm Income and Expenses.*)

Construction

Code
0018 Operative builders (for own account)

General contractors
0034 Residential building
0059 Nonresidential building
0075 Highway and street construction
3889 Other heavy construction (pipe laying, bridge construction, etc.)

Building trade contractors, including repairs
0232 Plumbing, heating, air conditioning
0257 Painting and paper hanging
0273 Electrical work
0299 Masonry, dry wall, stone, tile
0414 Carpentering and flooring
0430 Roofing, siding, and sheet metal
0455 Concrete work
0885 Other building trade contractors (excavation, glazing, etc.)

Manufacturing, Including Printing and Publishing
0638 Food products and beverages
0653 Textile mill products
0679 Apparel and other textile products
0695 Leather, footwear, handbags, etc.
0810 Furniture and fixtures
0836 Lumber and other wood products
0851 Printing and publishing
0877 Paper and allied products
1032 Stone, clay, and glass products
1057 Primary metal industries
1073 Fabricated metal products
1099 Machinery and machine shops
1115 Electric and electronic equipment
1883 Other manufacturing industries

Mining and Mineral Extraction
1511 Metal mining
1537 Coal mining
1552 Oil and gas
1719 Quarrying and nonmetallic mining

Agricultural Services, Forestry, Fishing
1933 Crop services
1958 Veterinary services, including pets
1974 Livestock breeding
1990 Other animal services
2113 Farm labor and management services
2212 Horticulture and landscaping
2238 Forestry, except logging
0836 Logging
2246 Commercial fishing
2469 Hunting and trapping

Wholesale Trade—Selling Goods to Other Businesses, Etc.

Durable goods, including machinery, equipment, wood, metals, etc.
2618 Selling for your own account
2634 Agent or broker for other firms— more than 50% of gross sales on commission

Nondurable goods, including food, fiber, chemicals, etc.
2659 Selling for your own account

2675 Agent or broker for other firms— more than 50% of gross sales on commission

Retail Trade—Selling Goods to Individuals and Households
3012 Selling door-to-door, by telephone or party plan, or from mobile unit
3038 Catalog or mail order
3053 Vending machine selling

Selling From Showroom, Store, or Other Fixed Location

Food, beverages, and drugs
3079 Eating places (meals or snacks)
3086 Catering services
3095 Drinking places (alcoholic beverages)
3210 Grocery stores (general line)
0612 Bakeries selling at retail
3236 Other food stores (meat, produce, candy, etc.)
3251 Liquor stores
3277 Drug stores

Automotive and service stations
3319 New car dealers (franchised)
3335 Used car dealers
3517 Other automotive dealers (motorcycles, recreational vehicles, etc.)
3533 Tires, accessories, and parts
3558 Gasoline service stations

General merchandise, apparel, and furniture
3715 Variety stores
3731 Other general merchandise stores
3756 Shoe stores
3772 Men's and boys' clothing stores
3913 Women's ready-to-wear stores
3921 Women's accessory and specialty stores and furriers
3939 Family clothing stores
3954 Other apparel and accessory stores
3970 Furniture stores
3996 TV, audio, and electronics
3988 Computer and software stores
4119 Household appliance stores
4317 Other home furnishing stores (china, floor coverings, etc.)
4333 Music and record stores

Building, hardware, and garden supply
4416 Building materials dealers
4432 Paint, glass, and wallpaper stores
4457 Hardware stores
4473 Nurseries and garden supply stores

Other retail stores
4614 Used merchandise and antique stores (except motor vehicle parts)
4630 Gift, novelty, and souvenir shops
4655 Florists
4671 Jewelry stores
4697 Sporting goods and bicycle shops
4812 Boat dealers
4838 Hobby, toy, and game shops
4853 Camera and photo supply stores
4879 Optical goods stores
4895 Luggage and leather goods stores
5017 Book stores, excluding newsstands
5033 Stationery stores
5058 Fabric and needlework stores
5074 Mobile home dealers
5090 Fuel dealers (except gasoline)
5884 Other retail stores

Finance, Insurance, Real Estate, and Related Services
5520 Real estate agents or brokers
5579 Real estate property managers
5710 Subdividers and developers, except cemeteries
5538 Operators and lessors of buildings, including residential
5553 Operators and lessors of other real property
5702 Insurance agents or brokers
5744 Other insurance services
6064 Security brokers and dealers
6080 Commodity contracts brokers and dealers, and security and commodity exchanges
6130 Investment advisors and services
6148 Credit institutions and mortgage bankers
6155 Title abstract offices
5777 Other finance and real estate

Transportation, Communications, Public Utilities, and Related Services
6114 Taxicabs
6312 Bus and limousine transportation
6361 Other highway passenger transportation
6338 Trucking (except trash collection)
6395 Courier or package delivery services
6510 Trash collection without own dump
6536 Public warehousing
6551 Water transportation
6619 Air transportation
6635 Travel agents and tour operators
6650 Other transportation services
6676 Communication services
6692 Utilities, including dumps, snowplowing, road cleaning, etc.

Services (Personal, Professional, and Business Services)

Hotels and other lodging places
7096 Hotels, motels, and tourist homes
7211 Rooming and boarding houses
7237 Camps and camping parks

Laundry and cleaning services
7419 Coin-operated laundries and dry cleaning
7435 Other laundry, dry cleaning, and garment services
7450 Carpet and upholstery cleaning
7476 Janitorial and related services (building, house, and window cleaning)

Business and/or personal services
7617 Legal services (or lawyer)
7633 Income tax preparation
7658 Accounting and bookkeeping
7518 Engineering services
7682 Architectural services
7708 Surveying services
7245 Management services
7260 Public relations
7286 Consulting services
7716 Advertising, except direct mail
7732 Employment agencies and personnel supply
7799 Consumer credit reporting and collection services

7856 Mailing, reproduction, commercial art and photography, and stenographic services
7872 Computer programming, processing, data preparation, and related services
7922 Computer repair, maintenance, and leasing
7773 Equipment rental and leasing (except computer or automotive)
7914 Investigative and protective services
7880 Other business services

Personal services
8110 Beauty shops (or beautician)
8318 Barber shop (or barber)
8334 Photographic portrait studios
8532 Funeral services and crematories
8714 Child day care
8730 Teaching or tutoring
8755 Counseling (except health practitioners)
8771 Ministers and chaplains
6882 Other personal services

Automotive services
8813 Automotive rental or leasing, without driver
8839 Parking, except valet
8953 Automotive repairs, general and specialized
8896 Other automotive services (wash, towing, etc.)

Miscellaneous repair, except computers
9019 TV and audio equipment repair
9035 Other electrical equipment repair
9050 Reupholstery and furniture repair
2881 Other equipment repair

Medical and health services
9217 Offices and clinics of medical doctors (MDs)
9233 Offices and clinics of dentists
9258 Osteopathic physicians and surgeons
9241 Podiatrists
9274 Chiropractors
9290 Optometrists
9415 Registered and practical nurses
9431 Other health practitioners
9456 Medical and dental laboratories
9472 Nursing and personal care facilities
9886 Other health services

Amusement and recreational services
8557 Physical fitness facilities
9597 Motion picture and video production
9688 Motion picture and tape distribution and allied services
9613 Videotape rental
9639 Motion picture theaters
9670 Bowling centers
9696 Professional sports and racing, including promoters and managers
9811 Theatrical performers, musicians, agents, producers, and related services
9837 Other amusement and recreational services

8888 Unable to classify

Fig. D.3 cont.

Schedule C, Form 1040.

---

probably to set up accounts to track each asset and liability that appears on the tax return. Another approach is to use accounts that can be combined to calculate the total asset or liability figure that needs to be entered on the tax return.

Fig. D.4.

The 1065 form indicates which income and expense categories partnerships use to report profits and losses.

Form **1065**	**U.S. Partnership Return of Income**	OMB No. 1545 0099
Department of the Treasury Internal Revenue Service	▶ See separate instructions.	**1989**

For calendar year 1989, or fiscal year beginning _____, 1989, and ending _____ 19 ___

A Principal business activity

Retail

B Principal product or service

Books

C Business code number

5942

Name

10-9876543   DEC89   D71

AbleBee Book Store
334 WEST MAIN STREET
ANYTOWN   MD   20904

I
R
S

D Employer identification number
10-9876543

E Date business started
10/1/78

F Total assets (see Specific instructions)
$ *45,691*

G Check applicable boxes: (1) ☐ Initial return   (2) ☐ Final return   (3) ☐ Change in address   (4) ☐ Amended return

H Enter number of partners in this partnership . . . . ▶ *2*

I Check this box if this is a limited partnership . . . . ▶ ☐

J Check this box if any partners in the partnership are also partnerships . . . . ▶ ☐

K Check this box if this partnership is a partner in another partnership . . . . ▶ ☐

See page 4, items L through T, for Additional Information Required.

Designation of Tax Matters Partner (See instructions.)

Enter below the general partner designated as the tax matters partner (TMP) for the tax year of this return:

Name of designated TMP ▶

Identifying number of TMP ▶

Address of designated TMP ▶

Caution: *Include only trade or business income and expenses on lines 1a–21 below. See the instructions for more information.*

Income

1a	Gross receipts or sales	1a *409,465*	
b	Less returns and allowances	1b *3,365*	1c *406,100*
2	Cost of goods sold and/or operations (Schedule A, line 7)		2 *267,641*
3	Gross profit (subtract line 2 from line 1c)		3 *138,459*
4	Ordinary income (loss) from other partnerships and fiduciaries (attach schedule)		4
5	Net farm profit (loss) (attach Schedule F (Form 1040))		5
6	Net gain (loss) (Form 4797, Part II, line 18)		6
7	Other income (loss)		7 *559*
8	**Total income (loss)** (combine lines 3 through 7)		8 *139,018*

Deductions (see instructions for limitations)

9a	Salaries and wages (other than to partners)	9a *29,350*	
b	Less jobs credit	9b	9c *29,350*
10	Guaranteed payments to partners		10 *25,000*
11	Rent		11 *18,000*
12	Interest (see instructions)		12 *451*
13	Taxes		13 *350*
14	Bad debts		14 *250*
15	Repairs		15 *1,125*
16a	Depreciation (attach Form 4562) (see instructions)	16a *1,174*	
b	Less depreciation reported on Schedule A and elsewhere on return	16b	16c *1,174*
17	Depletion (**Do not deduct oil and gas depletion.**)		17
18a	Retirement plans, etc.		18a
b	Employee benefit programs		18b
19	Other deductions (attach schedule)		19 *13,948*
20	**Total deductions** (add lines 9c through 19)		20 *89,648*
21	Ordinary income (loss) from trade or business activities (subtract line 20 from line 8)		21 *49,370*

Please Sign Here

Under penalties of perjury, I declare that I have examined this return, including accompanying schedules and statements, and to the best of my knowledge and belief, it is true, correct, and complete. Declaration of preparer (other than general partner) is based on all information of which preparer has any knowledge.

▶ *Frank W. Able*
Signature of general partner

▶ Date *4/3/90*

Paid Preparer's Use Only

Preparer's signature ▶	Date	Check if self-employed ▶ ☐	Preparer's social security no.
Firm's name (or yours if self-employed) ▶ and address		E.I. No. ▶	
		ZIP code ▶	

For Paperwork Reduction Act Notice, see page 1 of separate instructions.   Form **1065** (1989)

This appendix contains copies of the 1989 federal income tax forms for businesses (see figs. D.1 through D.7). You can use these forms to build your lists of required categories and accounts. The forms, however, change almost every year. Unfortunately—and thank your congressman for this—the forms are not finalized until late in the year. You cannot

Form 1065 (1989)   Page 2

Schedule A Cost of Goods Sold and/or Operations

1	Inventory at beginning of year	1	18,125
2	Purchases less cost of items withdrawn for personal use	2	268,741
3	Cost of labor	3	
4a	Additional section 263A costs (see instructions—attach schedule)	4a	
b	Other costs (attach schedule)	4b	
5	Total (add lines 1 through 4b)	5	286,866
6	Inventory at end of year	6	19,225
7	Cost of goods sold (subtract line 6 from line 5). Enter here and on page 1, line 2	7	267,641

8a Check all methods used for valuing closing inventory:

    (i) ☐ Cost

    (ii) ☑ Lower of cost or market as described in Regulations section 1.471-4

    (iii) ☐ Writedown of "subnormal" goods as described in Regulations section 1.471-2(c)

    (iv) ☐ Other (specify method used and attach explanation) ▶ . . . . ▶ ☐

    b Check if the LIFO inventory method was adopted this tax year for any goods (if checked, attach Form 970) . . . . ▶ ☐

    c Do the rules of section 263A (with respect to property produced or acquired for resale) apply to the partnership? . . . ☐ Yes ☑ No

    d Was there any change in determining quantities, cost, or valuations between opening and closing inventory? . . . . ☐ Yes ☑ No

    If "Yes," attach explanation.

Schedule H Income (Loss) From Rental Real Estate Activities

1 In the space provided below, show the kind and location of each rental property. Attach a schedule if more space is needed.

    Property A ....

    Property B ....

    Property C

Rental Real Estate Income		Properties			Totals (add columns A, B, C, and amounts from any attached schedules)
		A	B	C	
2 Gross income	2				2
Rental Real Estate Expenses					
3 Advertising	3				
4 Auto and travel	4				
5 Cleaning and maintenance . .	5				
6 Commissions	6				
7 Insurance	7				
8 Legal and other professional fees	8				
9 Interest	9				
10 Repairs	10				
11 Taxes	11				
12 Utilities	12				
13 Wages and salaries	13				
14 Depreciation from Form 4562 .	14				
15 Other (list) ▶	15				
16 Total expenses. Add lines 3 through 15	16				16
17 Net income (loss) from rental real estate activities. Subtract line 16 from line 2. Enter net income (loss) from the total column on Schedule K, line 2 .	17				17

Fig. D.4. cont.

Form 1065.

know with certainty which income and expense categories or which asset and liability accounts you should be using until the year is almost over. The 1989 versions of these income tax forms, for example, appeared in November, 1989. The practical approach is to use the categories and accounts indicated by the preceding year and to make adjustments when the new forms come out.

Fig. D.4. cont.

Form 1065.

Form 1065 (1989)			Page 3
Schedule K Partners' Shares of Income, Credits, Deductions, Etc.			

	(a) Distributive share items		(b) Total amount
Income (Loss)	1 Ordinary income (loss) from trade or business activities (page 1, line 21)	**1**	49,370
	2 Net income (loss) from rental real estate activities (Schedule H, line 17)	**2**	
	3a Gross income from other rental activities **3a**		
	b Less expenses (attach schedule) **3b**		
	c Net income (loss) from other rental activities	**3c**	
	4 Portfolio income (loss) (see instructions):		
	a Interest income.	**4a**	
	b Dividend income	**4b**	150
	c Royalty income	**4c**	
	d Net short-term capital gain (loss) (Schedule D, line 4)	**4d**	100
	e Net long-term capital gain (loss) (Schedule D, line 9)	**4e**	200
	f Other portfolio income (loss) (attach schedule)	**4f**	
	5 Guaranteed payments to partners	**5**	25,000
	6 Net gain (loss) under section 1231 (other than due to casualty or theft) (see instructions) .	**6**	
	7 Other income (loss) (attach schedule)	**7**	
Deduc-tions	8 Charitable contributions (attach list)	**8**	650
	9 Section 179 expense deduction (attach Form 4562)	**9**	
	10 Deductions related to portfolio income (do not include investment interest expense) . . .	**10**	
	11 Other deductions (attach schedule)	**11**	
Credits	12a Credit for income tax withheld	**12a**	
	b Low-income housing credit: (1) Partnerships to which section 42(j)(5) applies	**12b(1)**	
	(2) Other than on line 12b(1).	**12b(2)**	
	c Qualified rehabilitation expenditures related to rental real estate activities (attach schedule)	**12c**	
	d Credits (other than credits shown on lines 12b and 12c) related to rental real estate		
	activities (attach schedule)	**12d**	
	e Credits related to other rental activities (see instructions) (attach schedule)	**12e**	
	13 Other credits and expenditures (attach schedule)	**13**	
Self-Employ-ment	14a Net earnings (loss) from self-employment	**14a**	74,370
	b Gross farming or fishing income.	**14b**	
	c Gross nonfarm income	**14c**	
Adjustments and Tax Preference Items	15a Accelerated depreciation of real property placed in service before 1987	**15a**	
	b Accelerated depreciation of leased personal property placed in service before 1987 . . .	**15b**	
	c Depreciation adjustment on property placed in service after 1986	**15c**	
	d Depletion (other than oil and gas)	**15d**	
	e (1) Gross income from oil, gas, and geothermal properties	**15e(1)**	
	(2) Deductions allocable to oil, gas, and geothermal properties	**15e(2)**	
	f Other adjustments and tax preference items (attach schedule)	**15f**	
Invest-ment Interest	16a Interest expense on investment debts.	**16a**	
	b (1) Investment income included on lines 4a through 4f above	**16b(1)**	450
	(2) Investment expenses included on line 10 above	**16b(2)**	
Foreign Taxes	17a Type of income		
	b Foreign country or U.S. possession		
	c Total gross income from sources outside the U.S. (attach schedule)	**17c**	
	d Total applicable deductions and losses (attach schedule)	**17d**	
	e Total foreign taxes (check one): ▶ ☐ Paid ☐ Accrued	**17e**	
	f Reduction in taxes available for credit (attach schedule)	**17f**	
	g Other foreign tax information (attach schedule)	**17g**	
Other	18a Total expenditures to which a section 59(e) election may apply (attach schedule)	**18a**	
	b Attach schedule for other items and amounts not reported above (see instructions) . . .		
Analysis	19a Total distributive income/payment items (combine lines 1 through 7 above)	**19a**	
	b Analysis by type of partner:		

	(a) Corporate	(b) Individual		(c) Partnership	(d) Exempt organization	(e) Nominee/Other
		i. Active	ii. Passive			
1. General partners		74,820				
2. Limited partners						

Sole proprietors must consider one other thing: you actually may need to complete more than one Schedule C form. You cannot aggregate a series of dissimilar businesses and report the consolidated results on one Schedule C. For example, if you own a tavern, practice law, and run a small manufacturing business, you must complete three Schedule C forms: one

Fig. D.4. cont.

Form 1065.

Form 1065 (1989) Page 4

Schedule L Balance Sheets

(See the instructions for Question N on page 8 of the Instructions before completing Schedules L and M.)

Assets	Beginning of tax year (a)	(b)	End of tax year (c)	(d)
1 Cash		3,455		4,650
2 Trade notes and accounts receivable	7,150		10,990	
a Less allowance for bad debts		7,150		10,990
3 Inventories		18,125		19,225
4a U.S. government obligations				
b Tax-exempt securities		1,000		1,000
5 Other current assets (attach schedule)				
6 Mortgage and real estate loans				
7 Other investments (attach schedule)		1,000		–
8a Buildings and other depreciable assets	15,000		15,000	
b Less accumulated depreciation	4,000	11,000	5,174	9,826
9a Depletable assets				
b Less accumulated depletion				
10 Land (net of any amortization)				
11a Intangible assets (amortizable only)				
b Less accumulated amortization				
12 Other assets (attach schedule)				
13 **Total assets**		41,730		45,691
Liabilities and Capital				
14 Accounts payable		10,180		10,462
15 Mortgages, notes, bonds payable in less than 1 year		4,000		3,600
16 Other current liabilities (attach schedule)				
17 All nonrecourse loans				
18 Mortgages, notes, bonds payable in 1 year or more		–		7,739
19 Other liabilities (attach schedule)				
20 Partners' capital accounts		27,550		23,890
21 **Total** liabilities and capital		41,730		45,691

Schedule M Reconciliation of Partners' Capital Accounts

(Show reconciliation of each partner's capital account on Schedule K-1 (Form 1065), Item K.)

(a) Partners' capital accounts at beginning of year	(b) Capital contributed during year	(c) Income (loss) from lines 1, 2, 3c, and 4 of Sch. K	(d) Income not included in column (c), plus nontaxable income	(e) Losses not included in column (c), plus unallowable deductions	(f) Withdrawals and distributions	(g) Partners' capital accounts at end of year (combine columns (a) through (f))
27,550		49,820	50	(650)	(52,880)	23,890

Additional Information Required (continued from page 1)

	Yes	No
L Check accounting method: (1) ☐ Cash (2) ☑ Accrual (3) ☐ Other		
M Check this box if this is a partnership subject to the consolidated partnership audit procedures of sections 6221 through 6233 (see instructions) ▶ ☐		
N Does the partnership meet **all** the requirements shown in the Instructions for **Question N**?		✓
O Was there a distribution of property or a transfer (for example, by sale or death) of a partnership interest during the tax year?		✓
If "Yes," see the instructions concerning an election to adjust the basis of the partnership's assets under section 754.		
P Does the partnership have any foreign partners?		✓
Q At any time during the tax year, did the partnership have an interest in or a signature or other authority over a financial account in a foreign country (such as a bank account, securities account, or other financial account)? (See the instructions for exceptions and filing requirements for form TD F 90-22.1.)		✓
If "Yes," write the name of the foreign country. ▶		
R Was the partnership the grantor of, or transferor to, a foreign trust which existed during the current tax year, whether or not the partnership or any partner has any beneficial interest in it? If "Yes," you may have to file Forms 3520, 3520-A, or 926		✓
S Check this box if the partnership has filed or is required to file **Form 8264**, Application for Registration of a Tax Shelter ▶ ☐		
T Check this box if the partnership is a publicly traded partnership as defined in section 469(k)(2) ▶ ☐		

for the tavern, one for the legal practice, and still another for the manufacturing firm. Quicken can handle this situation, but you need to account for each business that needs a separate Schedule C in its own account group. (Chapter 2 describes how to set up and select different account groups.)

Fig. D.4. cont.

Form 1065.

SCHEDULE D (Form 1065)	Capital Gains and Losses	OMB No. 1545-0099
Department of the Treasury Internal Revenue Service	▶ Attach to Form 1065.	1989

Name of partnership: AbleBee Book Store

Employer identification number: 10-9876543

Part I Short-Term Capital Gains and Losses—Assets held one year or less

(a) Description of property (Example, 100 shares 7% preferred of "Z" Co.)	(b) Date acquired (mo., day, yr.)	(c) Date sold (mo., day, yr.)	(d) Sales price (see instructions)	(e) Cost or other basis (see instructions)	(f) Gain (loss) (d) minus (e)
1 XYZ Chemical Co. 20 shares common	12/5/88	5/1/89	600	500	100

2 Short-term capital gain from installment sales from Form 6252, line 22 or 30

3 Partnership's share of net short-term capital gain (loss), including specially allocated short-term capital gains (losses), from other partnerships and from fiduciaries

4 Net short-term capital gain (loss)—Combine lines 1 through 3. Enter each partner's share on Schedule K-1 (Form 1065), line 4d ... **100**

Part II Long-Term Capital Gains and Losses—Assets held more than one year

| 5 ABC Motors Inc. 10 shares common | 12/7/87 | 6/5/89 | 700 | 500 | 200 |

6 Long-term capital gain from installment sales from Form 6252, line 22 or 30

7 Partnership's share of net long-term capital gain (loss), including specially allocated long-term capital gains (losses), from other partnerships and from fiduciaries

8 Capital gain distributions

9 Net long-term capital gain (loss)—Combine lines 5 through 8. Enter each partner's share on Schedule K-1 (Form 1065), line 4e ... **200**

General Instructions

(Section references are to the Internal Revenue Code.)

Caution: At the time these instructions were printed, Congress was considering tax legislation that would change the treatment of certain dispositions of property that qualify as long-term capital gains. If this legislation is passed, we will take the steps necessary to publicize the final rules.

Purpose of Schedule.—Use Schedule D (Form 1065) to report sales or exchanges of capital assets, except capital gains (losses) that are specially allocated to any partners.

Specially allocated capital gains (losses) received by the partnership as a partner in other partnerships and from fiduciaries are to be entered on Schedule D, line 3 or 7, whichever applies. Capital gains (losses) of the partnership that are specially allocated to partners should be entered directly on line 4d of Schedules K and K-1 or line 4e of Schedules K and K-1, whichever applies. Do not include these amounts on Schedule D. See **How Income is Shared Among Partners** in the General Instructions for Schedules K and K-1 of the Instructions for Form 1065 for more information.

General Information.—To report sales or exchanges of property other than capital assets, including the sale or exchange of

property used in a trade or business and involuntary conversions (other than casualties and thefts), see **Form 4797**, Sales of Business Property, and related instructions.

For amounts received from an installment sale, the holding period rule in effect in the year of sale will determine the treatment of the amounts received as long-term or short-term capital gain.

Report every sale or exchange of property in detail, even though there is no gain or loss.

For more information, see **Publication 544**, Sales and Other Dispositions of Assets.

Note: For information on liquidations of corporations, see **Publication 542**, Tax Information on Corporations, and Publication 544.

What Are Capital Assets?—Each item of property the partnership held (whether or not connected with its trade or business) is a capital asset **except**:

1. Assets that can be inventoried or property held mainly for sale to customers.

2. Depreciable or real property used in the trade or business.

3. Certain copyrights; literary, musical, or artistic compositions; letters or memorandums; or similar property.

4. Accounts or notes receivable acquired in the ordinary course of trade or business for services rendered or from the sale of property described in 1 above.

5. A U.S. Government publication (including the Congressional Record) received from the Government or any of its agencies in a manner other than by buying it at the price offered for public sale, which is held by a taxpayer who received the publication or by a second taxpayer in whose hands the basis of the publication is determined, for purposes of determining gain from a sale or exchange, by referring to its basis in the hands of the first taxpayer.

Items for Special Treatment and Special Cases.—The following items may require special treatment:

• Transactions by a securities dealer.

• Bonds and other debt instruments.

• Certain real estate subdivided for sale that may be considered a capital asset.

• Gain on the sale of depreciable property to a more than 50% owned entity, or to a trust in which the partnership is a beneficiary, is treated as ordinary gain.

• Gain on disposition of stock in an Interest-Charge Domestic International Sales Corporation or a Foreign Sales Corporation.

For Paperwork Reduction Act Notice, see the instructions for Form 1065. Schedule D (Form 1065) 1989

Tips for Lawyers, Consultants, and Other Professionals

Probably the simplest kind of business for which to perform accounting is a professional service business. You should be able to run your accounting records out of a checkbook. As long you record an income category when

Form 1120-A
Department of the Treasury
Internal Revenue Service

U.S. Corporation Short-Form Income Tax Return
Instructions are separate. See them to make sure you qualify to file Form 1120-A.
For calendar year 1989 or tax year beginning .... , 1989, ending .... , 19 .....

OMB No. 1545-0890

1989

A Check this box if corp. is a personal service corp. (as defined in Temp. Regs sec. 1.441-4T— see instructions) ▶ ☐	Use IRS label. Otherwise, please print or type.

Name
10-2134657   DEC 89   D89   5995
ROSE FLOWER SHOP, INC.
38 SUPERIOR LANE
FAIR CITY, MD   20715

B Employer identification number
10-2134657
C Date incorporated
7-1-82
D Total assets (see Specific Instructions)
$ 65,987

E Check applicable boxes: (1) ☐ Initial return (2) ☐ Change in address
F Check method of accounting: (1) ☐ Cash (2) ☑ Accrual (3) ☐ Other (specify) ▶

Income

1a Gross receipts or sales **248,000** b Less returns and allowances **7,500** c Balance ▶	1c	240,500
2 Cost of goods sold and/or operations (see instructions)	2	144,000
3 Gross profit (line 1c less line 2)	3	96,500
4 Domestic corporation dividends subject to the 70% deduction	4	
5 Interest	5	942
6 Gross rents	6	
7 Gross royalties	7	
8 Capital gain net income (attach Schedule D (Form 1120))	8	
9 Net gain or (loss) from Form 4797, Part II, line 18 (attach Form 4797)	9	
10 Other income (see instructions)	10	
11 Total income—Add lines 3 through 10 ▶	11	97,442

Deductions (See instructions for limitations on deductions.)

12 Compensation of officers (see instructions)	12	23,000
13a Salaries and wages **24,320** b Less jobs credit c Balance ▶	13c	24,320
14 Repairs	14	
15 Bad debts	15	
16 Rents	16	6,000
17 Taxes	17	3,320
18 Interest	18	1,340
19 Contributions (see instructions for 10% limitation)	19	1,820
20 Depreciation (attach Form 4562)	20	
21 Less depreciation claimed elsewhere on return	21a	21b
22 Other deductions (attach schedule) *(Advertising)*	22	3,000
23 Total deductions—Add lines 12 through 22 ▶	23	62,800
24 Taxable income before net operating loss deduction and special deductions (line 11 less line 23)	24	34,642
25 Less: a Net operating loss deduction (see instructions) 25a		
b Special deductions (see instructions) 25b	25c	
26 Taxable income—Line 24 less line 25c	26	34,642
27 Total tax (Part I, line 7)	27	5,196

Tax and Payments

28 Payments:		
a 1988 overpayment credited to 1989 28a		
b 1989 estimated tax payments 28b **6,000**		
c Less 1989 refund applied for on Form 4466 28c ( ) Bal ▶ 28d **6,000**		
e Tax deposited with Form 7004 28e		
f Credit from regulated investment companies (attach Form 2439) 28f		
g Credit for Federal tax on fuels (attach Form 4136) 28g		
h Total payments—Add lines 28d through 28g	28h	6,000
29 Enter any penalty for underpayment of estimated tax—Check ▶ ☐ if Form 2220 is attached	29	
30 Tax due—If the total of lines 27 and 29 is larger than line 28h, enter amount owed	30	
31 Overpayment—If line 28h is larger than the total of lines 27 and 29, enter amount overpaid	31	804
32 Enter amount of line 31 you want: Credited to 1990 estimated tax ▶ **804** Refunded ▶	32	

Please Sign Here
Under penalties of perjury, I declare that I have examined this return, including accompanying schedules and statements, and to the best of my knowledge and belief, it is true, correct, and complete. Declaration of preparer (other than taxpayer) is based on all information of which preparer has any knowledge.

George Rose   2/14/90   *President*
Signature of officer   Date   Title

Paid Preparer's Use Only
Preparer's signature ▶   Date   Check if self-employed ☐   Preparer's social security number
Firm's name (or yours if self-employed) and address ▶   E.I. No. ▶   ZIP code ▶

For Paperwork Reduction Act Notice, see page 1 of the instructions.   Form **1120-A** (1989)

Fig. D.5.

The 1120-A form indicates which income and expense categories small corporations should use to report profits and losses.

you make deposits and an expense category when you write checks or withdraw money, you can produce helpful financial reports that enable you to gauge your performance.

If you sell services, think about your billing. Billing produces what is probably your other major asset besides cash—receivables—in addition to determining your cash inflow.

Fig. D.5. cont.

Form 1120-A

Form 1120-A (1989)   Page **2**

Part I   Tax Computation

1	Income tax (see instructions to figure the tax) Check this box if the corp. is a qualified personal service corp. (see instructions). ▶ ☐	**1** 5,196
2a	General business credit. Check if from ☐ Form 3800 ☐ Form 3468 ☐ Form 5884 ☐ Form 6478 ☐ Form 6765 ☐ Form 8586 **2a**	
b	Credit for prior year minimum tax (attach Form 8801) **2b**	
3	Total credits—Add lines 2a and 2b	**3**
4	Line 1 less line 3	**4** 5,196
5	Recapture taxes. Check if from ☐ Form 4255 ☐ Form 8611	**5**
6	Alternative minimum tax (attach Form 4626)	**6**
7	Total tax—Add lines 4 through 6. Enter here and on line 27, page 1 . . .	**7** 5,196

Additional Information (See instruction F.)

G   Refer to the list in the instructions and state the principal:

(1) Business activity code no. ▶ 5995

(2) Business activity ▶ .... *Flower Shop*

(3) Product or service ▶ .... *Flowers*

H   Did any individual, partnership, estate, or trust at the end of the tax year own, directly or indirectly, 50% or more of the corporation's voting stock? (For rules of attribution, see section 267(c).)   Yes ☐   No ☑
If "Yes," attach schedule showing name, address, and identifying number.

I   Enter the amount of tax-exempt interest received or accrued during the tax year . . . . ▶ |$ – 0 –

J   (1) If an amount for cost of goods sold and/or operations is entered on line 2, page 1, complete (a) through (c):

(a) Purchases (see instructions) . .		134,014
(b) Additional sec. 263A costs (see instructions —attach schedule) . .		
(c) Other costs (attach schedule) . .		9,466

(2) Do the rules of section 263A (with respect to property produced or acquired for resale) apply to the corporation? . . . Yes ☐   No ☑

K   At any time during the tax year, did you have an interest in or a signature or other authority over a financial account in a foreign country (such as a bank account, securities account, or other financial account)? (See instruction F for filing requirements for form TD F 90-22.1.) . . . . Yes ☐   No ☑
If "Yes," enter the name of the foreign country ▶ ....

L   Enter amount of cash distributions and the book value of property (other than cash) distributions made in this tax year ▶ |$ – 0 –

Part II   Balance Sheets

		(a) Beginning of tax year	(b) End of tax year
1	Cash	20,540	18,498
2a	Trade notes and accounts receivable		
b	Less allowance for bad debts	( )	( )
3	Inventories	2,530	2,010
4	U.S. government obligations	13,807	45,479
5	Tax-exempt securities (see instructions) . . .		
6	Other current assets (attach schedule) . .		
7	Loans to stockholders		
8	Mortgage and real estate loans		
9a	Depreciable, depletable, and intangible assets		
b	Less accumulated depreciation, depletion, and amortization . .	( )	( )
10	Land (net of any amortization)		
11	Other assets (attach schedule)		
12	Total assets	36,877	65,987
13	Accounts payable	6,415	6,079
14	Other current liabilities (attach schedule)		
15	Loans from stockholders		
16	Mortgages, notes, bonds payable		
17	Other liabilities (attach schedule)		
18	Capital stock (preferred and common stock)	20,000	20,000
19	Paid-in or capital surplus		
20	Retained earnings	10,462	39,908
21	Less cost of treasury stock	( )	( )
22	Total liabilities and stockholders' equity	36,877	65,987

(Left margin labels: Assets; Liabilities and Stockholders' Equity)

Part III   Reconciliation of Income per Books With Income per Return (Must be completed by all filers)

1	Net income per books	29,446	5	Income recorded on books this year not included on this return (itemize) ....
2	Federal income tax	5,196		
3	Income subject to tax not recorded on books this year (itemize)		6	Deductions on this return not charged against book income this year (itemize) ....
4	Expenses recorded on books this year not deducted on this return (itemize)		7	Income (line 24, page 1). Enter the sum of lines 1 through 4 less the sum of lines 5 and 6 34,642

If your volumes are low—in the number of invoices and clients—you probably can perform billing and collecting by using a combination of manual techniques and Quicken. You may be able to track the hours you spend with various clients in an appointment calendar.

Form **1120S**
Department of the Treasury
Internal Revenue Service

U.S. Income Tax Return for an S Corporation
For the calendar year 1989, or tax year beginning .... 1989, ending .... 19 ....
► For Paperwork Reduction Act Notice, see page 1 of separate instructions.

OMB No. 1545-0130
1989

A Date of election as an S corporation
12-1-88

B Business code no. (see Specific Instructions)
5008

Use IRS label. Otherwise, please print or type.

10-4487965   DEC89   D74   3070
ESTEX, INC.
482 WINSTON ST.
METRO CITY   OH   43705

C Employer Identification number

D Date incorporated
3-1-72

E Total assets (see Specific Instructions)
$ *825,714*

F Check applicable boxes: (1) ☑ Initial return (2) ☐ Final return (3) ☐ Change in address (4) ☐ Amended return

G Check this box if this is an S corporation subject to the consolidated audit procedures of sections 6241 through 6245 (see instructions before checking this box) ► ☑

H Enter number of shareholders in the corporation at end of the tax year . . . . ► *6*

Caution: Include **only** trade or business income and expenses on lines 1a through 21. See the instructions for more information.

Income

1a Gross receipts or sales *1,545,700* b Less returns and allowances *21,000* c Bal ►	1c	*1,524,700*
2 Cost of goods sold and/or operations (Schedule A, line 7)	2	*954,700*
3 Gross profit (subtract line 2 from line 1c)	3	*570,000*
4 Net gain (or loss) from Form 4797, line 18 (see instructions)	4	*-0-*
5 Other income (see instructions—attach schedule)	5	*-0-*
6 Total income (loss)—Combine lines 3, 4, and 5 and enter here . . . . . . ►	6	*570,000*

Deductions (See instructions for limitations.)

7 Compensation of officers	7	*170,000*
8a Salaries and wages *144,000* b Less jobs credit *6,000* c Bal ►	8c	*138,000*
9 Repairs	9	*800*
10 Bad debts (see instructions)	10	*1,600*
11 Rents	11	*9,200*
12 Taxes	12	*15,000*
13 Interest (see instructions)	13	*24,200*
14a Depreciation (attach Form 4562) (see instructions) . . . 14a *5,200*		
b Depreciation reported on Schedule A and elsewhere on return . . 14b *-0-*		
c Subtract line 14b from line 14a	14c	*5,200*
15 Depletion (**Do not deduct oil and gas depletion. See instructions.**)	15	*-0-*
16 Advertising	16	*8,700*
17 Pension, profit-sharing, etc. plans	17	*-0-*
18 Employee benefit programs	18	*-0-*
19 Other deductions (attach schedule)	19	*78,300*
20 Total deductions—Add lines 7 through 19 and enter here . . . . ►	20	*451,000*
21 Ordinary income (loss) from trade or business activities—Subtract line 20 from line 6 .	21	*119,000*

Tax and Payments

22 Tax:		
a Excess net passive income tax (attach schedule) 22a		
b Tax from Schedule D (Form 1120S) 22b		
c Add lines 22a and 22b (see instructions for additional taxes)	22c	*-0-*
23 Payments:		
a Tax deposited with Form 7004 . . . . 23a		
b Credit for Federal tax on fuels (attach Form 4136) 23b		
c Add lines 23a and 23b	23c	*-0-*
24 Tax due—If line 22c is larger than line 23c, enter amount owed. See instructions for Paying the Tax	24	*-0-*
25 Overpayment—If line 23c is larger than line 22c, enter amount overpaid . . . . . ►	25	*-0-*

Under penalties of perjury, I declare that I have examined this return, including accompanying schedules and statements, and to the best of my knowledge and belief, it is true, correct, and complete. Declaration of preparer (other than taxpayer) is based on all information of which preparer has any knowledge.

Please Sign Here
► *John H. Anders*
Signature of officer

Date *3-10-90*

Title *President*

Paid Preparer's Use Only

Preparer's signature ►

Date

Check if self-employed ☐

Preparer's social security number

Firm's name (or yours if self-employed) and address ►

E.I. No. ►

ZIP code ►

Form **1120S** (1989)

Fig. D.6.

The 1120S form indicates which expense categories S corporations should use to report profits and losses.

If your volumes are high, you need a fast way to accumulate the amounts your clients owe you, to aggregate these amounts, and to produce an invoice. You also need an easy way to track outstanding invoices. If you are not happy with the way your current billing and receivables tracking

Fig. D.6. cont.

Form 1120S.

Form 1120S (1989)   Page 2

Schedule A Cost of Goods Sold and/or Operations (See instructions for Schedule A.)

1	Inventory at beginning of year	1	126,000
2	Purchases	2	1,127,100
3	Cost of labor	3	-0-
4a	Additional section 263A costs (attach schedule) (see instructions)	4a	-0-
b	Other costs (attach schedule)	4b	-0-
5	Total—Add lines 1 through 4b	5	1,253,100
6	Inventory at end of year	6	298,400
7	Cost of goods sold and/or operations—Subtract line 6 from line 5. Enter here and on line 2, page 1	7	954,700

8a Check all methods used for valuing closing inventory:
    (i) ☐ Cost
    (ii) ☑ Lower of cost or market as described in Regulations section 1.471-4
    (iii) ☐ Writedown of "subnormal" goods as described in Regulations section 1.471-2(c)
    (iv) ☐ Other (specify method used and attach explanation) ▶
  b Check this box if the LIFO inventory method was adopted this tax year for any goods (if checked, attach Form 970) . . . ▶ ☐
  c If the LIFO inventory method was used for this tax year, enter percentage (or amounts) of closing inventory computed under LIFO . . . . | 8c |
  d Do the rules of section 263A (with respect to property produced or acquired for resale) apply to the corporation? . . . ☐ Yes ☑ No
  e Was there any change in determining quantities, cost, or valuations between opening and closing inventory? . . . . ☐ Yes ☑ No
    If "Yes," attach explanation.

Additional Information Required (continued from page 1)

		Yes	No
I	Did you at the end of the tax year own, directly or indirectly, 50% or more of the voting stock of a domestic corporation? For rules of attribution, see section 267(c). If "Yes," attach a schedule showing: (1) name, address, and employer identification number; and (2) percentage owned.		✔
J	Refer to the listing of business activity codes at the end of the Instructions for Form 1120S and state your principal (1) Business activity ▶ *5008 – Distributor* (2) Product or service ▶ *Heavy equipment*		
K	Were you a member of a controlled group subject to the provisions of section 1561?		✔
L	At any time during the tax year, did you have an interest in or a signature or other authority over a financial account in a foreign country (such as a bank account, securities account, or other financial account)? (See instructions for exceptions and filing requirements for form TD F 90-22.1.)		✔
	If "Yes," enter the name of the foreign country ▶		
M	Were you the grantor of, or transferor to, a foreign trust which existed during the current tax year, whether or not you have any beneficial interest in it? If "Yes," you may have to file Form 3520, 3520-A, or 926		✔
N	During this tax year did you maintain any part of your accounting/tax records on a computerized system?		✔
O	Check method of accounting: (1) ☐ Cash (2) ☑ Accrual (3) ☐ Other (specify) ▶		
P	Check this box if the S corporation has filed or is required to file **Form 8264**, Application for Registration of a Tax Shelter ▶ ☐		
Q	Check this box if the corporation issued publicly offered debt instruments with original issue discount ▶ ☐		
	If so, the corporation may have to file **Form 8281**, Information Return for Publicly Offered Original Issue Discount Instruments.		
R	If the corporation: (1) filed its election to be an S corporation after December 31, 1986, (2) was a C corporation prior to making the election, and (3) at the beginning of the tax year had net unrealized built-in gain as defined in section 1374(d)(1), enter the net unrealized built-in gain (see instructions) ▶ *37,200*		

Designation of Tax Matters Person (See instructions.)

Enter below the shareholder designated as the tax matters person (TMP) for the tax year of this return:

Name of designated TMP ▶	*John H. Anders*	Identifying number of TMP ▶	*458 - 00 - 0327*
Address of designated TMP ▶	*4340 Holmes Parkway* *Metro City, OH 43704*		

works, consider acquiring one of the stand-alone billing packages available. One popular package is Timeslips III, which provides a convenient way to record the hours you spend on a client's behalf, account for the out-of-pocket expenses you incur, and generate invoices at the end of the month.

Form 1120S (1989)   Page **3**

Schedule K	Shareholders' Shares of Income, Credits, Deductions, Etc. (See Instructions.)		
	(a) Pro rata share items		(b) Total amount

Income (Loss) and Deductions

1	Ordinary income (loss) from trade or business activities (page 1, line 21)	1	119,000
2a	Gross income from rental real estate activities — 2a		
b	Less expenses (attach schedule) — 2b		
c	Net income (loss) from rental real estate activities	2c	
3a	Gross income from other rental activities — 3a		
b	Less expenses (attach schedule) — 3b		
c	Net income (loss) from other rental activities	3c	
4	Portfolio income (loss):		
a	Interest income	4a	4,000
b	Dividend income	4b	16,000
c	Royalty income	4c	
d	Net short-term capital gain (loss) (Schedule D (Form 1120S))	4d	
e	Net long-term capital gain (loss) (Schedule D (Form 1120S))	4e	
f	Other portfolio income (loss) (attach schedule)	4f	
5	Net gain (loss) under section 1231 (other than due to casualty or theft) (see instructions)	5	
6	Other income (loss) (attach schedule)	6	
7	Charitable contributions (attach list)	7	24,000
8	Section 179 expense deduction (attach Form 4562)	8	
9	Expenses related to portfolio income (loss) (attach schedule) (see instructions)	9	
10	Other deductions (attach schedule)	10	

Credits

11a	Credit for alcohol used as a fuel (attach Form 6478)	11a	
b	Low-income housing credit: (1) From partnerships to which section 42(j)(5) applies	11b(1)	
	(2) Other than on line 11b(1)	11b(2)	
c	Qualified rehabilitation expenditures related to rental real estate activities (attach schedule)	11c	
d	Credits (other than credits shown on lines 11b and 11c) related to rental real estate activities (attach schedule)	11d	
e	Credits related to other rental activities (see instructions) (attach schedule)	11e	
12	Other credits and expenditures (attach schedule) *Jobs Credit*	12	6,000

Investment Interest

13a	Interest expense on investment debts	13a	3,000
b	(1) Investment income included on lines 4a through 4f above	13b(1)	20,000
	(2) Investment expenses included on line 9 above	13b(2)	

Adjustments and Tax Preference Items

14a	Accelerated depreciation of real property placed in service before 1987	14a	
b	Accelerated depreciation of leased personal property placed in service before 1987	14b	
c	Depreciation adjustment on property placed in service after 1986	14c	
d	Depletion (other than oil and gas)	14d	
e	(1) Gross income from oil, gas, or geothermal properties	14e(1)	
	(2) Deductions allocable to oil, gas, or geothermal properties	14e(2)	
f	Other adjustments and tax preference items (attach schedule)	14f	

Foreign Taxes

15a	Type of income		
b	Name of foreign country or U.S. possession		
c	Total gross income from sources outside the U.S. (attach schedule)	15c	
d	Total applicable deductions and losses (attach schedule)	15d	
e	Total foreign taxes (check one): ▶ ☐ Paid ☐ Accrued	15e	
f	Reduction in taxes available for credit (attach schedule)	15f	
g	Other foreign tax information (attach schedule)	15g	

Other Items

16	Total property distributions (including cash) other than dividends reported on line 18 below	16	65,000
17	Other items and amounts not included on lines 1 through 16 above, that are required to be reported separately to shareholders (attach schedule)		
18	Total dividend distributions paid from accumulated earnings and profits contained in other retained earnings (line 27, Schedule L)	18	

Fig. D.6. *cont.*

Form 1120S.

Tips for Restaurants

You can use Quicken for restaurant accounting. As part of closing out the cash register, you can record the daily cash and credit-card sales as a deposit transaction into your register. You also can record expenses directly into Quicken as they occur by categorizing any checks you write.

Fig. D.7.

The 1120 form indicates which income and expense categories some corporations should use to report profits and losses.

Form 1120 — Department of the Treasury, Internal Revenue Service

U.S. Corporation Income Tax Return

For calendar year 1989 or tax year beginning _____ 1989, ending _____ 19 ____
► Instructions are separate. See page 1 for Paperwork Reduction Act Notice.

OMB No. 1545-0123

1989

Check if a—
A Consolidated return ☐
B Personal holding co. ☐
C Personal service corp.(as defined in Temp. Regs. sec. 1 441-4T—see instructions) ☐

Use IRS label. Otherwise, please print or type.

Name: 10-0395674 DEC89 071 3998
TENTEX TOYS, INC.
36 DIVISION STREET
ANYTOWN, IL 60930

D Employer identification number: 10-0395674
E Date incorporated: 3-1-72
F Total assets (see Specific Instructions): $ 879,417

G Check applicable boxes: (1) ☐ Initial return (2) ☐ Final return (3) ☐ Change in address

Income

1a	Gross receipts or sales $2,010,000	b Less returns and allowances $20,000
1c	c Bal ►	1,990,000
2	Cost of goods sold and/or operations (Schedule A, line 7)	1,520,000
3	Gross profit (line 1c less line 2)	470,000
4	Dividends (Schedule C, line 19)	10,000
5	Interest	4,500
6	Gross rents	
7	Gross royalties	
8	Capital gain net income (attach Schedule D (Form 1120))	
9	Net gain or (loss) from Form 4797, Part II, line 18 (attach Form 4797)	
10	Other income (see instructions—attach schedule)	1,000
11	Total income—Add lines 3 through 10	485,500

Deductions (See instructions for limitations on deductions.)

12	Compensation of officers (Schedule E, line 4)	70,000
13a	Salaries and wages 44,000	b Less jobs credit 6,000	c Balance ►
13c		38,000
14	Repairs	800
15	Bad debts	1,600
16	Rents	9,200
17	Taxes	15,000
18	Interest	27,200
19	Contributions (see instructions for 10% limitation)	23,150
20	Depreciation (attach Form 4562) 17,600	
21a	Less depreciation claimed on Schedule A and elsewhere on return 12,400	
21b		5,200
22	Depletion	
23	Advertising	8,700
24	Pension, profit-sharing, etc., plans	
25	Employee benefit programs	
26	Other deductions (attach schedule)	78,300
27	Total deductions—Add lines 12 through 26 ►	277,150
28	Taxable income before net operating loss deduction and special deductions (line 11 less line 27)	208,350
29	Less: a Net operating loss deduction (see instructions) 29a	
	b Special deductions (Schedule C, line 20) 29b 8,000	
29c		8,000
30	Taxable income—Line 28 less line 29c	200,350
31	Total tax (Schedule J, line 10)	55,387

Tax and Payments

32	Payments: a 1988 overpayment credited to 1989 32a	
	b 1989 estimated tax payments 32b 69,117	
	c Less 1989 refund applied for on Form 4466 32c ( ) d Bal ► 32d 69,117	
	e Tax deposited with Form 7004 32e	
	f Credit from regulated investment companies (attach Form 2439) 32f	
	g Credit for Federal tax on fuels (attach Form 4136) 32g	
32h		69,117
33	Enter any penalty for underpayment of estimated tax—Check ► ☐ if Form 2220 is attached	
34	Tax due—If the total of lines 31 and 33 is larger than line 32h, enter amount owed	
35	Overpayment—If line 32h is larger than the total of lines 31 and 33, enter amount overpaid	13,730
36	Enter amount of line 35 you want: Credited to 1990 estimated tax ► 13,730 Refunded ►	

Please Sign Here

Under penalties of perjury, I declare that I have examined this return, including accompanying schedules and statements, and to the best of my knowledge and belief, it is true, correct, and complete. Declaration of preparer (other than taxpayer) is based on all information of which preparer has any knowledge.

► *James Q. Barclay* (Signature of officer) Date 3/7/90 Title President

Paid Preparer's Use Only

Preparer's signature ► _____ Date _____ Check if self-employed ☐ Preparer's social security number _____
Firm's name (or yours if self-employed) and address ► _____ E.I. No. ► _____ ZIP code ► _____

Although you may be tempted to carry your inventory in an account because inventory is an asset, this method is probably not worth the effort. Food inventories are too short-lived. What you record on Monday as food inventory, you probably use up or throw out by the following

Form 1120 (1989)   Page **2**

Schedule A Cost of Goods Sold and/or Operations (See instructions for line 2, page 1.)

1 Inventory at beginning of year	**1**	126,000
2 Purchases	**2**	1,127,100
3 Cost of labor	**3**	402,000
4a Additional section 263A costs (see instructions—attach schedule)	**4a**	
b Other costs (attach schedule)	**4b**	163,300
5 Total—Add lines 1 through 4b	**5**	1,818,400
6 Inventory at end of year	**6**	298,400
7 Cost of goods sold and/or operations—Line 5 less line 6. Enter here and on line 2, page 1	**7**	1,520,000

8a Check all methods used for valuing closing inventory:

(i) ☐ Cost (ii) ☑ Lower of cost or market as described in Regulations section 1.471-4 (see instructions)

(iii) ☐ Writedown of "subnormal" goods as described in Regulations section 1.471-2(c) (see instructions)

(iv) ☐ Other (Specify method used and attach explanation.) ▶ _____ ☐

b Check if the LIFO inventory method was adopted this tax year for any goods (if checked, attach Form 970) . . . . . ☐

c If the LIFO inventory method was used for this tax year, enter percentage (or amounts) of closing inventory computed under LIFO **8c**

d Do the rules of section 263A (with respect to property produced or acquired for resale) apply to the corporation? . . ☑ Yes ☐ No

e Was there any change in determining quantities, cost, or valuations between opening and closing inventory? If "Yes," attach explanation . . . . ☐ Yes ☑ No

Schedule C Dividends and Special Deductions (See instructions.)

	(a) Dividends received	(b) %	(c) Special deductions: (a) × (b)
1 Dividends from less-than-20%-owned domestic corporations that are subject to the 70% deduction (other than debt-financed stock)		70	
2 Dividends from 20%-or-more-owned domestic corporations that are subject to the 80% deduction (other than debt-financed stock)	10,000	80	8,000
3 Dividends on debt-financed stock of domestic and foreign corporations (section 246A)		see instructions	
4 Dividends on certain preferred stock of less-than-20%-owned public utilities		41.176	
5 Dividends on certain preferred stock of 20%-or-more-owned public utilities		47.059	
6 Dividends from less-than-20%-owned foreign corporations and certain FSCs that are subject to the 70% deduction		70	
7 Dividends from 20%-or-more-owned foreign corporations and certain FSCs that are subject to the 80% deduction		80	
8 Dividends from wholly owned foreign subsidiaries subject to the 100% deduction (section 245(b))		100	
9 Total—Add lines 1 through 8. See instructions for limitation			8,000
10 Dividends from domestic corporations received by a small business investment company operating under the Small Business Investment Act of 1958		100	
11 Dividends from certain FSCs that are subject to the 100% deduction (section 245(c)(1))		100	
12 Dividends from affiliated group members subject to the 100% deduction (section 243(a)(3))		100	
13 Other dividends from foreign corporations not included on lines 3, 6, 7, 8, or 11			
14 Income from controlled foreign corporations under subpart F (attach Forms 5471)			
15 Foreign dividend gross-up (section 78)			
16 IC-DISC and former DISC dividends not included on lines 1, 2, or 3 (section 246(d))			
17 Other dividends			
18 Deduction for dividends paid on certain preferred stock of public utilities (see instructions)			
19 Total dividends—Add lines 1 through 17. Enter here and on line 4, page 1. ▶	10,000		
20 Total deductions—Add lines 9, 10, 11, 12, and 18. Enter here and on line 29b, page 1 . . . . ▶			8,000

Schedule E Compensation of Officers (See instructions for line 12, page 1.)

Complete Schedule E only if total receipts (line 1a, plus lines 4 through 10, of page 1, Form 1120) are $500,000 or more.

(a) Name of officer	(b) Social security number	(c) Percent of time devoted to business	Percent of corporation stock owned		(f) Amount of compensation
			(d) Common	(e) Preferred	
1 James Q. Barclay	581·00·0936	100 %	45 %	%	40,000
		%	%	%	
George M. Collins	447·00·2604	100 %	15 %	%	21,000
		%	%	%	
Samuel Adams	401·00·2611	50 %	2 %	%	9,000
2 Total compensation of officers					70,000
3 Less: Compensation of officers claimed on Schedule A and elsewhere on return					( )
4 Compensation of officers deducted on line 12, page 1					70,000

Fig. D.7. cont.

Form 1120.

Monday. Categorize food purchases in an expense category rather than by setting up a food inventory account that you must adjust every time you calculate your profits. You need to calculate an inventory balance for your income tax return, but only once per year.

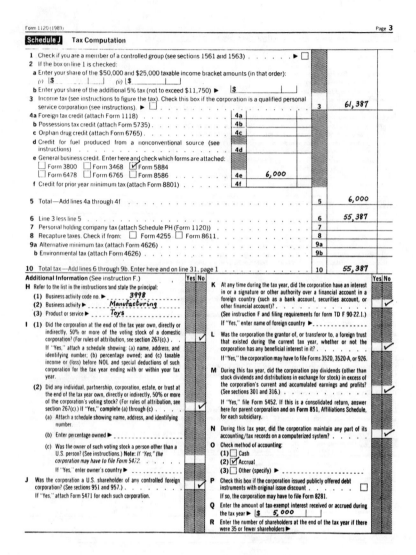

Fig. D.7. cont.

Form 1120.

Tips for Retailers

Retail businesses, especially those that do not have to prepare invoices or statements, also can use Quicken with good results. You need a point-of-sale system like a cash register to ring up sales, make change, and so forth. At the end of the day, you can enter the total sales for the day as a deposit transaction into your check register.

Form 1120 (1989)					Page 4
Schedule L Balance Sheets		Beginning of tax year		End of tax year	
Assets		(a)	(b)	(c)	(d)
1 Cash			14,700		28,331
2a Trade notes and accounts receivable . . .		98,400		103,700	
b Less allowance for bad debts			98,400		103,700
3 Inventories			126,000		298,400
4 U.S. government obligations					
5 Tax-exempt securities (see instructions) .			100,000		120,000
6 Other current assets (attach schedule) . .			26,300		17,266
7 Loans to stockholders					
8 Mortgage and real estate loans					
9 Other investments (attach schedule) . . .			100,000		80,000
10a Buildings and other depreciable assets . .		272,400		296,700	
b Less accumulated depreciation		88,300	184,100	104,280	192,420
11a Depletable assets					
b Less accumulated depletion					
12 Land (net of any amortization)			20,000		20,000
13a Intangible assets (amortizable only) . . .					
b Less accumulated amortization					
14 Other assets (attach schedule)			14,800		19,300
15 Total assets			684,300		879,417
Liabilities and Stockholders' Equity					
16 Accounts payable			28,500		34,834
17 Mortgages, notes, bonds payable in less than 1 year			4,300		4,300
18 Other current liabilities (attach schedule) .			6,800		7,400
19 Loans from stockholders					
20 Mortgages, notes, bonds payable in 1 year or more			176,700		264,100
21 Other liabilities (attach schedule)					
22 Capital stock: a Preferred stock					
b Common stock		200,000	200,000	200,000	200,000
23 Paid-in or capital surplus					
24 Retained earnings—Appropriated (attach schedule)			30,000		40,000
25 Retained earnings—Unappropriated . . .			238,000		328,783
26 Less cost of treasury stock			( )		( )
27 Total liabilities and stockholders' equity . .			684,300		879,417

Fig. D.7. cont.

Form 1120.

Schedule M-1 Reconciliation of Income per Books With Income per Return (You are not required to complete this schedule if the total assets on line 15, column (d), of Schedule L are less than $25,000.)

1 Net income per books	147,783	7 Income recorded on books this year not included on this return (itemize):		
2 Federal income tax	55,387			
3 Excess of capital losses over capital gains .	3,600	a Tax-exempt interest $ 5,000		
4 Income subject to tax not recorded on books this year (itemize): _____		b Insurance Proceeds 9,500		14,500
		8 Deductions on this return not charged against book income this year (itemize):		
5 Expenses recorded on books this year not deducted on this return (itemize):		a Depreciation . . . $ 1,620		
a Depreciation . . . $ _____		b Contributions carryover $ _____		
b Contributions carryover $ 850		_____		
c Travel and entertainment . $ _____		_____		
See Itemized		_____		
Statement Attached $ 16,850	17,700	9 Total of lines 7 and 8		16,120
6 Total of lines 1 through 5	224,470	10 Income (line 28, page 1)—line 6 less line 9 .		208,350

Schedule M-2 Analysis of Unappropriated Retained Earnings per Books (line 25, Schedule L) (You are not required to complete this schedule if the total assets on line 15, column (d), of Schedule L are less than $25,000.)

1 Balance at beginning of year	238,000	5 Distributions: a Cash		65,000
2 Net income per books	147,783	b Stock		
3 Other increases (itemize):		c Property		
Refund of 1987 Income Tax		6 Other decreases (itemize): _____		
Due to IRS Examination		Reserve for Contingencies		10,000
_____	18,000	7 Total of lines 5 and 6		75,000
4 Total of lines 1, 2, and 3	403,783	8 Balance at end of year (line 4 less line 7)		328,783

One weakness in using Quicken for a retail business holding extensive inventory is that you do not have a good way to track the units and dollars of inventory you hold. You may want to implement a manual inventory-tracking system and use a common tool for setting priorities: ABC Analysis and Classification.

ABC Analysis and Classification is a common-sense approach to breaking down your inventory into classes—A, B, or C—to show their relative value to you. Items in the A class are the most valuable, and items in the C class are the least valuable. After categorizing items in the three classes, you decide which control and management procedures are appropriate and cost-effective for each class.

Typically, class A items constitute 20 percent of the total number of items in your inventory and make up 80 percent of your inventory's dollar value. You may want or be required by law, therefore, to count class A items on a weekly or daily basis and to maintain precise manual records of balances and changes in the balances.

Class B items are at the next level of importance and value. These items usually constitute 40 to 50 percent of the total number of items in inventory, but they may account for less than 15 percent of the dollar value of your inventory. Accordingly, you may want to use a periodic inventory approach for class B items and take a physical count of your inventory once per quarter or month.

For some retailers and manufacturers, class C items may be as much as 40 percent of the total number of items in inventory, although they account for less than 5 percent of the inventory's value. Naturally, the effort expended on controlling this inventory is considerably less than the effort connected with classes A and B. For example, you may decide to count class C items annually.

ABC Analysis and Classification is a straightforward approach of setting priorities in your inventory control and management efforts. Although every item in your inventory may be important, do not succumb to the temptation to classify all your items as class A. Categorize your inventory holdings into meaningful and manageable groups.

Summary

This appendix gives you some tips and ideas for using Quicken in specific business situations. Not all the material covered applies to your business, but the information presented should make using Quicken easier.

Index

341

Free Catalog!

Mail us this registration form today, and we'll send you a free catalog featuring Que's complete line of best-selling books.

Name of Book _____

Name _____

Title _____

Phone (_____) _____

Company _____

Address _____

City _____

State _____ ZIP _____

Please check the appropriate answers:

1. Where did you buy your Que book?
   ☐ Bookstore (name: _____)
   ☐ Computer store (name: _____)
   ☐ Catalog (name: _____)
   ☐ Direct from Que
   ☐ Other: _____

2. How many computer books do you buy a year?
   ☐ 1 or less
   ☐ 2-5
   ☐ 6-10
   ☐ More than 10

3. How many Que books do you own?
   ☐ 1
   ☐ 2-5
   ☐ 6-10
   ☐ More than 10

4. How long have you been using this software?
   ☐ Less than 6 months
   ☐ 6 months to 1 year
   ☐ 1-3 years
   ☐ More than 3 years

5. What influenced your purchase of this Que book?
   ☐ Personal recommendation
   ☐ Advertisement
   ☐ In-store display
   ☐ Price
   ☐ Que catalog
   ☐ Que mailing
   ☐ Que's reputation
   ☐ Other: _____

6. How would you rate the overall content of the book?
   ☐ Very good
   ☐ Good
   ☐ Satisfactory
   ☐ Poor

7. What do you like *best* about this Que book?
   _____
   _____

8. What do you like *least* about this Que book?
   _____
   _____

9. Did you buy this book with your personal funds?
   ☐ Yes   ☐ No

10. Please feel free to list any other comments you may have about this Que book.
    _____
    _____
    _____

que

Order Your Que Books Today!

Name _____

Title _____

Company _____

City _____

State _____ ZIP _____

Phone No. (_____) _____

Method of Payment:

Check ☐   (Please enclose in envelope.)

Charge My: VISA ☐   MasterCard ☐

American Express ☐

Charge # _____

Expiration Date _____

Order No.	Title	Qty.	Price	Total

You can **FAX** your order to 1-317-573-2583. Or call **1-800-428-5331, ext. ORDR** to order direct.
Please add $2.50 per title for shipping and handling.

Subtotal _____

Shipping & Handling _____

Total _____

que

BUSINESS REPLY MAIL

First Class Permit No. 9918   Indianapolis, IN

Postage will be paid by addressee

que®

11711 N. College
Carmel, IN 46032

NO POSTAGE
NECESSARY
IF MAILED
IN THE
UNITED STATES

BUSINESS REPLY MAIL

First Class Permit No. 9918   Indianapolis, IN

Postage will be paid by addressee

que®

11711 N. College
Carmel, IN 46032

Main

1. Write/P▮
2. Check ▮
3. Reports
4. Reconc
5. Change
E. Exit

Change Settings Menu

1. Screen Colors
2. Monitor Speed
3. Set Up Printer 1
4. Set Up Printer 2
5. Other Settings
6. Bank Account Activities

Reports Menu

1. Transaction Repo▮
2. @Category Repor
3. Budget Report
4. Reconciliation Rep
5. Memorized Transa
6. @Category Repor

Bank Account Activities Menu

1. Select Bank Account (Ctrl-A)
2. Set Up New Bank Account
3. Set Bank Account Location
4. Back Up/Restore Bank Account
5. Delete Bank Account
6. Rename Bank Account
7. Copy Bank Account

Using Q

Quicke
Menu

que®

11711 N. College Ave.
Carmel, IN 46032

Menu

nt Checks —
egister —

e
Settings

ort
ction List

Quicken

n 2.0
Map

F3—Edit/Find Menu

1. Record Transaction (Ctrl-Enter)
2. Delete Transaction (Ctrl-D)
3. Find (Ctrl-F)
4. Repeat Find (previous) (Ctrl-←)
5. Repeat Find (next) (Ctrl-→)
6. Go To Date (Ctrl-G)
7. Split Transaction (Ctrl-S)

F4—Quick Entry Menu

1. Recall Transaction (Ctrl-T)
2. Memorize Transaction (Ctrl-M)
3. Recall Category (Ctrl-C)
4. Memorize Category (Ctrl-L)
5. Execute Transaction Group
6. Set Up Transaction Group

F5—Print

1. Print (Ctrl-P)
2. Set Up Printer 1
3. Set Up Print 2

F6—Activities

1. Check Register (Ctrl-R)*
   -or-
   Write Checks (Ctrl-W)
2. Reports
3. Reconcile
4. Order Supplies
5. Use DOS

*Depends on which menu option you select F6 from.